THE NEGRO AND FUSION POLITICS
IN NORTH CAROLINA
1894–1901

THE NEGRO
AND FUSION POLITICS
IN NORTH CAROLINA

1894-1901

By

HELEN G. EDMONDS

Chapel Hill
THE UNIVERSITY OF NORTH CAROLINA PRESS

To

MR. AND MRS. JAMES H. CARTER
whose generosity inspired me in
my college days.

ACKNOWLEDGMENTS

THE HUMBLEST ATTEMPT at historical writing finds an author indebted to the present and the past, to the living and the dead. While bibliographical references herein cited bear mute recognition of the debt of gratitude to some, I want and must express my obligation to a number of individuals whose help has gone beyond the ordinary courtesy of formal response.

My sincere thanks are expressed to Dr. Albert N. Newsome and Dr. Hugh T. Lefler, Chairman of the Department and Professor of History, respectively, University of North Carolina, who offered important suggestions in matters of detail and general organization for the improvement of this work. They read the many revisions in their entirety with a critical eye and helpful spirit. Dr. Henry H. Simms, Associate Professor of History at Ohio State University, offered many discriminating criticisms which were invaluable. It was in his classes that I became inspired, my historical insight enriched, and my attention focused on Southern history. I am indebted to Dr. John Hope Franklin, Professor of History, Howard University, and Mr. J. MacLeod, Department of History, University of North Carolina, for their time in reading parts of this manuscript which fell within their particular areas of research. While this work was read and advised by these scholars, it is to be understood, however, that I absolve them from the responsibility for any errors which may have crept into it.

I am grateful for the cooperative and courteous services rendered me personally by the staffs of the libraries of Duke University, North Carolina College at Durham, the University of North Carolina, North Carolina State Department of Archives and History, North Carolina State Library, and Congress. Mrs. Parepa W. Jackson, former Librarian, North Carolina College at Durham, reduced the necessity of some travel thereby minimizing expense by assembling some materials through inter-library loan. Miss Helen Oyler of Duke University Library provided a cordial academic atmosphere for the use of those materials which could not be taken from a library. I am equally anxious to pay some tribute to my sister-in-law, Mrs. Rebecca Palmer Edmonds, for laborious hours of retyping and helpful suggestions.

Persons interviewed are thanked for their time and the rendition of their experiences. It is my hope that they will not be shocked by the omission of some of their contributions. It was found necessary to use only information which coincided with available data.

While the completion of this treatise involved the academic aid of many persons, the financial assistance cannot be ignored. I express appreciation to the General Education Board for the fellowship which enabled me to complete my academic training at Ohio State University in 1946 and simultaneously undertake the writing of this book. Dr. James E. Shepard, deceased president of North Carolina College at Durham, kindly relieved me of classroom teaching in order that I could give greater concentration to composition.

To the members of my household goes my highest esteem for their herculean forbearance during those times when research began to collect from me its toll of human energy. May they breathe a sigh of relief.

HELEN G. EDMONDS

April 3, 1951
Durham, N. C.

CONTENTS

MAPS

TABLES

THE NEGRO AND FUSION POLITICS
IN NORTH CAROLINA
1894–1901

CHAPTER ONE

INTRODUCTION

IT IS OFTEN STATED that North Carolina is dominantly a one-party state. The history of the past fifty years bears testimony to the fact that the Democratic party has been in control of government of this state more often than any other party. The historian is compelled to analyze the factors which gave rise to that domination. The North Carolina pattern cannot be fitted into the single formula that the Reconstruction Period, which followed the War Between the States, solidified the Democratic whites against the Republican blacks and thereby created a Democratic state beyond peradventure. The unique forces and circumstances which contributed to the one-party system in this state warrant the analysis of a more recent historical period than Reconstruction.

The Democratic party has, from 1870 to 1951, had a majority representation in the North Carolina legislature, with but one exception. That exception is the brief interlude, 1895-1901, commonly termed the Fusion Period. This treatise, in analyzing the Fusion Period, involved first, the rise of a third party in the state, the People's party; second, the "fusion" of that party with the Republican party; third, the Fusion's overthrow of the Bourbon Democratic party; and, fourth, Democratic restoration. Fusion politics in this study means the strategy employed and the results attained by the Populists and Republicans in their ascendancy, domination, and decline. It means a redefining of the political role of the Negro in the period.

Any writer who deals with the turbulent 1890's in this state's history will find that there are two schools of opinion relative to the interpretation of Fusion politics: the old and the new. There will also be found numerous shades of opinion between the two points of view. Those writers who have maintained a condemnation of the Fusion administration constitute the old. The few writers and statesmen who have given some credit to the period constitute the new.

Some of the possible determinants which have established the old school point of view and perpetuated it are: First, most of the earlier writers were staunch Democrats; hence, they were anti-Republican, anti-Populist, anti-Negro participation in politics, and unscientific in the evaluation of data.[1] Second, more recent writers, in treating this period in their general histories of the state, have leaned heavily upon Democratic source materials and have accepted the decade of the 1890's as a terrible political era, a near replica of Reconstruction days.[2] Third, many Democratic campaign speakers, at that

3

time and until 1930, resurrected the activities of the Fusion Period to illustrate the necessity of "white supremacy," although the majority of Negroes had been disfranchised by constitutional amendment in 1901 and fraudently disfranchised by intricate election laws before 1901.[3] Fourth, such source materials as private papers, campaign literature, newspapers, periodicals, and memoirs which set forth the Democratic side of the question are in greater abundance and are more centrally located than those materials which present the Fusion side.[4]

The new school of interpretation of Fusion is small and comparatively recent. The decades of the 1930's and 1940's found the emotional attitudes of the Democratic party more receptive to any analysis which was at variance with the established Democratic hypotheses. Pioneer attempts by the students of the University of North Carolina, Duke University, and the University of Chicago have re-examined some aspects of the period. As J. D. Hicks in *The Populist Revolt* exposed many unjust condemnations which anti-Populist propaganda has assigned to the national movement, so has the new group of writers in North Carolina, by the more thorough use of source materials, attempted to see Populism in its true light. The new school has focused its attention first upon the economic implications involved in Fusion; secondly, upon the racial constituency of the Fusion parties; and thirdly, upon the Democratic techniques employed in the overthrow of Fusion.

Fusion included three factors: the Populist party, the Republican party, and the Negro. It is necessary to analyze critically the existing works which treat each factor separately and the three factors collectively in terms of new points of view. Simeon Delap was the first writer to see in Populism any benefits to this state.[5] His work is superficial in treatment, but it was a pioneer attempt in a neglected phase of state history. Florence E. Smith sought to justify the righteousness of the Populist party and ignored the truth or falsity of the factors involved in the race question.[6]

There is no separate treatment of the Republican party. The Negro as a component part of the Republican party is also a neglected phase. William A. Mabry, in recording the political activities of the Negro, devoted some attention to the Negro in Fusion politics. He believed that there was no threat of Negro domination, yet he concerned himself more with exposing the effects of Negro office-holding on race relations than ascertaining the number and quality of positions held by Negroes.[7]

Others of the recent writers on state history, as a whole, have introduced new appraisals on Fusion politics and the Negro. Albert R. Newsome and Hugh T. Lefler have modified some of the points of view on the period by showing that the rule of the Populists and the Republicans pleased the people in some respects. They have eliminated some of the Negro-phobia from Fusion politics by the use of the terms "some" and "few" in reference to

Negro officeholders.[8] Lefler has opened other new vistas to future writers through his compilation of documentary data which show both sides of the Fusion picture.[9] The best, most authentic and dispassionate interpretation of the Fusion election of 1896 made thus far has been done by Phillip J. Weaver.[10] His work asserts that Fusion was the reaction against the Democratic party's failure to meet the new challenge for reform and advancement. While the writers of the old school contend that the Negro vote was responsible for Fusion victory in 1896, Weaver states that victory was assured without the Negro vote. His estimate of the race question in the background of Fusion politics shows that he was not unduly influenced by the racial propaganda of the period.

Recent memoirs, personal correspondence, and autobiographies have contributed some either towards new points of view or towards the furthering of the new points of view. The Clawson Memoirs add a small bit of clarity to the Wilmington Race Riot in that the writer (white) owned the press with which Alex Manly (Negro) printed the Negro newspaper.[11] The private correspondence of one Negro sheds much light on the duplicity of some of the Republican leaders.[12] The first two volumes of Josephus Daniels' autobiography are indispensable for an analysis of the atmosphere of the 1890's.[13] These volumes are intensely Democratic, and the author lets this fact be known without apologies. Some of his conclusions are new points of view, as he writes them in retrospect. It is primarily because of Daniels' retrospective writings that one may assume that the time seems at hand when the emotional attitude of North Carolina historians will permit a dispassionate appraisal of the tempestuous 1890's. This tendency is well illustrated when this energetic Democratic participant, opponent of the Negro in politics, and enemy of Fusion, says, in 1941:

I made enemies and I garnered friends, and my vehemence of denunciation of opponents was not always tempered with charity.... But I look back, also, amazed at my own editorial violence at times, even when I understood the circumstances which surrounded it.... The poverty of the South, the poverty of my State, and resentment at the Politics of Reconstruction, bred a violence in insecurity which reduced to pure bitterness the contest between men and groups and races.[14]

There are certain handicaps inherent in the study of Fusion politics. There are few county histories. Of the ninety-six counties of the state in this period, only six have written histories.[15] Only one of the six discussed Fusion.[16] There is a scarcity of source materials on Negro officeholders. The House and Senate *Journals* and *Public Documents* make no distinction between white and colored members of the legislature. The most useful aid in identifying them was the North Carolina Manual, 1913, but this work failed to designate several Negro members. Personal interviews, newspapers, relatives, and secondary materials are the chief means of determining racial identity. The *Congressional Record* and House *Journals* (North Carolina General Assembly) are the basic sources for the activities of George H. White and James H. Young, respectively, two Negroes who figured prominently in the period.

The Democratic newspapers of the period were more numerous and had wider circulation; in them, however, one has to wade through vitriolic and partisan propaganda. The Republican party had no official press at the time, and this makes difficult a nonpartisan study of the period. The Populists relied upon the *Progressive Farmer* and the *Caucasian* to carry their message.

This work attempts to pursue the path of the new school of interpretation, taking into consideration certain points of view of the old. It aims to investigate the bases of Fusion in each election from 1894 to 1900; to appraise those aspects of Fusion legislation which bear relationship to the Negro; to examine the facts concerning the cry of "Negro domination" through an analysis of Negro office-holding with regard to federal, state, county, and municipal positions; to see the industrial and commercial forces at work behind the issue of race; and to estimate the Democrats' use of the race question as an instrument in making North Carolina a one-party state.

NOTES TO CHAPTER ONE

1. Samuel A. Ashe, *History of North Carolina*, Vol. II.
   Fred Rippy, (ed.), *Furnifold Simmons, Statesman of the New South; Memoirs and Addresses*.
   James Sprunt, *Chronicles of the Cape Fear River 1660-1916*, Second ed.
   Alfred M. Waddell, *Some Memories of My Life*.
2. R. D. W. Connor, *North Carolina: Rebuilding an Ancient Commonwealth, 1584-1925*, Vol. II.
   R. D. W. Connor and Clarence Poe, *The Life and Speeches of Charles Brantley Aycock*.
   J. G. deR. Hamilton, *History of North Carolina Since 1860* (*History of North Carolina*, Vol. III).
   Archibald Henderson, *North Carolina, The Old North State and the New*, Vol. II.
3. Charles B. Aycock, Josephus Daniels, Locke Craig, Robert Glenn, T. J. Jarvis, Claude Kitchin, Cameron Morrison, George Rountree, Furnifold Simmons, Francis Winston.
4. Duke University Library (Durham, North Carolina), State Department of Archives and History (Raleigh, North Carolina), State Library (Raleigh, North Carolina), University of North Carolina Library (Chapel Hill, North Carolina).
5. Simeon Delap, "The Populist Party in North Carolina," *Trinity College Historical Papers*, Series XXIV (1922), 40-74.
6. Florence E. Smith, Populism and Its Influence in North Carolina (Unpublished Ph.D. dissertation, University of Chicago, 1929).
7. William A Mabry, "The Negro in North Carolina Politics Since Reconstruction," *Historical Papers of Trinity College Historical Society*, Series XXIII (1940).

8. Albert R. Newsome and Hugh T. Lefler, *The Growth of North Carolina.*

9. Hugh T. Lefler, (ed.), *North Carolina History Told by Contemporaries.*

10. Phillip J. Weaver, The Gubernatorial Election of 1896 in North Carolina (Unpublished M.A. thesis, University of North Carolina, 1937).

11. Clawson Memoirs. Retelling the Story of the Wilmington Race Riot, North Carolina Historical Commission, Raleigh, North Carolina, deposited May 26, 1944.

12. Private Correspondence of John Dancy, Collector of Customs, Wilmingon, North Carolina. Correspondence in possession of John Dancy, Jr., Director of Urban League, 606 E. Vernor, Detroit, Michigan.

13. Josephus Daniels, *Tar Heel Editor,* 1939; *Editor in Politics,* 1941.

14. Daniels, *Editor in Politics,* 623.

15. Clarence Griffin, *History of Old Tryon or Rutherford County, 1730-1936.*
Joseph Separk, *History of Gastonia and Gaston County.*
Forster A. Sondley, *Buncombe County.*
Joseph K. Turner and John Bridges, *History of Edgecombe County.*
A. M. Waddell, *History of New Hanover County,* Vol. I.
Sherrill L. Williams, *Lincoln County.*

16. Turner and Bridges, *History of Edgecombe County.*

CHAPTER TWO

THE FACTORS UNDERLYING FUSION

THE THREADS OF SOUTHERN HISTORY weave a very confusing web, during and immediately after the period of Reconstruction, when writers attempt to characterize the Negro in Southern politics. It is historically unsound to categorize the Negro in Southern politics. Political activities of the Negro in the post-bellum South varied according to localities and ratio in the population. The approach must be specific, confined to state and county areas, and fundamentally localized in nature. The evidence thus secured would then present a more accurate picture than is possible from the general approach. Just as methods of slave discipline, black codes, and master-slave relations differed vastly in Southern areas before the Civil War, so did Bourbon tolerance of Negroes in politics differ in the post-bellum period.

The Reconstruction left in its wake in North Carolina two distinct political parties: the Republican and the Conservative (later called Democratic).[1] The Republican party was composed of carpetbaggers, scalawags, and Negroes. The Conservative party was composed of white men whose desire was to drive out the Northern "foreigners" who had manipulated their Negro cohorts and to return the control of state government exclusively to whites. The rivalry of these two parties, the Republican to maintain control and the Conservative to obtain it, is roughly the story of Reconstruction in North Carolina. The Conservatives captured the legislature in 1870 and the gubernatorial election in 1876. North Carolina was Democratic from 1876 to 1894. The Negro was less active in politics. The Negro and the Republican party as political factors reappeared in 1894. The strengthening of the Republican party in the 1890's is closely linked with the appearance of the People's party (a third party); hence, an examination of these three parties between 1877 and 1894 is important.

THE DEMOCRATIC PARTY

It is reasonably safe to assume that when Congress removed the political disabilities from many North Carolinians in 1872, the "restored" whites joined the Democratic party. The psychological aftermath of the Civil War gave impetus to the growth of the Democratic party, for the whites suffered not only military defeat, but Reconstruction made voting Republicans of the Negroes. The Democratic legislature of 1874 chafed under the Reconstruction Constitution which had been saddled on the state in 1868. The Constitution of 1868 was condemned on the basis of "its origin in a military

8

despotism, and on its lack of suitability to the needs of the State."[2] A new constitutional convention met on September 5, 1875. The Conservative party secured a majority, but one so narrow that the path of the convention was fraught with difficulties. Among the vast number of amendments proposed, only thirty were adopted.[3] Those were ratified in 1876.

While it is needless to go into a survey of the thirty amendments, there are two which claim attention because of their relation to partisan politics and the Negro. The first pertained to suffrage and eligibility to office and stipulated that the residence requirement for voting in any county would be ninety days rather than the previous requirement of sixty days, and that any person convicted of a felony would be debarred.[4] The second amendment gave to the General Assembly full power to modify, change, or abrogate county government.[5] Future legislative assemblies, by these constitutional changes, could regulate and control elections and county government.

The repercussions of the presidential election of 1876 also aided the Conservatives in securing a firmer grip on North Carolina. The Hayes-Tilden election of 1876 produced disputed returns from South Carolina, Louisiana, and Florida. Congress created an Electoral Commission of fifteen—five members each from the House, Senate, and the Supreme Court—to count the disputed returns. The Commission voted 8-7 for Republican Hayes. The decision was not entirely satisfactory. The Commission was accused of voting strictly along party lines.[6] On February 26, 1877, Republican and Democratic politicians held three conferences, the last of which took place at Wormley's Hotel, Washington, D. C. The outcome of these conferences was to all intents and purposes an agreement by which "the Republicans, while expressly disclaiming any authority to speak for him in effect guaranteed that Mr. Hayes, when he became president, would, by a gradual process of non-interference and withdrawal of troops, allow the Republican governments in the two states [South Carolina and Louisiana] to disappear."[7] Hayes won the election. He removed the federal troops from the three states in question in March and April of the same year. The policy of removal became universal in all the formerly seceded states.[8] The Conservative victory of 1876 in the state and the removal of federal troops from the South signalled the end of Reconstruction in North Carolina.

The Conservatives became the Democratic party in 1876, and how they became so is interesting speculation. An authority on the Reconstruction period states this historical probability:

But for Reconstruction, the State would today, so far as one can estimate human probabilities, be solidly Republican. This was clearly evident in 1865 when the attempted restoration of President Johnson put public affairs in the hands of former Whigs who had no thought of joining in politics their old opponents, the Democrats. So strong was the opposition to such a thing that it was eight years before there was an avowed Democratic Party in the State, the Whigs who formed and led the conservative Party having so decided a detestation for the very name.[9]

The association of the Negro with the Republican party had supplied the Democratic party with a fighting weapon. Zebulon Baird Vance and the Democratic ticket vanquished Judge Thomas Settle and the Republican ticket in 1876. The Democrats hailed Vance for the redemption of the state from Yankees and Negroes.

The industrial growth of North Carolina in the 1880's and 1890's was reflected in the growth of the Democratic party into whose ranks came many lawyers, textile mill owners, and railroad magnates. While the leadership of the party was not captured by the industrial or capitalistic element until the 1890's, its presence gave the party in the 1880's a "pro-corporation" attitude which was further enhanced by "machine politics."[10] Prior to 1894, the Democratic triumvirate included Zebulon B. Vance, the "war governor," redeemer of the state, and United States senator; T. J. Jarvis, governor from 1880 to 1884 and later United States senator; and, Matthew Ransom, state Democratic leader and later United States senator. There was no doubt that old men assumed the leadership of the party.

Among the lesser lights were railroad magnates and newspaper editors. Samuel A'Court Ashe was editor of the Raleigh *News,* precursor to the Raleigh *News and Observer,* and a staunch party man. His paper failed to recognize the full implications of the agrarian movement in North Carolina and thereby ignored the farmers' grievances. The editor was anti-Negro and anti-Populist. Julian S. Carr, of Durham, was a wealthy industrial magnate who also had political aspirations. Carr was one of the Democratic possibilities for governor in 1892. Colonel Alexander B. Andrews was a "corporation" Democrat of the first order, vice president of the Southern Railroad. Andrews owned a Democratic paper in Raleigh, *The Morning Post,* a vigorous champion of the railroad interest in politics. There was Elias Carr who possessed enough dual characteristics to be pleasing to the "corporation" element as well as the agricultural element of the party. By 1894, the Democratic party stood for laissez faire policies, no governmental regulation of railroads, and favoritism to business. A party so large, yet governed by so few, was bound to direct party efforts toward self-preservation. The national issues of the 1880's centered around the regulation of railroads, currency fluctuation, tariffs, control of monopolies, and agricultural demands made by a vocal West. The masses of the Democratic party in North Carolina were never sufficiently informed on the real issues of the day. A cursory examination of the leaders and policies before 1894 shows that no attempts were made to foster social and economic reforms in the Assembly or to agitate it in the state, for reforms were opposed by the industrial and railroad interests.

John T. Crowell, president of Trinity College, a Democrat, a plain citizen, and a close observer of the political lethargy of the day, urged that the legislature increase progressively the appropriations for public schools, encourage immigration, appropriate funds for a systematic and scientific improvement of highways, appoint a board of commissioners of transportation and provide for the construction of dikes along the lowlands and rivers, render more efficient the Bureau of Industrial Statistics, authorize an economic and geological survey of the state, abolish the discrediting homestead law, and establish credit banks for farmers.[11] This implied criticism of the political and legislative lethargy of North Carolina confirms Weaver's contention that the Democrats had failed to offer the state a vitalized program.[12] The leadership of the Democratic party was at a low ebb in 1892. If the leaders could complacently evade the vital issues of the day and retain the support of the unknowing masses, so much the better. It has been said that "evasion of issues was most often accomplished by reminding the voters of Negro rule under the Republican party during Reconstruction."[13] When economic grievances arose, the Democratic leaders attributed them to the policies of the national government, especially those of the Republican administration of Harrison, 1889-93.[14] Any serious attempt to regulate railroads or any other big business in the state was considered at that time as dangerous and radical. The national government had paid lip service to regulation through the creation of the Inter-State Commerce Commission in 1887[15] and the enactment of the Sherman Anti-Trust Law in 1890,[16] but they were largely ineffective.

Another factor solidified the party in the state. Northern Republicans in Congress agitated in 1890 for a Federal Election Law which would extend the long arm of the federal government into state politics. This bill, commonly referred to as the "Force Bill," proposed that in response to a petition from five hundred persons in a district or fifty in a county, federal election officers would be supplied, and the arrangement would control federal elections only.[17] While the bill was designed to supervise federal elections only, it was bound to have influence on state politics, as federal and state elections were held at the same time and the same place. The possibility of the Force Bill "proved a spur to unity among southern Democrats who regarded white supremacy as an issue more important than all others."[18] The state legislature of 1891 urged its United States senators, Ransom and Vance, and its nine representatives to vote against the Force Bill. It resolved:

That we applaud the patriotic efforts of our United States Senators and representatives in Congress to secure the defeat of the bill now pending in the Congress of the United States and known as the Federal Election Law or "Force Bill." That the South has passed through a period during which the antagonism of the races and the suspicions engendered in the minds of the colored people by designing, unprincipled and unpatriotic men placed in jeopardy the stability of society and the lives and property of the people, but now happily that period has passed and comparative contentment, confidence and repose have been established in all parts of the southern States. This has been accompanied by an improvement in the material conditions of both races, by the establishment of schools and education of the people, by the opening of mines, the building of factories; the construction of railroads, and generally by an immense development of the moral, intellectual and material resources of a dozen states peopled by millions of citizens and forming a vast empire, claiming the fostering care of our national legislature. In this advancing prosperity northern and foreign capital has had its share, has largely contributed, northern citizens have sought among us profitable investment for their surplus means and have invested hundreds of millions in our industrial enterprises, to say nothing of the obligations arising from the business dealings between the different sections of our common country. We cannot contemplate the disturbance of these relations in business, prosperous and promising yet greater developments, and as to the sections, fraternal and tending to promote broad patriotism without great concern as citizens, and particularly as residents of that section whose best interests are threatened by the measure in question.[19]

The resolutions reflected certain Democratic party attitudes. First, the views of the business or capitalistic element of the party were emphasized, and the use of such terms as "railroads," "factories," "mines," and "material resources" demonstrated the industrial atmosphere of North Carolina at that time. Second, there was a subtle reminder to Northern Republicans who might support the bill that their money was invested in the state, a warning which was tantamount to the economic threat: "support the Force Bill and we will sever our financial arrangements." Third, it was singular for its omission of reference to the agricultural situation, rather centering its attention on industrial enterprises. Fourth, the North Carolina legislature seemed to have considered the resolution a "Southern Manifesto" incorporating the opinion of all the Southern states which participated in the war. Fifth, its reference to the race question was predicated upon the statement that the period of the former antagonism of the races had happily passed and had been accompanied by the material improvement of both races. One cannot always be safe in making conclusions about a party solely on the basis of its official expressions; but if the Negro people had improved materially, morally, and intellectually before 1891, then they speedily degenerated into a "beast" according to the party newspapers, speakers, pamphleteers, and politicians of 1895-1901.

More recent historical evidence throws light upon the activities of another element in the Democratic party. There were the Prohibitionists in the 1880's who sought to outlaw the saloon. Sentiment for state prohibition was crystallized by certain religious groups, chief among which were the Baptists and the Methodists. The party was divided on the issue. The prohibition election of 1881 returned an overwhelming victory for the anti-prohibition forces.[20] The nature of the campaign bears out the contention that the Democratic party did not want to make the whiskey issue political.[21] It is held that the Republican leaders saw the split in the Democratic ranks as an opportunity for their party to emerge victorious in subsequent political elections and thus threw their weight with the anti-prohibition forces.[22] The Republicans' attempt to capitalize on the anti-prohibition sentiment was a fiasco. The Prohibitionists, a remnant group in the Democratic party, had decreased in numbers at the close of the 1880's.

The Democratic party had, in 1890, two elements: a dominant conservative Bourbon wing (pro-business, anti-reform) led by a few leaders who controlled the complacent rank and file by appeals to party loyalty and fears of Republican-Negro rule; and a minority liberal agrarian anti-corporation wing with such spokesmen as Josephus Daniels, Walter Clark, and Leonidas Lafayette Polk. While the minority liberal element of the party grew into strength in the late 1880's, because of mounting agrarian revolt, criticism of the Railroad Commission, and the anti-prohibition sentiment, the self-confident Bourbon leaders of the party did not doubt their ability to maintain party unity and control.

United States Senator Vance died in 1894. Matthew Ransom, the younger senator, was not considered for re-election by a Fusionist legislature in 1895. Jarvis was now merely the former governor. With the decline of the triumvirate's political influence, a more vocal group of young men came to the front in the party. These young men were predominantly lawyers, with the exception of Josephus Daniels. Daniels, an ardent party man, assumed editorship of the Raleigh *News and Observer* in 1894 and wielded immeasurable influence through his paper which was anti-Populist and anti-Negro. There was no man more responsible for shaping public opinion against Fusion than he. The following lawyers rose to influence in the party: Furnifold M. Simmons, Henry G. Connor, Locke Craig, Robert Glenn, Charles B. Aycock, Cameron Morrison, George Rountree, William W. Kitchin, Claude Kitchin, Alfred M. Waddell, and Walter Clark. This infusion of young and vigorous blood was there in 1894 but was not decisive.

In comparing the Democratic party with the Republican party, there is no doubt that political experience was on the side of the Democratic party. The Negro cohorts of the Republican party discredited the party in the estimation of the majority of white North Carolinians because "their [Negro] participation in politics gave the Democratic party a safe majority of white voters."[23]

In 1894, "the Democratic party was a white man's party. . . . And as such demanded and received the allegiance of those who were opposed to universal suffrage upheld by the Republicans and provided for in the Constitution of 1868. The question of the Negro in politics was the dominant issue in all party affiliations."[24] The majority of the Democratic leaders were "not farmers who had suffered from the severe agrarian depression, but were men engaged in other businesses that had been less affected."[25] In reference to their lack of progressiveness, Henderson states that "in many respects they were apathetic and hostile toward the introduction of new ideas."[26] Democratic election law, Democratic control of county government, gerrymandering, intimidation, manipulation, and corruption had kept the Democratic party in control from 1876 to 1894.

THE REPUBLICAN PARTY

The Republican party in North Carolina increased in numbers as a result of the Act of Reconstruction enacted by Congress, March 2, 1867. General Canby, the military governor, called a constitutional convention in Raleigh. Pursuant to the call, one hundred and seven Republicans and thirteen Conservatives appeared as delegates.[27] After fifty-five days of deliberation, the Constitution of 1868 emerged. It was ratified. William W. Holden, of Wake County, was elected Republican governor in that year. White and Negro Republicans dominated the legislature for the next two years. The Conservatives captured the legislature in 1870 and from that time until 1894 there was a recession in the activities of the Republican party. The party was held together chiefly because the "machinery fell into the hands of Federal office-holders."[28]

The constituency of the Republican party in 1868 included carpetbaggers, scalawags, and Negroes. The excessive influence of the Northerners declined rapidly after 1870 and the leadership of the party passed into the hands of native whites. They cannot be classified as Yankees seeking to impose "foreign" customs and political mores on a local people.

The geography of the state played its part in the development of the party. A few extreme western counties were centers of Republican strength. The background of the western counties bore, and bears today, testimony to the clash between the seaboard and the frontier. Lack of equitable representation in the General Assembly, together with the contempt with which the western, nonslaveholding white farmers were treated by the slave owners of the lowland, had incited sectional hostility before the Civil War. Perhaps with some modification as to solidarity, the opinion can be accepted that "when the war came the mountaineers stood loyally by the Union and rendered most efficient service to the armies through the long contest. When the war ended, they entered the Republican party *en masse*."[29]

The geographical distribution of the party as revealed by the gubernatorial elections from 1876 through 1896 shows that ten counties in the western third of the state voted Republican in each election.[30] There were sixteen counties in the central and eastern thirds which voted Republican during the same period.[31] There were then in the east and west definite centers of Republican strength. The geographical distribution of the party cannot be ascertained from these twenty-six counties alone. A better indication of the opposition strength to the Democratic party is shown through an analysis of those counties which polled from 40 to 49 per cent of the total vote in each election from 1876 through 1896. There were forty-seven counties with this type of Republican strength.[32] Many of these forty-seven often switched clearly over into the Republican columns.[33] The ten sure counties in the west, sixteen in the center and east, plus forty-seven counties garnering between 40 and 49 per cent of the total vote, made the Republican party in North Carolina a definite force to be reckoned with. This potential strength, though the party was out of power from 1876 to 1894, was sufficient to warrant the comment that "the party has always been able to put their opponents on the mettle and, more often than not, divide congressional representation with them."[34]

There were certain factors inherent in the geographical distribution of the party. The ten western Republican counties were based on the votes of adult white males since the Negro ratio in population ranged from only 2.7 in Cherokee to 20.1 in Montgomery County.[35] There were in central and eastern North Carolina sixteen "black counties" in 1890, so designated because the Negro population exceeded 50 per cent.[36] Fourteen of these "black counties" voted solidly Republican from 1876 through 1896,[37] with but one election as an exception.[38] Two of the "black counties" went Democratic in each election, though the Republicans polled over 40 per cent of the votes.[39] Three "white counties" in the east voted solidly the Republican ticket, with the exception of one county in one election.[40] While it is obvious that the Republican party was the choice of the Negro, there is to be considered also the general geographical distribution of the party. It was scattered throughout the state, showing safe returns in ten counties of the west, sixteen counties of the east, and from 40 to 49 per cent of the total vote in forty-seven counties. Its geographical diversity is sufficient to indicate that the principles and democratic policies of the Republican party appealed to many whites throughout the state. A comparative vote of the Republicans and Democrats in each election from 1876 through 1900 reveals that before 1892 the margin of Democratic victory ranged from 2,000 to 20,000, that in 1892 the Republicans lost by 40,000, but the third party's vote of 47,840 indicated an anti-Democratic vote of 142,524 to 135,519 for the victorious Democrats.[41]

It is reasonable to assume that Negroes formed a large element in the

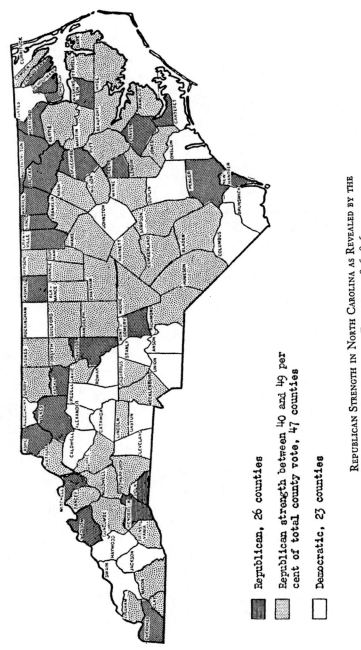

Republican Strength in North Carolina as Revealed by the Gubernatorial Elections, 1876-1896

Variations in 1892 when a third party appeared are not recorded on this chart. (*North Carolina Manual*, 1913, 1002-1996)

▨ Republican, 26 counties

▨ Republican strength between 40 and 49 per cent of total county vote, 47 counties

☐ Democratic, 23 counties

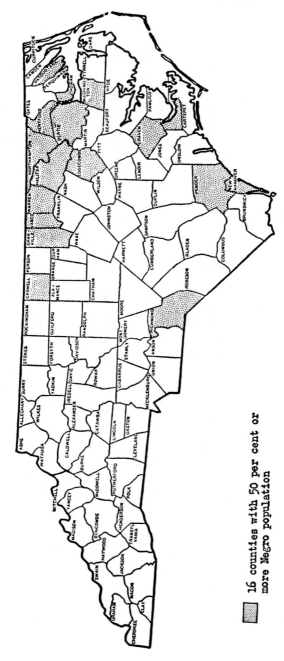

BLACK COUNTIES, 1890

(United States Bureau of Census, *Negro Population, 1790-1915*, 784-85)

16 counties with 50 per cent or
more Negro population

Republican party. Most writers have made different estimates of the number of Negro voters in the 1890's. The election returns of 1894, 1896, 1898, and 1900 did not make the distinction of race in the total count. The impossibility of ascertaining even the approximate number of Negro voters becomes increasingly apparent as one handles the materials of the period. Estimates were made by leading representatives of each party. Jeter C. Pritchard, Republican United States senator, said in 1899 that there were 60,000 white Republicans and 80,000 Negro Republicans.[42] Eugene Holton, state chairman of the Republican party during Fusion, stated that there were 73,000 white Republicans and 92,600 Negro Republicans.[43] One of the chief Democratic newspapers stated that 120,000 Negroes and 30,000 whites voted solidly the Republican ticket.[44] The *Democratic Handbook* of 1898 gave the same figures;[45] but the editor of the *News and Observer* drew up almost all the material for the *Handbook*.[46] The census shows that there were 109,000 male Negroes over the age of twenty-one in 1890,[47] and the larger portion of these was in the sixteen "black counties" in the state.[48] The number indicated by the census bears no accurate relationship to the number of voters, for there is no proof that the total adult male Negro population voted. The largest Republican vote between 1872 and 1892 was 134,026 in 1888, and this included whites and Negroes.[49] The accepted figure in the majority of the literature on the period is the Democratic estimate of 120,000 Negro voters. Just why writers have accepted the Democrats' estimate is difficult to understand since by doubtful logic the basis of the Democratic estimate is that "it is possible, upon a full vote, to poll 360,000. It is certain, therefore, that there is at least 120,000 negro voters in the State; and it is rare that one of them fails to vote."[50] The assumption is that the Negro was one-third of the total population and that he cast one-third of the votes in each election. It was a fact that the Negro was one-third of the population.[51] Whether the potential male Negro voters represented one-third of all the ballots cast may or may not be a fact. Chairman Holton's figures of 73,000 white Republicans and 92,600 Negro Republicans were given on the eve of the election of 1896 in reply to a reporter's inquiry. United States Senator Pritchard gave his estimate on the floor of Congress at a time when the North Carolina legislature had framed a suffrage bill to disfranchise the Negro, and he was attempting to convince the nation that Negro domination did not exist in his state. The *Democratic Handbook* gave its figure in the heat of the "white supremacy" campaign when the Democratic party was determined to convince the state that Negro domination did exist. It is sufficient to repeat that no specific number can be assigned, that the Negro did form a large element of the Republican party, and that such an association of the Negro with the party was always fuel for Democratic propaganda.

The leadership of the Republican party after 1865 fell into the hands of

W. W. Holden, R. P. Dick, and Thomas E. Settle.[52] These men had varied political experiences between 1865 and 1890. Holden of Wake County served as Reconstruction governor from 1868-70, and was impeached and removed from office.[53] Dick of Guilford County was associate justice of the state Supreme Court, 1868-76.[54] Settle of Rockingham County served as a member of the Reconstruction Convention in 1865, and associate justice of the state Supreme Court, and gubernatorial candidate in 1876.[55] The oratorical magnetism of Settle in the campaign of 1876 was reputed to have been quite a match for Zebulon B. Vance, the Democratic nominee.[56] While Holden was disgraced, and Dick retired from active politics, Settle's political popularity continued into the 1890's.

The second and third decades after the Civil War found new leaders in the party, but they were not new in politics. Oliver H. Dockery of Richmond County had served in Congress, 1867-71, and as gubernatorial candidate in 1880, when he was defeated by his Democratic opponent with a majority of only 14,380.[57] Dockery was high in party politics to 1900. W. T. Faircloth of Wayne County, a successful lawyer, was an associate justice of the state Supreme Court from 1876 to 1879 and chief justice from 1895 to 1901.[58] David Furchess of Iredell County served as a judge of the superior court, 1875-79, as gubernatorial candidate in 1892, as an associate justice of the State Supreme Court, 1895-1901, and became chief justice in 1901.[59] Daniel L. Russell of New Hanover County was a member of the Constitutional Convention of 1875 and also of the General Assembly of 1876.[60] Russell later became the first and only Republican governor in the state's history since 1876. Jeter C. Pritchard, of Madison County, was the leading Republican in the western part of the state and had performed well in keeping the party organization alive while it was out of power. Pritchard, later a United States senator, was one of the realists of the 1890's who saw the rise of a third party in the state as advantageous to his party.[61] Robert M. Douglas, of Rockingham County, who was appointed a colonel in the State Militia in 1868,[62] had become associate justice of the state Supreme Court in 1896. Tyre York, of Wilkes County, congressman from 1883 to 1884, was the gubernatorial candidate in 1884 and lost to his Democratic opponent by a bare 9,320 votes.[63] His political ambitions had waned by 1890. J. H. Loge Harris, of Wake County, lawyer, was instrumental in the 1890's in holding the Fusion forces together. His political opponents styled him as a clever politician.[64]

There were prominent Negro party leaders. James H. Harris, of Wake County, educated in Ohio, who had figured conspicuously in Reconstruction politics and in the 1870's, along with J. E. O'Hara, of Halifax County, had suffered political eclipse by 1890.[65] Younger and more vigorous Negro leaders appeared. Henry P. Cheatham, of Vance County, served as United States congressman from the Second District from 1889 to 1893 and contested

the election of 1892 for the same honor and lost.[66] Cheatham was not of weak
caliber, and his political opponents measured him as a man of good graces
and intellectual stature.[67] James Hunter Young, of Wake County, was easily
the outstanding Negro in state influence; while George H. White, of
Edgecombe County, stood second. Thomas O. Fuller, of Warren County,
kept the party together in Vance and Warren counties. John C. Dancy, of
New Hanover County, by virtue of federal patronage, wielded immense
influence in his county as collector of customs at the port of Wilmington.
Alex Manly, also of New Hanover County, used his pen in behalf of the
Negro members of his party through his paper, *The Wilmington Record*.

The Republican party on the eve of the 1894 election was headed by native
white North Carolinians. The critics of the Republican regime could point
to only two leftovers of the Reconstruction Republicans: Major Hiram L.
Grant, postmaster at Goldsboro and recognized party leader in eastern North
Carolina; and G. Z. French, federal officeholder, of Wilmington. The quality
of Republican leadership was attested by one state historian, who rarely sees
anything good in the Republican party's activities in the entire South, when
he said that "the Republican party in North Carolina, however, differed
from the organization in other Southern States in that it had always a larger
number of able and respectable members."[68] The party, in and out of power,
championed local self-government and a free and untrammeled election law.

The Populist Party

The third party movement which came to North Carolina had its origin
among the vast number of wheat and corn farmers of the Western and
Middle-Western states. There was a growing feeling among these farmers in
the 1880's that the national government favored the industrial East at the
expense of the agrarian West. The farmers began to organize. They established Granges, Farmers' Alliances, and Farmers' Clubs which were symp-
tomatic of agrarian discontent. That it was essentially a farmer's movement,
evolved from the various farmers' organizations, has been attested by several
writers.[69] No one could have prophesied in the 1870's and 1880's that the
farmers' picnics, excursions, and social gatherings would have crystallized
into a national political party. Yet the outcome was natural. It is very difficult to discuss grievances, whether they be real or apparent, without suggesting "what ought to be done."

The Western farmers saw products selling below production costs; the
lack of cash money as an artificial barrier to consumption; railroads receiving more in rates than the growers received in profit; monopolies operating
to increase prices; the practice of stock watering which resulted in inflated
railroad securities; railroads giving rebates to favored customers and none
to individual farmers who shipped; preferential treatment by the national

government to big business through land grants, protective tariffs, and absence of regulation of these businesses; some state and local governments extending tax exemption and low valuation to railroads; state debts incurring from helping railroads while the farmers had to pay higher taxes to the state; an inadequate system of credit; and withal the profits of the middlemen steadily rising.[70] Thus was born in the United States a movement which began as a social group, developed into a political party, and placed its first presidential candidate in the field in 1892. Whether the farmers' grievances were real or imaginary or whether the farmers failed to understand the intricacies of a highly developed economic order which involved production, distribution, and consumption, it is sufficient to say that they considered themselves the victims of real grievances, and their subsequent actions were in accordance with the state of their feelings.

The farming South shared the sad plight of the West in the general agricultural depressions of the 1880's and 1890's. The Southern farmers' grievances differed in degree but not in kind. They saw the Southern railroads levying freights and fares at pleasure; excessive railroad influence in state legislatures; free passes handed out to legislators; trusts selling to farmers at high prices agricultural machinery, fertilizer, cotton bagging, plows, materials for barns and fences, and clothing; the protective tariff forcing them to pay higher prices for purchases; lack of cash; crop-liens and mortgages.[71] Hallie Farmer contends that the resentment of the Southern farmer was directed against three groups—the middleman, whose debtor he was; the government, in which he had too little voice; and the political party, which placed the interests of other groups above his.[72] Southern farmers heaped condemnations upon the heads of the merchants and their crop-lien procedure. The crop-lein procedure involved a commercial contract under which both merchants and farmers formed a joint partnership to do business. The merchants, however, were organized as well as informed concerning business procedures, whereas the farmers were not.[73] The merchants were taking the risk; hence, they exacted the lien. Crop failure and fluctuation of market price often cost the farmer his land and thereby the merchant became the landowner and a competitor with his debtor.

The North Carolina farmers' grievances were in part the grievances of the Western farmers but more those of the Southern farmers. There were, however, unique factors in this state not apparent in other Southern states. The Civil War and Reconstruction left this agricultural state with smaller farm units,[74] little capital, very little credit, and the problem of labor.[75] In 1887, roughly 75 per cent of the total population was engaged in farming.[76] One-third of the farms were operated by tenants.[77] Cotton and tobacco shaped the life and fortune of the farmer, and there was always a ready market for cotton. This crop became the stipulated one in the crop-lien procedure.

The North Carolina farmers saw the price of cotton go lower and lower during the depression which followed the panic of 1893, so much so that "on the bulk of the crop of 1894 and 1895 the farmer realized not more than five cents, while much was sold below this price, which was less than the average cost of production. Low prices for tobacco, corn, and wheat accompanied the ruinous price of cotton."[78] There stood out clearly in the North Carolina farmer's mind the conviction that the prices of the things he sold were too low and that the prices of the things he bought were too high.

The farmers of the state suffered from high rates of interest.[79] The Democratic legislatures had refused to accord them a uniform legal rate of interest. Too, Southern banks were not in a position to carry the entire agrarian credit of the South.[80] The farmer was left to merchant and banker with no regulation on the lenders.

The farmers' fight against the Southern, Seaboard, and Atlantic Coast Line railroads in North Carolina was long and heoric. There was a bitter fight in the 1880's to end the giving of passes to legislators and public officials, to eliminate tax exemptions to railroads, to reduce rates, to create a railroad commission, and to overthrow railroad control of the Democratic party.[81] The farmers sent their leaders to the legislature to see them constantly outvoted by the railroad interests on measures calculated to remedy the farmers' plight. It was not until 1891 that a railroad commission was established, and even then it was disappointing to the people of the state.

Another signal grievance of the North Carolina farmers was that in the 1880's they were faced by competitors in the rise of textile mills. Urban life, and the certainty of the Saturday pay envelope lured their children, and sometimes themselves, from the farms. The farmer saw the little mill double and treble in size; the ease with which capital came in increasing amounts to start a mill; Northern interests buy, build, and combine mills to form big businesses; and the selling and buying of shares on the exchange.[82] So anxious were many towns to have mills that civic leaders agitated for the organization of small corporations. The Reverend Mr. F. J. Murdock of Salisbury is reputed to have said, "what Salisbury needs most, next to the grace of God, is a cotton mill."[83] While the number of mills constantly increased, the tendency in the state was toward smaller establishments employing a greater number of operatives and with a vastly increased product.[84]

Rising prosperous industry was the beneficiary of the dominant Democratic party and of local state government. Boundary lines were often changed to throw a proposed establishment outside the town limits thereby letting the mill escape the payment of town taxes until it was well established, and often for a considerable period thereafter.[85] Although the North Carolina law required that all property be assessed at its true value, the actual assessment of mills and other real property was less than the true value. It has been stated that the average net profits for the mills from 1880 to 1900 were about 15 per cent and that instances of 40 to 60 per cent dividends were not unknown.[86] There were textile mills located in fifty-four of the ninety-seven counties of the state.[87] The industrialization of North Carolina in the 1880's and 1890's held the farmer in its grip. He could not understand these economic forces beyond his control. Thompson's appraisal is that "granted that many ills were due to the ignorance, inertia or stupidity of the farmers themselves, intolerable grievances did exist."[88]

The owners of the textile mills looked prosperous. While the Western farmers of the United States were far removed from the Eastern capitalists, the North Carolina farmer rubbed shoulders with the millowners weekly, and his visits to town brought before his very eyes how much greater the rewards of manufacture were than those of agriculture.[89] The farmers also suffered a decline in social prestige because they were no longer the dominant class. Social prestige depended upon "ownership of a merchandising house, city real estate, stock in a manufacturing enterprise or bank, or even upon a managerial or technological position in one of these establishments. . . . The very mechanics or factory operatives, descendants for the most part of the despised poor whites, yielded nothing of social prestige to the farmer."[90]

These grievances caused the farmers to organize themselves in this state. The first Grange was established in 1873, and by January, 1875, there were 477 Granges in the state with a membership of 10,000. During the next fifteen years other groups appeared with various names. While some were short lived and some lasted, none was powerful enough to mold public opinion. What the farmer lacked during these years was intelligent leadership and state-wide organization.[91]

The man who gave his genius of organization to the farm groups in this state was Leonidas Lafayette Polk. He became a member of the Pond Mill Grange, No. 471, in 1875, later its master, and rapidly rose to positions of Grange leadership in the county, district, and state.[92] It was chiefly through Polk's efforts and the influence of the Grange that there was established the state Department of Agriculture in 1877. Polk, at the age of forty, was North Carolina's first Commissioner of Agriculture and served from 1877 to 1880. Under his commission, the quality of commercial fertilizers was improved, preparation of home fertilizers stimulated, hatcheries were established, fish culture received attention, artificial propagation was begun, crop bulletins issued, and the cause of the farmers championed.[93]

Simultaneously with the growth of the Grange movement in the state were other farm groups. The Farmers' Alliance was organized in 1887 and by the next year had 1,018 subordinate alliances and a membership of 42,000 scattered over fifty-two counties.[94] Polk called two mass conventions in

Raleigh in 1887 for the chief purpose of discussing the farmers' plight and devising means of influencing legislation. At the second meeting, irrespective of the names of the individual groups, it was decided that the farmers assembled should be organized under the name the North Carolina Farmers' Association.[95] Within two years, Polk's leadership had welded the majority of the farm groups together, and they began operation in 1889 united under a liberal charter as the Farmers' State Alliance of North Carolina.[96] Membership in the Alliance was opened to "white persons only, with the exception of Cherokee Indians in Clay, Graham, Haywood, Jackson, Macon and Swain Counties if they are of pure Indian blood and not less than half white."[97] Croatan Indians were in the same category. Negroes were not permitted under any circumstances.

There has been much discussion as to whether the Alliance in this state had political motives. Its constitution prohibited religious and political discussions. Professor Hamilton holds that, inasmuch as their aims were all in the direction of correcting outstanding abuses, their entrance into politics was inevitable.[98] The Alliance was interested in politics and what political parties were doing, but the inevitability of entrance into politics does not mean that the farmers intended to form a separate political party. In reality, "the Alliance wanted to work through both of the old parties, but naturally expected more from the Democrats since they were in power in the State."[99] The Alliance demands were: recognition of the subtreasury scheme by the state and national legislatures, creation of a state railroad commission, the ending of railroad influence in politics, and a uniform rate of interest.[100] So popular were these demands that the state legislature chosen in 1890 found a substantial number of farmers present and an Alliance leader as speaker of the House of Representatives. So popular were the Alliance demands that the Democratic party incorporated them in essence in its platforms of 1888 and 1890. In reality, what provoked the Alliance to send farmers to the 1891 legislature was the fact that the Democratic platform of 1888 endorsed an effective railroad commission and the legislature of 1888 defeated the proposal. The Alliance soon learned that there was a vast gap between campaign pledges and legislative fulfillment, for the Democratic party did nothing about their demands.

It was Harry Skinner, a North Carolinian, who captured the imagination of the farmers nationally through his subtreasury idea (later perfected by Charles Macune of Texas). The plan was to induce the national government to build a great system of warehouses in which the farmers could store such products as cotton and tobacco as security on which to borrow from the government, at low rates of interest, 80 per cent of the market value of these products in legal tender notes.[101] The North Carolinia Alliance had asked Senator Vance to present the plan on the floor of the United States Senate.

Vance presented the plan but did not support it; hence, the Alliance men felt that the Democrats had conspired against them.[102] It is held that by 1890 the North Carolina Alliance wanted to enter politics as a separate group, but again its devotion to the "white man's party" had been made acute by the threat of the Force Bill and such precluded all possibility of separate political action in that year.[103] The above thesis is highly debatable for 1890, but there is no doubt that by 1892, "this organization had abandoned all hope of reform through either of the old parties, and the radical wing of the Alliance was demanding separate political action."[104] The year of 1892 marked a split in the Alliance. The more conservative wing—loyal to the Democratic party and fearful of the Negroes and the Republicans—remained with the Democratic party. The radical wing formed the Populist party in North Carolina (a counterpart of the national People's party organized by the Western farmers). It was against the Democratic party that the Alliance in North Carolina made its political revolt.[105] The farmers believed that state laws could remedy some of their ills, but as long as lawyers, corporation interests, banking influence, and merchants controlled the state, no help was forthcoming.

Leonidas L. Polk, the signal leader of the agrarian movement, kept the North Carolina farmers advised through his publication, the *Progressive Farmer*. He favored the formation of a third party in the state.[106] This founder of the North Carolina Populist party died in 1892, and his mantle of leadership fell upon Marion Butler, of Sampson County. Butler became president of the Farmers' Alliance in this state and chairman of the Populist National Committee. His political activities covered the period 1891-1900, including a term as state Senator in 1891 and as United States senator in 1895. His paper, *The Caucasian,* extolled the Populists' views. Thus "a country editor, sprung from the plain people and reared on a farm, at 33 this young man finds himself in control of the party machinery of a political organization larger in numbers than that which elected Lincoln for the first time."[107] Harry Skinner, of Pitt County, who had represented his county as a Democrat in the state legislature in 1891, and whose subtreasury idea had added to his stature in the Alliance, stood staunchly as a member of the new party in 1892. In this position, he was supported by many other former Democrats, including J. L. Ramsey, of Wake County, who became editor of the *Progressive Farmer* in 1892; Charles H. Mebane, of Catawba County, a public school official; Dr. Cyrus Thompson, of Onslow County, an eloquent orator and scholar; Hal Ayer, of Wake County, a newspaper man; and William H. Worth, of Guilford County, who later became state auditor. There was at least one notable Republican who joined the party and helped to spread its influence, namely, W. A. Guthrie, a lawyer from Durham County. While the leadership of the party had had scant political experience, the men at the helm were by no means "wool hat boys." There is no doubt that there were a number who joined the party only to secure place and preferment for themselves, but "the rank and file of the Third Party men were enlisted like crusaders to battle for a cause, regardless of the difficulties that beset their way."[108]

As the election of 1892 approached, it was clear that the third party men were determined to enter the race. The Populist party held its first state convention on August 16 in Raleigh. The party put full state and local tickets in the field, chose electors-at-large, pledged support to the national ticket, and endorsed a platform of free coinage of silver, railroad regulation, graduated income tax, uniform rate of interest, and local self-government.[109] Marion Butler and Harry Skinner were the guiding lights. Skinner was the first choice for the gubernatorial candidacy; but he informed the convention that, should it appear that "white supremacy" was threatened, he would withdraw.[110] Skinner was replaced by W. P. Exum, of Wayne County.

The Democrats met in convention in Raleigh August 17, 1892. They feared the growing strength of Populism and hastened to reduce the potency of the party by selecting Elias Carr, of Edgecombe County, as their standard-bearer. Carr was former president of the state Alliance, still active in the work, but opposed to the third party movement.[111] The Democrats pledged allegiance to the national ticket and to Cleveland, reminded voters of the Force Bill, prophesied the return of Reconstruction should the Republican party and the Negro return to power, and made no serious effort to placate the Populists.

The Republicans met in Raleigh and selected D. M. Furchess, of Iredell County, as gubernatorial candidate. They pledged to support the national ticket, put up state and local tickets, and endorsed a state platform calling for fair election laws and local self-government.[112] The Republican leaders felt that the party would draw the greater part of the Negro vote and even secure a goodly number of the farmers from the Colored Alliance.[113]

The election of 1892 was like a political barometer in several ways. It revealed that in spite of the Democratic bait to restore the disaffected farm element to the fold, 47,840 went their independent way in 1892.[114] The Republicans garnered 94,684, and the Democrats rode into victory with a total of 135,519.[115] The Populist vote comprised approximately 18 per cent of the total votes cast.

An analysis of the Populist returns showed that Chatham, Nash, and Sampson counties registered victories for the new party. The Populist party garnered 49 per cent of the total vote of Brunswick and Hyde, 40 per cent in Wake, and 30 per cent in Cumberland and Franklin. The vote of 47,840 may be an inaccurate measure of true Populist strength because of three distinct reasons: first, Colonel Polk, the strong man of the party, died in

1892 previous to the election; second, General J. B. Weaver, the national party's presidential candidate in 1892, was unpopular in North Carolina because of his hostile attitude toward the South after the Civil War; and third, the fear that "white supremacy" might be threatened caused some either to refrain from voting or to support the Democratic ticket. It was very evident that had the Populists fused with the Republicans in 1892 there would have been anti-Democratic victories in twenty-six counties,[116] and a Populist-Republican victory in the state.[117]

The Populists sent to the legislature fourteen members: three to the Senate; eleven to the House of Representatives.[118] The fight of 1892 had been to hold in the Democratic party the allegiance of the bulk of the farmers.[119] The Populists claimed that their votes had not been counted fully by the Democratic election officials. The Republicans of the state had been using the charge of Democratic fraud as one of their campaign issues for years. Nor was this charge without foundation as a prominent Democratic newspaper confessed that "in a few negro counties it may be that the negro vote has sometimes been partially suppressed, but this has never occurred in more than eight or ten counties in the State."[120]

The charge was made repeatedly that the Republican National Committee assisted materially in financing the third party campaign in North Carolina.[121] Professor Hamilton feels that the Republicans aided and abetted the Populist movement in a gleeful sort of way, and that, with a third party in the field, they saw a possibility of success.[122] Local Republicans would sacrifice much to oust the Democrats from control of the state, and the national leaders were not unwilling to help the Populists against the Democrats in the South in order to offset the inroads which the new party was sure to make upon Republican majorities in the Northwest.[123] But Republican campaign literature made no bid for Populist support in 1892.

The Democratic legislature of 1893 gave a mortal blow to whatever sympathy the Populists may have had for the old party by placing so many limitations on the Alliance's charter that its effectiveness was hampered.[124] By 1894, the gap between the Populists and the Democrats seemed irreparable. The Populists faced the choices of remaining a separate party with no assurance of political victory, which policy would at the same time so weaken the Democratic vote that the Republicans might return to power; of returning to the Democratic fold despite the Democrats' past offenses; or of fusing with the Republican party and facing squarely the resurrected ghost of Negro office-holding.

By 1894, the talk of Fusion was real in North Carolina and "the lack of a real opposition party since Reconstruction had given the Democrats a false sense of security. Frequent reminders of the turbulent era of carpetbaggers and scalawags had for years kept the mass of white men voting

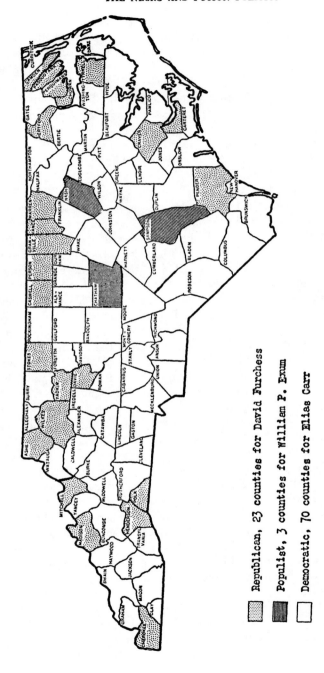

GUBERNATORIAL ELECTION, 1892
(*North Carolina Manual*, 1913, 1005-6)

Republican, 23 counties for David Furchess

Populist, 3 counties for William P. Exum

Democratic, 70 counties for Elias Carr

solidly Democratic."[125] But to many white farmers, by 1894, the familiar cry of defending the state against Negro rule was becoming an outworn shibboleth.

NOTES TO CHAPTER TWO

1. J. G. deR. Hamilton, "Reconstruction in North Carolina," *Columbia University Studies in History, Economics, and Political Law,* LVIII, No. 141 (1914), 631-67.

2. *Ibid.,* 631.

3. *Ibid.,* 642.

4. *Constitution of the State of North Carolina as amended by the Constitutional Convention of 1875,* Article VI, Sections 1, 2; *Public Laws and Resolutions of the State of North Carolina Passed By the General Assembly at its Session 1876-77,* 25-26.

5. *Constitution of the State of North Carolina as amended by the Constitutional Convention of 1875,* Article VII, Section 14, 29.

6. Paul L. Haworth, *The Hayes-Tilden Disputed Presidential Election of 1876,* 243-44.

7. *Ibid.,* 269-70.

8. *Ibid.,* 304.

9. Hamilton, "Reconstruction in North Carolina," 663.

10. Daniels, *Editor in Politics,* 235.

11. John F. Crowell, "A Program of Progress: An Open Letter to the General Assembly of North Carolina of 1891," *Trinity College Publication No. 3,* 3-35.

12. Phillip J. Weaver, The Gubernatorial Election of 1896 (Unpublished M.A. thesis, University of North Carolina, 1937), 64.

13. *Ibid.,* 10.

14. *State Democratic Executive Committee to the People of North Carolina,* October 6, 1892.

15. *United States Statutes at Large,* XXIV, 379.

16. *Ibid.,* XXVI, 209.

17. *Congressional Record,* Fifty-first Congress, Second Session, XXI, Part 7, 6114, 6286.

18. Archibald Henderson, *North Carolina, The Old North State and The New,* II, 388.

19. *Public and Private Laws and Resolutions,* 1891, 653.

20. *North Carolina Manual,* 1913, 1019-20.

21. Daniel Whitener, "North Carolina Prohibition Election of 1881 and its Aftermath," *The North Carolina Historical Review,* XI, No. 2 (1934), 71-93.

22. *Ibid.,* 91.

23. Hamilton, "Reconstruction in North Carolina," 663.

24. Florence E. Smith, The Populist Movement and Its Influence in North Carolina (Unpublished Ph.D. dissertation, University of Chicago, 1929), 29.

25. Weaver, *op. cit.,* 8.

26. Henderson, *op. cit.,* II, 372.

27. Hamilton, "Reconstruction in North Carolina," 253.

28. *Ibid.,* 665.

29. *The Outlook,* LXV, No. 15 (1900), 841.

30. Ashe, Cherokee, Davidson, Henderson, Madison, Mitchell, Montgomery, Polk, Wilkes, and Yadkin.

31. Caswell, Chowan, Craven, Edgecombe, Granville, Greene, Halifax, Hertford,

New Hanover, Northampton, Pasquotank, Pender, Perquimans, Vance, Warren, and Washington.

32. See map, 16.

33. Citations showing counties (which amassed between 40 and 49 per cent Republican vote from 1876 through 1896) which voted Republican at intervals. (Unless otherwise noted, these counties voted Republican the years indicated.)

Beaufort—1880, 1896
Bertie—1876, 1880, 1884, 1896
Bladen—1880, 1884
Brunswick—1876, 1880, 1884, 1896
Buncombe—1896
Camden—1888, 1892, 1896
Chatham—(Populist) 1892, 1896
Cumberland—1896
Dare—1884, 1892, 1896
Davie—1888, 1892, 1896
Forsyth—1876, 1880, 1888, 1896
Graham—1896
Harnett—1888
Jones—1876, 1880, 1884, 1896

Lenoir—1876, 1880
Moore—1896
Pamlico—1896
Person—1892, 1896
Randolph—1888, 1896
Richmond—1876, 1880, 1896
Robeson—1896
Rutherford—1880
Stokes—1892, 1896
Surry—1884, 1896
Transylvania—1888, 1896
Tyrrell—1892, 1896
Wake—1876, 1880, 1888, 1896
Watauga—1888, 1896

34. Hamilton, "Reconstruction in North Carolina," 666.

35. United States Bureau of Census, *Negro Population in the United States 1790-1915*, 774-75. Negro ratio in population:

Cherokee, 2.7
Ashe, 3.8
Madison, 4.0
Mitchell, 4.3
Wilkes, 9.0

Yadkin, 9.9
Henderson, 10.9
Davidson, 16.3
Polk, 18.5
Montgomery, 20.1

36. See map, 17.

37. Caswell, Chowan, Craven, Edgecombe, Granville, Halifax, Hertford, New Hanover, Northampton, Pasquotank, Pender, Warren, Washington, and Vance. Vance had its first election in 1884.

38. The election of 1892 found Edgecombe, Halifax, New Hanover, Northampton, and Washington in the Democratic column. A third party entered the election of 1892, and the combined votes of the Republican party and the third party showed an anti-Democratic majority.

39. Bertie and Richmond.

40. Greene, Jones, and Perquimans. Jones went Democratic in 1892; yet, anti-Democratic forces outnumbered the Democrats.

41. Total gubernatorial vote, 1876-1900, showing comparative vote of the parties, *North Carolina Manual*, 1913, 1001-6.

Year	Democrat	Republican	Populist
1876	118,258	104,330	......
1880	121,832	115,589	......
1884	143,249	122,914	......
1888	148,406	134,026	......
1892	135,519	94,684	47,840
1896	145,266	153,787	31,143
1900	186,650	126,296	......

42. *Congressional Record*, Fifty-Sixth Congress, First Session, XXXIII, Part 2, 1034.

43. *Charlotte Observer*, October 18, 1896.

44. *News and Observer*, October 30, 1898.

45. *Democratic Handbook*, 1898, 37.

46. Daniels, *Editor in Politics*, 288-89, 295; also Fred Rippy (ed.), *Furnifold Simmons, Statesman of the New South; Memoirs and Addresses*, 57.

47. *United States Department of Commerce, Bureau of Census, Eleventh Census*, I (1890), 693.

48. Appendix, 225-27.

49. *North Carolina Manual*, 1913, 1004.

50. *Democratic Handbook*, 1898, 37.

51. United States Bureau of Census, *Negro Population in the United States 1790-1915*, 774.

52. Hamilton, "Reconstruction in North Carolina," 244.

53. *North Carolina Manual*, 1913, 419.

54. *Ibid.*, 447.

55. *Ibid.*

56. Hamilton, "Reconstruction in North Carolina," 649-54.

57. *North Carolina Manual*, 1913, 1004.

58. *Ibid.*, 446-47.

59. *Ibid.*, 446, 450, 1005.

60. *Public Laws*, 1876-1877, xiv.

61. Daniels, *Editor in Politics*, 133.

62. Hamilton, "Reconstruction in North Carolina," 346.

63. *North Carolina Manual*, 1913, 942, 1004.

64. Daniels, *Editor in Politics*, 227-29.

65. Hamilton, "Reconstruction in North Carolina," 648; *North Carolina Manual*, 1913, 942-43.

66. United States Congress, *Biographical Directory of the American Congress, 1774-1927*, 805.

67. Daniels, *Tar Heel Editor*, 176.

68. Hamilton, "Reconstruction in North Carolina," 665.

69. Solon J. Buck, *The Agrarian Crusade, The Granger Movement;* F. E. Haynes, *Third Party Movements in the United States;* J. D. Hicks, *The Populist Revolt, A History of the Farmers' Alliance and the People's Party.*

70. Hicks, *op. cit.*, 54-95.

71. *Ibid.*

72. Hallie Farmer, "The Economic Background of Southern Populism," *The South Atlantic Quarterly*, XXIX, No. 1 (January, 1930), 89.

73. Charles H. Otken, *The Ills of the South*, 22-24.

74. John Spencer Bassett, "Slavery in the State of North Carolina," *Johns Hopkins University Studies in Historical and Political Science*, XVII, 71-82; also Rosser Taylor, "Slaveholding in North Carolina: An Economic View," *The James Sprunt Historical Publications*, XVIII, Nos. 1-2 (1926), 81-96.

75. Florence E. Smith, The Populist Movement and Its Influence in North Carolina (Unpublished Ph.D. dissertation), 37.

76. *Report of the Bureau of Labor Statistics*, 1887, 76.

77. *Ibid.*, 1889, 87.

78. Holland Thompson, *From Cotton Field to Cotton Mill: A Study of the Industrial Transition in North Carolina*, 69.

79. *Progressive Farmer*, August 18, 1890.

80. Farmer, *op. cit.*, 93.

81. Daniels, *Tar Heel Editor*, 388-416.

82. Holland Thompson, "The Southern Textile Situation," *South Atlantic Quarterly*, XXIX, No. 2 (April, 1930), 117.

83. Broadus Mitchell, "The Rise of Cotton Mills in the South," *Johns Hopkins University Studies in Historical and Political Science*, XXXIX, No. 2, 135; cited from *North Carolina Herald*, November 9, 1887.

84. Henderson, *op. cit.*, II, 379.

85. Thompson, *From Cotton Field to Cotton Mill: A Study of the Industrial Transition in North Carolina*, 86.

86. *Ibid.*, 87-89.

87. *Report of the Bureau of Labor Statistics*, 1900, 117.

88. Thompson, "The Southern Textile Situation," *South Atlantic Quarterly*, XXIX, No. 2 (April, 1930), 117.

89. Samuel A. Ashe, *History of North Carolina*, II, 1187.

90. Benjamin B. Kendrick, "Agrarian Discontent in the South, 1880-1900," *American Historical Review* (1920), 269.

91. Delap, "The Populist Party in North Carolina," *Trinity College Historical Papers*, XXIV (1922), 40-42.

92. Stuart Noblin, "Leonidas Lafayette Polk," *North Carolina Historical Review*, XX, No. 2 (1943), 116.

93. *Ibid.*, No. 3, 197-218.

94. Delap, *op. cit.*, 43.

95. *Progressive Farmer*, February 6, 1877.

96. *Private Laws*, 1889, Chap. 105, 692-95.

97. *Constitution of the Farmers' State Alliance of North Carolina*, 1889, Article 3, 14-15, Edwards and Broughton Printers, Raleigh, 1890, *Pamphlets 1890-95*, Duke University Library.

98. J. G. deR. Hamilton, *History of North Carolina Since 1860 (History of North Carolina*, Vol. III), 226, 234.

99. Weaver, *op. cit.*, 7.

100. J. D. Hicks, "Farmers' Alliance in North Carolina," *North Carolina Historical Review*, II (1925), 177-83.

101. *Progressive Farmer*, April 29, May 13, December 2, 1890.

102. *Ibid.*, July 8, 1890.

103. Hicks, "Farmers' Alliance in North Carolina," 181.

104. Hugh T. Lefler (ed.), *North Carolina History Told by Contemporaries*, 375.

105. Weaver, *op. cit.*, 10.

106. *Progressive Farmer*, March 22, April 5, 1892.

107. Carl Snyder, "Marion Butler," *Review of Reviews*, XIV, 429.

108. Hicks, "Farmers' Alliance in North Carolina," 181.

109. *Progressive Farmer*, August 28, 1892.

110. Hicks, "Farmers' Alliance in North Carolina," 183.

111. Daniels, *Tar Heel Editor*, 489-505.

112. *Republican Handbook*, 1892, 44.

113. *Charlotte Observer*, September 1, 14, 1892.

114. *North Carolina Manual*, 1913, 1006.

115. See map, 28, for individual counties.

116. Alexander, Bladen, Brunswick, Cabarrus, Cumberland, Duplin, Durham,

Franklin, Gates, Hyde, Jones, Lincoln, Montgomery, Moore, Northampton, Orange, Pamlico, Pitt, Randolph, Rutherford, Swain, Tyrrell, Wake, Washington, Watauga, and Wayne.—*North Carolina Manual,* 1913, 1005-6. See map, 28.

117. See Appendix, 232.

118. *House Journal,* 1893, 3-5; *Senate Journal,* 1893, 5-6; and Turner's *Almanac,* 1894, 37-39.

119. Daniels, *Tar Heel Editor,* 489-505.

120. *News and Observer,* August 18, 1894.

121. *Greensboro Patriot,* July 20, August 3, 1892.

122. Hamilton, *History of North Carolina Since 1860,* 235.

123. Hicks, "Farmers' Alliance in North Carolina," 182.

124. *Public Laws,* 1893, Chap. 137, 193-95.

125. William A. Mabry, "The Negro in North Carolina Politics Since Reconstruction," *Historical Papers of Trinity College Historical Society,* Series XXIII (1940), 32.

CHAPTER THREE

TRIUMPH OF FUSION, 1894-1895

THE YEAR 1894 opened with the political air tense irrespective of the fact that it was not a gubernatorial election year. Marion Butler, made chairman of the State Populist Executive Committee in 1893, addressed a letter to the voters of North Carolina early in January condemning President Cleveland for the panic of 1893 and damning his party's activities in the state.[1] The Populist party ignored the Democratic assertion that Republican-Populist fusion would be a certainty in 1894. The Populists' evasion on the issue of fusion was because, perhaps, of two reasons: first, there had been no decision on fusion in early 1894; and, second, evasion appeared to be sound strategy designed to win more Democrats to the Populist cause—Democrats who were victims of the agrarian depression, who believed in Populism, and who detested the Republican party's principles and constituency. All three parties prepared, to some degree, for the election of 1894; and midsummer found the political kettle brewing.

The Populist convention was scheduled for August 1. On the eve of the convention, July 30, certain leaders of the Populist and Republican parties held a secret meeting in Raleigh. The following Republicans, Dr. J. J. Mott, V. S. Lusk, G. Roberts of the Asheville *Register*, Hiram L. Grant, Claude M. Bernard, R. S. McCall, A. R. Middleton (Negro), and Richmond Pearson, conferred with the following Populists, Marion Butler, Harry Skinner, and W. W. Kitchin.[2] There must have been some talk or plan of fusion because such a preconvention meeting of the leading elements of both parties could have had nothing else for its aim. The Democrats thought as much when the chief press stated in reference to the secret meeting "to fuse or not to fuse—that is the question. . . . The Populists are, we surmise, ready to fuse for they find their party dwindling and without the hope of any stand up fight."[3]

The Populist convention met first, August 1, 1894, in Raleigh. A religious and patriotic fervor dominated the meeting. Populist orators compared the tyranny of the Bourborn Democratic machine in the state with the tyranny of England over the early American colonies. Harry Skinner was so overwhelmed with the fervor of the occasion that he hinted at the divinity and historic purpose in the Populist party's mission. James Lloyd, temporary chairman, challenged the group with the reminder that "there are here today men who have imbibed the same spirit of the men of 1776, and are determined that by the ballot, though not by the bullet, we would achieve independence again from England, by destroying her influence in this country."[4] W. A. Guthrie explained why he had changed from a Republican to a Populist. He contended that he had followed the former party until the best element in it was dead, adding that "now we propose to have fair election laws in North Carolina if we have to fight for them. The interests of the black man and the white man are identical."[5] The emotional background of the meeting was so great that little was done on the first day except to hear testimonials on "why I am a Populist" and to select Marion Butler as permanent chairman.

The officers to be chosen in 1894 were a state treasurer, chief justice of the Supreme Court, and three associate justices. The Populist-endorsed slate for the Supreme Court included W. T. Faircloth (Republican) as chief justice; Walter Clark (Democrat), D. M. Furchess (Republican), W. Montgomery (Populist), and H. G. Conner (Democrat) as associate justices. The slate, including membership from all three parties, evidenced the "party's desire to lift the judicial ermine above the contaminating influence of partisan politics,"[6] as well as the results of the secret meeting with the Republicans on July 30. The Populist platform insisted that, whenever the state and national platforms came into conflict, Populist representatives be bound by the state platform. It pledged itself to operate the public schools of the state for four months in every year for both races, recommended a state reformatory for youthful criminals, promised a uniform rate of interest, and condemned the Democratic party for not passing anti-monopolistic measures. The convention closed its platform with two ringing denunciations: one condemned the Democratic election procedures, insisting that many Populists' votes in 1892 had been destroyed and Democratic ballots substituted; and the other condemned the Democratic system of county government. The convention adjourned with the promises that it stood "four square" for fairness in election law, local self-government, education, and a nonpartisan Supreme Court.[7]

The Democratic convention met August 8. The Democrats were confused by the fact that the Populists had gone their independent way and had amassed a substantial vote in 1892 which might be larger should there be fusion between the Populists and the Republicans in 1894. Democratic fusion with the Populists was impossible, although sentiment for such may have been present, because the Democratic leaders had ridiculed, jeered, chided, and shown extreme hostility to the Populists. Furnifold M. Simmons, state chairman of the Executive Committee, boldly opened the convention with a glorification of the party's accomplishments and admonished his party to fear nothing as he had just read the news from the state of Alabama in the morning papers where fusion had been tried and the result was a 40,000 Democratic majority.[8] Much time was spent trying to show that the hard times were not the fault of the Democratic Cleveland but of the Republican Harrison before him. The convention renominated the incumbents in office: Samuel McD. Tate, state treasurer; James E. Shepherd, chief justice; Walter Clark, James MacRae, and Alphonso C. Avery, associate justices. The democratic platform championed national policies such as the free coinage of silver and reduction of the tariff. Its state planks were but the expressed endorsement of past Democratic rule. The platform did not endorse a single progressive state measure. It was evident that the party had turned its back on reform. The convention adjourned with the feeling that the party's past was sufficient to stand on.

The Republicans met last, August 30, in Raleigh. All the Republican leaders, who had secretly met with the Populist leaders on July 30, were present. Negro leaders James Young, E. A. Johnson, George H. White, John C. Dancy, Isaac Smith, and James E. Shepard were present to assist either as generals to guide the plans of the meeting or as lieutenants to carry out the plans decided upon. The suggestion of fusion with the Populists arose and Chairman J. B. Eaves held that the independent vote of the Republicans in 1892 was a sufficient political barometer to indicate that 1894 might be a banner year for the party regardless of cooperation. Jeter Pritchard and Oliver H. Dockery favored some form of cooperation. The question was not settled.

The convention, however, with an eye toward fusion, endorsed the Populists' candidate, W. H. Worth, as state treasurer, and the Populists' slate for the Supreme Court (H. G. Conner, Democrat, refused to let his name remain on the Populists' judicial ticket; and the Republicans then endorsed the Populists' next choice, Alphonso C. Avery). The Republicans framed a state platform pledging a repeal of the present Democratic system of county government to be accompanied by a restoration of local self-government, and a fair election law guaranteeing to every qualified voter the privilege of casting one ballot and having that ballot count as cast.[9] While there was no official endorsement of fusion, two things were obvious. First, the Populists and Republicans had endorsed the same slate of state officials; and, second, the Populist and Republican platforms called for a fair election law and restoration of local self-government. The state executive committees of both parties met in early fall and jointly endorsed a cooperative ticket. Soon joint tickets for state senators and representatives were formed in the senatorial districts and counties, respectively, for the election of the new legislature.[10] It is believed that the master draftsman of the cooperative ticket was Hiram L. Grant, of Wayne County. He is reputed to have suggested to Butler the strategy that both parties draw up one ticket for both county and state officers and apportion party representation on these tickets in accordance with the relative strength of each party.[11]

The issue of official endorsement of fusion had been a meticulous one to decide because there were elements in both parties which opposed it. There were Populists who realized that they had sentimental connections and warm personal friendships with the Democratic party and that the status of their party as a white man's party was at stake. There were those who were influenced by Colonel Polk's stand, before his death, "the more I think of it the more I am convinced, that the only true and manly course to take, is to strike out boldly on our own hook."[12] Irrespective of dissenting opinions, the die had been cast, and if the ghost of Negro rule was still faintly visible to Butler,[13] it was not so to the majority of the Populists. To them, economic and political issues and Democratic defeat seemed paramount.

The Populists launched their campaign on reform, and the Democrats counterattacked with a glorification of their past and even prophesied that the People's party had dug its grave.[14] The Democrats lost no time during the campaign in playing up the fear that the Force Bill would be revived in Congress, a step which would mean federal authority at every polling place.[15] The Democrats drew comparisons between Reconstruction rule and Democratic rule and stated that a Fusion victory in 1894 would usher in a return of the conditions which had harassed the state from 1868 to 1876.[16]

Populist-Republican fusion meant that the race question had entered upon the stage of party politics. As Negroes formed a large element in the Republican party, and, as there were sixteen "black counties" in 1894, it was quite logical that "some" Negroes were placed on county tickets. In eastern North Carolina a number of Negroes were nominated for the House of Representatives; and while some Populists opposed the Negro as an officeholder, there was some degree of unity in 1894 for the sake of holding the ticket together. A contemporary states that "men who a few years before had been the most bitter in denunciation of the Republican party and its Negro cohorts, actually joined hands and defended the nomination of Negroes for office."[17] As the election day approached, the Democrats referred to the Republicans as pie-eaters, pie-hunters, and hungry men at the pie counter ever anxious to manipulate their Negro followers to the end of office-seeking.[18] The Populists stuck to their guns, refused any public endorsement of Negro officeholders, and blasted away on the inertia of the Democratic party.

The Fusion ticket carried the election of 1894. It was almost a clean sweep, much greater than the leaders of the party had expected. The Fusion victory stunned the Democrats. The House and Senate of the General Assembly were overwhelmingly Fusionist. The Democrats retained forty-six seats in the House and eight in the Senate, whereas the Populists garnered thirty-six seats in the House and twenty-four in the Senate, and the Republicans increased to thirty-eight in the House and eighteen in the Senate.[19] The Fusionists elected their Supreme Court ticket [20] and their state treasurer.

If the Republicans got the lion's share of offices, as some think,[21] the Populists had representation where they wanted it most, in the state legislature.

A further analysis of the election of 1894 reveals that twenty-three counties returned Republican majorities, thirty-three Populist, thirty-four Democrat, four with Republican-Populist fusion, and two with Republican-Democrat fusion.[22] Six "black counties" were found in the Democratic columns,[23] and two "black counties" had fused with the Democrats.[24] It may be safely concluded that the Negro vote was not the prime factor in determining the election of 1894.

While one Democratic paper, blinded by partisan loyalty, was stunned at the Fusion victory and candidly admitted "that it was a great surprise to everyone, and no politician was able to foresee it," [25] another sensed the tempo of the spirit and conditions in the state and did not hesitate in the following language to lay its indictment on the Democratic party: "Eighty-five per cent of the voters of North Carolina are farmers. The scheme to mobilize them, and line them up before the ballot box, there to do their work and against their former trusted friends, was not so difficult after all. The farmers at first had a grievance; it was presented to the Democratic party and a remedy denied; railroads were painted as great extortioners; they were impoverishing agriculture; the banks were impoverishing the people. All mercantile concerns, except those run by the Farmers' Alliance were making great profit [a point of view held by the farmers], and some were using false weights and measures. The farmer of North Carolina was driven to a state of frenzy that would have been creditable to a French Revolutionist in the days of Danton." [26]

With political victory tucked beneath their belts, the Fusion leaders faced the task of harmonious and constructive cooperation in the General Assembly of 1895 which met on January 9. Z. V. Walser, Republican, was elected speaker of the House. The legislature was concerned in the opening days with the choice of two United States senators. The six-year term of Ransom had expired. The death of Vance in 1894 provided a short-term vacancy to be filled. This situation would test the ability of the Republicans and the Populists to stick together. Butler was the Populists' choice, and Pritchard was the Republicans' choice. Butler's preeminence as the Fusion strategist in the election of 1894 engendered enough support for him to secure the nomination for the long term. Pritchard was satisfied with the nomination for the short term on the assumption that if Fusion were maintained in 1896 he could seek a long term. The Democratic minority pitted Thomas W. Mason against Butler and Lee S. Overman against Pritchard. The contest between the Fusionist candidates and the Democratic candidates symbolized at the very opening of the legislature the type of contest to be expected during the entire legislative session of 1895, a contest of partisanship.

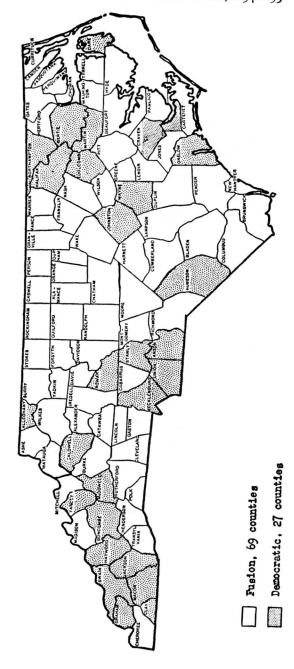

VOTE FOR CHIEF JUSTICE AND ASSOCIATE JUSTICES IN 1894 ON A FUSION TICKET
Candidates: Chief Justice, W. T. Faircloth (Republican);
Associate Justice, D. M. Furchess (Republican);
Associate Justice, W. A. Montgomery (Populist).
(*Caucasian*, November 22, 1894)

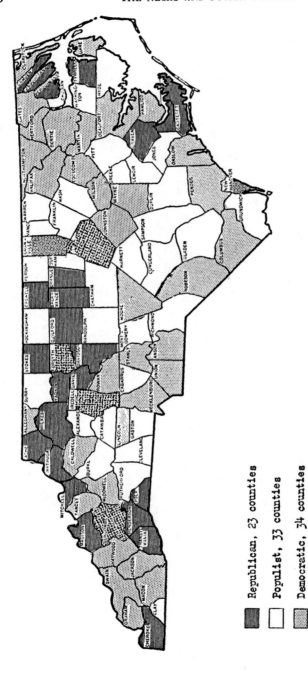

FUSION STATE ELECTION TO THE NORTH CAROLINA HOUSE OF REPRESENTATIVES, 1894

(*Caucasian*, December 6, 1894)

The Democrats realized that they would be outnumbered; hence, they resorted to dilatory tactics. Frank Ray introduced a resolution favoring "the election of Senators by the people of the State."[27] It was both interesting and humorous to see a Democrat championing the popular election of senators when his party had practiced legislative election of local officials from 1872 to 1894. The resolution was lost. Butler won the long term and Pritchard the short term.[28]

The Fusion legislature of 1895 set its face towards fulfilling the platform promises of 1894. The farmer as victim of the merchant and banker looked forward to a uniform rate of interest which would free him of exploitation. The legislature formulated an act which stated that 6 per centum was to be the legal rate of interest per annum and that a greater rate of interest knowingly would forfeit the entire interest, and the person paying a greater rate could recover twice the amount of interest paid.[29] In conformity with the pledge of a four months' school term, the legislature provided that a school tax of twenty cents be levied on every one hundred dollars worth of taxable property and sixty cents on the poll to supplement the public school funds in such counties as did not meet those requirements,[30] and that twenty-five thousand dollars of the money refunded to North Carolina by act of Congress on account of direct land tax be credited to the public school fund.[31] The mutilations of the Farmers' Alliance charter by the Democratic legislature of 1893 were removed.[32] The denominational groups lobbying in the legislature did not prevent the Fusionists from granting the usual biennial appropriation to the University of North Carolina and adding more money for equipment, repairs, and improvement.[33] The legislature crowned its achievements by the passage of an election law[34] and a change in the system of county government.[35] The former guaranteed representation to all parties at the polls, and the latter made county offices elective rather than appointive. Along with the popular election of county officials went the popular election of county school officials.[36] With these major platform promises realized in public laws, the Fusionists had leaped their legislative hurdles.[37]

The faces of three Negroes blurred the appearance of the "lily white" legislature of 1895. Fusion had brought James Young, of Wake County, and William H. Crews, of Granville County, to the House of Representatives and A. R. Middleton to the position of assistant door-keeper. Their very appearance evoked once more the Negro question. Two events of the session of 1895 projected still further the race issue and bore heavily upon the Fusionists' career. They were the Frederick Douglass Resolution and the Abe Middleton Affair.

The Frederick Douglass affair began when William H. Crews, Negro legislator from Granville County, introduced on February 21 a resolution of respect to Frederick Douglass.[38] This resolution was adopted. The House consented to adjourn in honor of the nationally-known Negro who had died. This simple observance would have had no political consequences had it not been for the fact that February 22 was George Washington's birthday and apparently no official action was taken by the House to honor him. The Democratic leaders and press used the Frederick Douglass Resolution to focus attention on the race question: "A Negro had been honored while Washington and Lee had been ignored." [39] In truth, Crews had asked the legislature to cut short a day's session, not to observe a whole day. The regular hour for adjournment was 2 P.M. On the particular day the legislature honored Crews' resolution, the House was in session until thirty-seven minutes past two o'clock.[40] Too, the House had voted to observe Lee's birthday; and, strangely enough, it was the Negro legislator James Young who proposed it. The House responded that "on the motion of Mr. Young of Wake, it being the birthday of Robert E. Lee, a day declared to be a public holiday by the laws of North Carolina, the House adjourn to meet at 3 P.M. Monday, January 21, 1895." [41] George Washington's birthday came on a Saturday at which time the House normally adjourned at one o'clock in the afternoon.

The Democrats raised the cry that the Fusionists had inaugurated social equality.[42] Their derisive party document aired the Douglass affair in these words: "If anybody had suggested that when this great disciple of intermarriage should be gathered to his fathers the Legislature of North Carolina would pass a resolution to adjourn in his honor he would have been regarded as an insane or imbecile person. And yet, after passing laws against intermarriage and mixed schools, and preserving the purity and unity of the two races, the spectacle was witnessed of a North Carolina Legislature paying a mark of respect to Fred Douglass which was denied to George Washington and Robert E. Lee." [43]

So much Democratic agitation required the Fusionists to explain their action. There was ordered spread upon the House Journal the Fusionists' declaration to the effect that the Democratic press had wilfully and maliciously charged and published that the General Assembly of 1895 refused to adjourn out of respect to the memory of Washington and Lee, and that "on January 19, after being in session less than a half hour the House adjourned out of respect to the memory of Robert E. Lee." Furthermore, a resolution was offered on February 21 to adjourn out of respect to Washington and it passed the House and was not concurred in by the Senate, but "the House met the next day as usual [February 22]; a motion was made by Mr. Lusk, to adjourn out of respect to the memory of George Washington, the same being his birthday, and the same was adopted unanimously." In reference to Douglass "the House did not adjourn until 37 minutes after the time required for adjournment." [44]

In spite of the Fusionists' declaration, the Democrats of the House insisted that their side of the story be spread on the *Journal*. They held, "that on the 18th of January [and] on the 20th of February the General Assembly refused to adopt a resolution to adjourn in the honor of Robert E. Lee and George Washington; [and] that on the 21st of February [it] resolved, that when this house adjourns, it adjourn in the memory of the deceased [Frederick Douglass] and said resolution was adopted." [45] The Democrats' declaration stated the particular days the two resolutions honoring Lee and Washington had been defeated. It is obvious that the declaration omitted the fact that on each respective birthday the House did adjourn, in honor of each, after the day's work had started.

So anxious was each opposing group to serve its cause that political leaders continued to explain through the press what each judged to be the true merits of the Douglass affair. Republican Lusk stated that, even if the Fusionists did honor Douglass, they were merely following a Democratic precedent because Frederick Douglass and his wife were guests of Grover Cleveland, the Democratic president. He insisted that Cleveland had done what no other President had ever done by sending a colored man to represent the United States at the court of France. Lusk's closing comment was "We are only following an example Cleveland set before us." [46]

The *News and Observer* would not let the Douglass affair drop, but insisted on rehashing it in the summer of 1895 and in the campaign of 1896; and echoes of it rumbled on into the "white supremacy" campaign of 1898. It was obvious that this Democratic newspaper was not anxious to clarify the political air over the incident. It should be remembered that its editor gave up a job in Washington to return to North Carolina with the avowed purpose of "joining in the fight for the redemption of the State." [47] In contrast to the *News and Observer*, another powerful Democratic paper mentioned the Douglass Resolution in its issues of February 22 and 23, carried the Fusionists' denial on February 26, and let the matter drop there. [48]

The Abe Middleton Affair was the second incident with racial implication which created public ill will for the legislature of 1895. The background of the "brawl" lies in the nature of Middleton's position and the attending activities. A. R. Middleton, Negro, in the humble position of assistant doorkeeper, became the victim of Democratic abuse. When the legislature of 1895 opened, A. J. Moye was elected door-keeper. [49] Middleton was accorded the position of assistant door-keeper through the insistence of James H. Young, Negro legislator. It was said that G. W. Justice, white, was the possible choice, but retired in favor of Middleton for the sake of party har-

mony.[50] The chief Democratic newspaper used Middleton's election as a
shining example of the Fusionists' preference for Negroes over whites.[51]
The Democratic party contended that the disgrace of the election was that
a one-legged Confederate veteran had been displaced by a Negro.[52] The
truth was that J. Reitzel, of Catawba County, the one-legged Civil War
veteran, had served as assistant door-keeper in the Democratic legislature of
1893, hence Middleton did not displace him. The Democratic legislature
had awarded its patronage to Democrats, and the Fusionist legislature had
followed the same rule: "to the victor belong the spoils." However, in the
selection of an assistant door-keeper, the ghost of the Negro question arose
to greet the Fusionists on the opening day. Republican V. S. Lusk rushed to
the defense of the election of Middleton by reminding the Democrats that
they had "in one legislature voted for a negro from Chatham area against a
one-legged confederate soldier" and that "the *House Journal* of 1873 shows
that the Democrats elected Christmas, negro, as assistant door-keeper," further adding "but when the Republicans follow them, then the hue and cry is
raised." [53]

Nothing more was heard of Middleton from the day of his election until
March 12, the closing day of the legislature of 1895. The session had been a
busy one. The legislature received more than one thousand eight hundred
bills and resolutions. Much time had been consumed by the Fusion forces
in making the bills acceptable to the two factions. The Republicans and
Populists held their caucuses separately. Much time was consumed by the
Democratic minority in efforts to stall, bungle, and delay Fusion legislation.
Frank Ray, the titular leader of the Democratic minority, was a man of
parliamentary skill. A Democratic reporter described him as a man "who
could introduce more dilatory motions and tie up legislation longer than
any man I have ever seen." [54] Many bills and resolutions were still in the
hands of committees in early March, and the latter days of the session found
the legislators working all day and holding special sessions at night.

The final day of March 12 was a full one, and the speaker in his attempt
to clear the House calendar bills urged all members to remain throughout
the last evening. He invoked the House rules and Middleton, assistant door-
keeper, was at his post. In the midst of this busy session, Captain R. B.
Peebles, of Northampton County, and W. T. Lee, of Haywood County—
both Democrats—approached the door and demanded to be let out. The
Negro refused. A struggle ensued. Several whites rushed to Peebles and Lee
and several Negroes rushed to Middleton. In the midst of the confusion, the
door flew open. The Raleigh *News and Observer* next day hailed the incident as "THE CROWNING INFAMY, A Burly Negro Forcibly Detains
Members of the House of Representatives." Then followed in small print:
"A burly negro apparently acting under the order of the Speaker stood at

the inside door and held it fast with both hands, refusing to allow either ingress or egress." [55] It did not matter to the chief Democratic press which side was right or who had started the physical violence. The fact that mattered was that a Negro, provoked or unprovoked, had laid hands on a white man. Captain Peebles stated that he informed the Negro that there had been no call of the House, and no one had a right to detain him. Ray, another Democrat, talked much of an investigation and offered a resolution that two of the Negroes be arrested and brought before the bar of the House.[56]

While the *News and Observer* was fanning the flames of racial hatred and condemning Middleton for his conduct, another powerful Democratic paper absolved him from guilt and placed the incident in a saner and more sober perspective. In part, it said "there is much indignation among Democrats at the action of the Speaker tonight in ordering the door locked and that no member be permitted to leave. This was done when no call of the House was ordered. The negro door-keeper, Abe Middleton, was pushed aside and the members left."[57] When the heat and glare of Fusion politics was over, Middleton was characterized by the editor of the *News and Observer* as "a smart Negro. He really had been one of the triumvirate of Butler, Grant, and Middleton, who had made it possible to fuse in the counties of Sampson and Duplin . . . and [ultimately] led his race in becoming productive citizens . . . organized the first Negro Farm Cooperative in the State."[58] It was the holding of political office which had transformed this leader of his race into "a burly negro." There was no doubt that the blackness of skin was enough in Southern politics.[59]

The issue of race had come to the fore and the legislature of 1895 came to a close. The Democrats hurriedly re-examined every activity of the Fusion legislature and wrote derisively *A History of the General Assembly of 1895* laying great emphasis upon the supposed failures of the body and upon Negro office-holding. A Republican paper praised the legislature of 1895 as accomplishing great and significant changes and leaving the Democrats nothing to criticize except the "Nigger."[60] Between the Democratic condemnation and the Republican exultation, lay the truth. The Fusionists had effected changes, and the merits of legislative enactments, either *pro or con,* could not be ascertained in early 1895. The subsequent years of Fusion rule would determine the application of the new measures.

NOTES TO CHAPTER THREE

1. *Caucasian,* January 11, 1894.
2. *News and Observer,* July 31, 1894.
3. *Ibid.*
4. *Caucasian,* August 2, 1894; *News and Observer,* August 2, 1894.
5. *News and Observer,* August 2, 1894.

6. *Caucasian*, August 8, 1894.

7. *News and Observer*, August 8, 1894; *Democratic Handbook*, 1894, 93-94; *Caucasian*, August 8, 1894.

8. *News and Observer*, August 9, 1894.

9. *News and Observer*, August 31, 1894; *Democratic Handbook*, 1894, 89.

10. William A. Mabry, "The Negro in North Carolina Politics Since Reconstruction," *Historical Papers of Trinity College Historical Society*, Series XXIII, 34.

11. Daniels, *Editor in Politics*, 123.

12. Hugh T. Lefler (ed.), *North Carolina History Told by Contemporaries*, 394. (Citation from Polk's letter in possession of Mrs. Denmark, Raleigh, N. C.)

13. William A. Mabry, "Negro Suffrage and Fusion Rule in North Carolina," *North Carolina Historical Review*, XII (1935), 83.

14. *Democratic Handbook*, 1894, 76.

15. *Ibid.*, 64.

16. *Ibid.*, 18.

17. Daniels, *Editor in Politics*, 123.

18. *News and Observer*, October 14, 1894.

19. *House Journal*, 1895, 4-7 (two Negroes); *Senate Journal*, 1895, 5-6.

20. See map, 39.

21. Hamilton, *History of North Carolina Since 1860*, 245.

22. See map, 40.

23. Bertie, Edgecombe, Halifax, Hertford, Northampton, and Pender.

24. Granville and New Hanover.

25. *News and Observer*, November 13, 1894.

26. *Charlotte Observer*, January 25, 1895.

27. *House Journal*, 1895, 37.

28. *Ibid.*, 85-87, 88-89.

29. *Public Laws*, 1895, Chap. 69, 75-76.

30. *Ibid.*, Chap. 297, 375-76.

31. *Ibid.*, Chap. 404, 436.

32. *Private Laws*, 1895, Chap. 12, 23.

33. *Public Laws*, 1897, Chap. 171, 293.

34. *Public Laws*, 1895, Chap. 159, 211-36; See *Infra*, Chap. V, for full discussion.

35. *Public Laws*, 1895, Chap. 135, 185-87; Chap. 157, 209-10; see *Infra*, Chap. VIII, for full discussion.

36. *Public Laws*, 1895, Chap. 439, 465-67.

37. The application of these public laws is a story unto itself, see Chaps. V, VI, and VII, VIII, *Infra*.

38. *House Journal*, 1895, 479.

39. *History of the General Assembly of 1895*, 37 (a derisive Democratic appraisal of the Fusion legislature).

40. *Appleton's Cyclopedia*, New Series, XX (1895), 556; *House Journal*, 1895, 546.

41. *House Journal*, 1895, 69, 71.

42. *Lenoir Topic*, February 27, 1895.

43. *History of the General Assembly of 1895*, 50, 63.

44. *House Journal*, 1895, 545-46.

45. *Ibid.*, 1084-86.

46. *Charlotte Observer*, February 26, 1895.

47. Daniels, *Editor in Politics*, 99.

48. *Charlotte Observer*.

49. *House Journal,* 1895, 12-13.
50. *Charlotte Observer,* January 12, 1895.
51. *News and Observer,* March 14, 1895.
52. *History of the General Assembly of 1895,* 23.
53. *Charlotte Observer,* February 26, 1895.
54. Daniels, *Editor in Politics,* 127.
55. *News and Observer,* March 13, 1895.
56. *Ibid.,* March 14, 1895.
57. *Charlotte Observer,* March 13, 1895.
58. Josephus Daniels, *Editor in Politics,* 126.
59. Jonathan Daniels, *Tar Heels: Portrait of A State,* 126.
60. *Elizabeth City North Carolinian,* March 13, 1895.

CHAPTER FOUR

THE COMPLETION OF FUSION, 1896-1897

THE CHALLENGING QUESTIONS raised among the North Carolina Populists in 1896 were: Would there be fusion again? If so, with which party? The Republicans wondered if they could hold the Populists to their side in another election. National party politics, conventions, and campaigns were bound to have repercussions in the state. North Carolina's politics in the summer of 1896 has to be viewed, first against the background of national politics; and, second, against the background of politics within the state.

The national Democratic convention met in July in Chicago. The party organization, controlled by the liberals, nominated William Jennings Bryan as its standard-bearer. It adopted a platform which incorporated agrarian demands and insisted upon the unlimited coinage of silver. Bryan's Western background, liberalism, political experience, and oratorical ability made him a worthy exponent of the agricultural and labor interests of the nation. Arthur M. Sewall of Maine, a banker, railway director, and shipbuilder, was nominated as vice-presidential candidate. It was obvious that Sewall had nothing whatever in common with the Populists except his belief in free silver.[1] A North Carolina Democrat who attended the national convention wrote that Sewall was reputed to be a very rich man, and his supporters thought he would finance the campaign if nominated.[2]

The national Populist party met later in the month in St. Louis. Its platform advocated unlimited coinage of silver, more effective antimonopolistic regulations, government ownership of railroads, popular election of United States senators, and a nonpartisan Supreme Court. The fact that the Democrats had already nominated their logical standard-bearer put them in a dilemma as to the choice of a presidential candidate. Bryan represented their beliefs, but to endorse him and the Democratic party might cause them to lose their separate identity. The strategy of the convention finally resulted in acceptance of Bryan as presidential candidate; but to accept Sewall, a reputed banker of high financial interests, was too much of a pill for the antimonopolistic Populists to swallow. Bryan did all he could, in an indirect way, to urge the Populists to accept Sewall. The Populists were not to be won over and proceeded to nominate their own vice-presidential candidate, Thomas Watson, from Georgia. Fusion of the Democrats and the Populists had been effected in the national arena, at least as far as the presidential nominee and parts of the platform were concerned.

It was obvious in the summer of 1896 that the majority of the Republicans wanted and needed fusion in North Carolina irrespective of how closely they veiled this secret at the time of their convention.[3] The Democrats, shocked by the Fusion victory of 1894, wanted and needed the support of the Populists.[4] The balance of power in 1896 lay in the hands of the third party. The Democrats and the Populists, in the national parties, were agreed on major issues; hence, the Democrats and the Populists in North Carolina made a fusion arrangement for the national tickets. But in August, 1895, the Democratic governor, Elias Carr, had sanctioned the leasing of the North Carolina Railroad to the Southern Railroad for ninety-nine years. This act, widely denounced by liberal Democrats and by the Populists who hated and feared the railroad interests, was an additional obstacle to Democratic-Populist fusion in state politics. State issues would be the basis of fusion in North Carolina.

The Republican state convention met May 14, 1896, in Raleigh. Eugene Holton acted as temporary chairman until Marshall Mott was chosen as permanent chairman. Three secretaries were chosen to handle the work, one of whom was a Negro, John C. Dancy. Chairman Mott appointed a committee on Order of Business which included Congressman Richmond Pearson, Congressman Thomas Settle, Hiram L. Grant, G. Z. French, and James Young, Negro. The committee reported that the order of business would be: first, seat the delegates; second, nominate a state ticket; and, third, organize a platform. The party met not knowing whether fusion with the Populists would be arranged. The party, however, stood behind the Republican Executive Committee which made a "proposition to the Populist committee on April 16 and 17 to the effect that the Republicans were to nominate the governor, auditor, attorney general, and one justice of the Supreme Court, and the Populists were to nominate the lieutenant governor, secretary of state, treasurer, superintendent of public instruction, and one justice; for cooperation congressional and legislative, as it was two years ago, each party was to have its own electoral ticket."[5] The Populists had declined, but the Republicans were willing and anxious to give them another chance to accept.[6] The air was tense and rightly so because two men were acceptable to large factions of the party for the gubernatorial nomination—Daniel L. Russell and Oliver H. Dockery. It was very difficult for the convention to get down to business as the choice of the candidate loomed high in the background. John Dancy summoned enough courage to mention Dockery on the first day of the convention, and the crowd went wild.[7] All day it was a question as to whether Russell or Dockery would be chosen. The Republican machine presumably had decided on Russell, yet various Negro elements were strong for Dockery. The question of which one would be chosen rested upon the likelihood of which sets of delegates would be seated. There were two delegations from ten counties.[8] Temporary Chairman Holton appointed the

Committee on Credentials on May 14. The fact that the Committee reportedly deliberated during the entire night of May 15 suggests something of the difficult problem they faced in deciding which delegations should be seated.

It was true that the Negroes were divided on the two men. Dr. James E. Shepard of Raleigh and John C. Dancy of Wilmington spoke in behalf of Dockery. James Young, the Negro member of the 1895 legislature, spoke for Russell. He said: "I wish we could get nine Russells on the Supreme Court Bench. He is the only judge who ever sat upon the bench, who had the courage and audacity to say the Constitution doesn't know the difference between the colored man or the white man. If you nominate Russell, fusion is assured."[9]

May 16 was the fateful day. There were thirty-four contesting delegates. Around the seating of these contesting delegates hangs the story of the Republican ticket. The Committee on Credentials brought in two reports: a majority one and a minority one. The majority report recommended the seating of eighteen delegates pledged to Dockery and sixteen pledged to Russell. The minority report recommended the seating of four delegates pledged to Dockery and thirty pledged to Russell. The convention accepted the minority report and the anti-Dockery delegates were seated. A Populist newspaper inferred that Dockery had been mistreated.[10] A pro-Dockery Republican paper felt the same way and insisted that Russell did not deserve the nomination because he had voted the Democratic ticket in 1888.[11]

The convention turned its attention towards the selection of a gubernatorial candidate. Again the contest centered between Russell and Dockery. A total of 117 of the convention vote of 232 was necessary for a choice. After seven separate ballots were cast, Russell emerged with a total of 119 3/7 as against Dockery's 112 4/7. Russell was declared the nominee for governor. Such outstanding Negroes as Dr. James E. Shepard, A. R. Middleton, A. L. Lloyd, John C. Dancy, L. A. Scruggs, E. A. Johnson, and Dr. Aaron McDuffie Moore were utterly disgusted at the nomination of Russell. Dr. Shepard said that those who tried to stifle the voice of the people would be doomed.[12] He was howled down and hissed. The confusion in the Republican convention gave the Democrats an opportunity to say that Russell had stolen the nomination, that the "skullduggery began in Wake County, where Parson Leak and the bulk of other Negro Republicans who were advocating Dockery were out-generalled by Jim Young and Loge Harris, Russell's leaders."[13] There are other writers who feel that these Democratic comments would probably have been uttered if Dockery had been nominated instead of Russell.[14] Russell, in accepting the nomination, said:

I entertain a sentiment of deep gratitude to the negroes. . . . I stand for the negroes' rights and liberties. I sucked at the breast of a negro woman. I judge from the adult development the milk must have been nutritious and plentiful. The negroes do not want control. They only demand, and they ought to have it, every right a white man has.[15]

After the exciting contest over the gubernatorial candidate, little time was spent on the slate of officers and the platform. Charles A. Reynolds, of Forsyth, was nominated as lieutenant governor; Z. V. Walser, of Davidson, as attorney general; Ruff Henderson, of Wake, as auditor; and R. M. Douglas as associate justice for the Supreme Court. The Republicans had refused to endorse anyone for the positions of secretary of state, state treasurer, and superintendent of public instruction. It was obvious that the party had placed a skeletal ticket in the field and the places were left open in case the Populists desired to share the ticket. The Populists were not unaware of what had happened because their chief publication stated that "this skeletal ticket was evidently a bid for the Democrats or Populists to join in with the Republicans and play a sort of I-tickle-you-you-tickle-me game. The *Caucasian* is certain that Populists will not play."[16]

The Republican platform of 1896 glorified the accomplishments of the election law and the county government system of 1895. It pledged support to an efficient state superintendent of education regardless of party and promised farmers and householders the same tax exemptions as were given to the bondholders. The platform closed with the warning to Republican voters that, if the Democrats got control of the state again, Negro Republicans would be disfranchised within sixty days.[17]

The Republicans wanted cooperation with the Populists again in 1896; but Butler had announced earlier that the Populists would fuse in 1896 if free silver were incorporated into the platforms of both parties.[18] Butler's insistence on this mutual agreement caused the Republicans, the gold party, to state that he made cooperation impossible. A Republican paper characterized Butler's delay in endorsing Republican-Populist fusion in these words: "No traitor in the opinions of the Republicans, since the days of Benedict Arnold will carry a more lasting mark than the foxey Marion Butler."[19] No formal vote was taken during the convention on the question; however, the very fact that a skeletal ticket was arranged has led some writers to believe, and with justification, that the Republicans had proceeded on the supposition that cooperation with the Populists would be finally arranged.[20]

The Negro leaders who felt that Dockery should have won the gubernatorial nomination also felt that United States Senator Pritchard had a hand in his defeat. These leaders met in Raleigh on May 19, two days after the convention had closed, to urge Dockery for the Senate in 1897 rather than Pritchard. They decided that they would support no man for the legislature who refused to pledge for Dockery.[21] They issued a call to all pro-Dockery

Negroes to meet in Raleigh on July 2. The rump convention, composed solidly of Negro voters, met and termed itself the State Convention of Colored Republicans. The Reverend Mr. W. H. R. Leak, of Raleigh, was chosen chairman and L. P. Berry, of Iredell County, was chosen secretary. Such statements circulated throughout the convention as "Russell's nomination was fraudulent," "We can't forget his reference to Negroes," and "Ninety per cent of the Republicans on May 16th wanted Dockery."[22] J. O. Nixon, colored alderman of Wilmington, went so far as to urge the group to delete Russell's name from the ticket. The chairman in opening the meeting stated that representatives from sixty-five counties were present to demonstrate against Russell. Dr. Aaron Moore, secretary of the committee on organization of the convention's activities, presented a new State Executive Committee of nine men from the nine Congressional districts. While there was no mention of whites in attendance, two of the nine suggested were whites: C. A. Reynolds, Eighth District, and J. M. Moody, of the Ninth.

The platform committee had two prominent Negro members: Professor L. B. Capehart, of Shaw University, and Professor W. G. Pearson, of Durham. Capehart read the following platform which was adopted:

We, the anti-Russell Republicans of the State of North Carolina, in convention assembled, appeal to honest self respecting negroes in the State to resent in every honorable way the cowardly insults that have been offered the race by Hon. D. L. Russell.

And we earnestly and conscientiously beseech every negro in whose heart there is still a spark of self respect and manhood to exert himslf to the utmost to defend the honesty and integrity of the race, by doing all in his power to defeat the election of D. L. Russell, whose name has become a stench to the humble, honest and intelligent negroes throughout the land and whose election would be a blot upon the fair name of North Carolina.[23]

There were planks expressing sympathy for the suffering Cubans, endorsing McKinley and the national ticket, demanding better schools and longer terms for both races, and reiterating the demand for honest election laws. The platform closed with the denunciation of Russell and the endorsement of W. A. Guthrie, of Durham County, as gubernatorial candidate.[24] By mid-July, 1896, there was a split in the Republican ranks.

The Democratic convention met on June 25 in Raleigh. The Democrats, stunned by the Fusion victory of 1894, had not pulled themselves out of their daze. Both national and state issues faced them, but the convention chose to deal only with national issues. An opposition newspaper described the convention as a collection of postmasters, revenue agents, federal officeholders, and lawyers. Humorously, the group was described as a congeries of "Gold bug Democrats, high tariff Democrats, low tariff Democrats, silver Democrats, corporation Democrats, anti-trust Democrats, my daddy was a Democrat, I was born a Democrat, I was rocked in the cradle of a Democrat, I didn't seek this nomination Democrat, I am willing to make any sacrifice Democrat, drunk Democrats and sober Democrats."[25]

The convention endorsed Cyrus Watson for governor, Thomas W. Mason for lieutenant governor, Charles M. Cooke for secretary of state, Frank Osborne for attorney general, Benjamin F. Aycock for state treasurer, Robert Furman for state auditor, and John C. Scarborough for superintendent of public instruction.[26]

Among the fourteen planks in the platform relating to national affairs were those condemning trusts, the gold standard, and the Republican party. Four planks on state affairs pointed with pride to the economic and stainless administration of the Democrats when they were in power; endorsed an election law which would secure purity of the ballot; praised the Democratic system of county government, and promised a just and impartial administration of the criminal law.[27] It was quite evident that the Democrats had no constructive program for the state and were content to rest in 1896, as in 1892, on their past record.

The Populist convention met on August 13 in Raleigh and had the advantage of knowing what both the Republicans and Democrats had done. The question of fusion was in the air, but no one dared put it to a vote in the convention. Harry Skinner was chosen chairman of the convention, and his selection was significant because he favored letting the party stand on its own merits in 1896.[28] Butler favored cooperation with the Republicans if free silver would be included in the agreement.

The Populists ignored completely the Republican slate of officers and proceeded to choose their own. W. A. Guthrie was chosen as gubernatorial candidate; O. H. Dockery, lieutenant governor; Dr. Cyrus Thompson, secretary of state; Young H. Cox, attorney general; W. H. Worth, state treasurer; Hal Ayer, state auditor; Charles H. Mebane, superintendent of public instruction; and Walter A. Montgomery, associate justice.[29] Whether the Populists were expressly bidding for Negro support is a matter if conjecture, but it was clear that the rump Negro Republican convention had endorsed Guthrie in July and that same gathering was a pro-Dockery faction, and the names of the Populist (formerly Republican) Guthrie and the Republican Dockery headed the Populist list of state officers.

The convention adopted its usual national platform and on state issues pledged the retention of the county government act and the election law of 1895, the abolition of free passes on railroads, the establishment of a reformatory for young criminals, the maintenance of a nonpartisan judiciary, and condemned the Democrats for the railroad lease of 1895.[30] The convention adjourned without any agreement on fusion for 1896.

The Populists released their ticket August 18, with the complete slate. The state Executive Committee of the Republican party, on the next day, hastened to fill in the vacant parts of the ticket with the nominees that the Populists had chosen, so stating at the time, "in testimony of our good faith with the Populists we accept on our ticket the candidates named by the late Populist State Convention."[31] It meant then that the Republican ticket included Daniel L. Russell (Republican) for governor; Charles A. Reynolds (Republican) for lieutenant governor; Zebulon V. Walser (Republican) for attorney general; Dr. Cyrus Thompson (Populist) for secretary of state; W. H. Worth (Populist) for state treasurer; Hal Ayer (Populist) for state auditor; and Charles H. Mebane (Populist) for superintendent of public instruction.[32]

Each party launched its campaign immediately after its state convention. The Republicans began first. They were divided. It is necessary to investigate the basis of Negro opposition to Russell. In commenting on him, Dr. James E. Shepard, one of the Negro leaders of the period, stated that "Russell is the meanest judge that ever sat on the bench in North Carolina and no self-respecting negro would vote for him."[33] Russell was reputed to have said of Negroes that they were savages who stole all week and prayed it off on Sunday, and that they were no more fit to govern than their brethren in the swamps of Africa.[34] While this statement is not found either in Russell's personal or executive papers, the rumor was well circulated in the Democratic newspapers of the period. Armond W. Scott, Negro lawyer of Daniel Russell's home, Wilmington, states that he was present at the trial in which Russell delivered these words and was the first to circulate them in his paper, The Wilmington Sentinel, when it was rumored in Republican circles that Judge Russell would seek the nomination. He states, also, that The Wilmington Messenger, Democratic paper, took the citation from his paper and that the Raleigh News and Observer played it up in the campaign.[35] With such a rumor astir, some Negroes felt that Russell's belated flattery to them, at the time of his acceptance of the nomination, was too much of an about-face position to be genuine. One white Republican suggested to Russell, "you issue a circular to the colored race setting forth the facts in the case . . . few of the colored men read and take any paper therefore I think a circular distributed among them would set them aright."[36] The job which faced James Young, Negro Republican leader, was to close the gap between the pro-Russell and the anti-Russell Negroes.

The Republicans proceeded with their campaign since no word of fusion had come from the Populists. There were those among the former who felt that the Populists, by their obstinancy, wanted to stick a gun in their backs. Congressman Pearson from the Eighth District wrote Russell that "the real trouble is and has been that the Populists are too exorbitant in their demands, insisting that we vote for a silver electoral ticket and in addition give them the Governor for the price of their cooperation."[37]

The Democrats approached the Populists to share with them the presidential electors since both parties from the standpoint of national politics had points in common. Both parties agreed that the Democrats were to have six electors and the Populists to have five.[38]

In September, the executive committees of the Republican and Populist parties reached a peculiar agreement on tactics. Neither party removed its state ticket from the field, but they agreed that the Populists should have Congressional candidates in four districts, the Republicans in five; that both parties would cooperate in the counties in electing members to the General Assembly and, in the event of victory, would support Jeter Pritchard for United States senator.[39] Irrespective of how the arrangement was worded, the machinery of both parties had effected fusion. In summarizing the Populists' situation, they were fused with the Democrats on the choice of Bryan and the division of presidential electors, were fused with the Republicans on Congressional candidates and county tickets, and were fused with a few local Democrats in one or two counties on the state ticket. The Populists realized their "tight rope walking circus act" when they stated, "we have undertaken a delicate yet Herculean task and while we want a genuine free silver man as president of the United States, we wish to defeat as disastrously as possible the Democratic organization in this State."[40]

The Democrats capitalized on the Russell-Dockery feud thereby hoping to widen the breach in the Republican party. They played up the charge that Russell might withdraw from the campaign. When discouraging Negroes from supporting Russell, they referred to his calling the Negroes savages. When discouraging the Populists from supporting him, they called him a "nigger lover." When rallying their own party, they charged the Fusionists with endorsing Negro rule. The Democrats were silent on the issues of Fusion reform, content to make Negro domination the chief issue.[41] The Democratic party used its choice invectives against the Republicans alone prior to the September endorsement of Republican-Populist fusion, with the hope of influencing the Populists against fusion, but began deriding the Populists in October.

The Populists staked their campaign on the accomplishment of the legislature of 1895 and ignored the Democratic accusation of Negro rule. The Republicans, however, contended that the Democrats sought Negro votes as enthusiastically as did any other party, and that Negro rule did not exist in North Carolina.[42] So anxious were the Republicans to win that they resorted in one county to a fictitious Negro sale. A Republican in describing the incident to Daniel L. Russell wrote:

The negro sale referred to was in a township in this country where the Democrats had created disaffection among the negroes, and they were going back on us. I went to this place the night before the election and spoke to them. I took a big black fellow, set him on a block and auctioneered him off at $1500.00. I then made appropriate references to their former state and the Democratic party. The negroes went wild and swore they would lynch any negro that votes the Democratic ticket.[43]

As the campaign was rapidly drawing toward the November election, W. A. Guthrie, the Populist convention's gubernatorial candidate exploded an eleventh hour bombshell by issuing a statement to his party that the Populists ought to fuse with the Democrats.[44] The September Republican-Populist accord had not touched Guthrie's nomination, but for all intents and purposes, Guthrie felt that he had been repudiated by his party.

Irrespective of the crisscross arrangement of all three parties, the election of 1896 was a victory for the Fusionists.[45] Republican Russell was elected governor with 153,787 votes carrying 49 counties, while Democratic Watson received 145,266 votes carrying 46 counties, and Populist Guthrie, 31,143 votes carrying one county.[46] The votes cast for Russell were 57,103 more than those cast for the Republican nominee in 1892. Watson received in defeat 9,747 more votes than the Democratic candidate did in victory in 1892. Guthrie received 16,697 votes less than the Populist candidate did in 1892.[47]

In comparing the Republican vote of 1896 with 1892, the party gained votes in 94 of the 96 counties. The gains ranged from 49 in Clay County to 3,118 in Wake County. The party witnessed a loss of five and eight votes in Person and Sampson counties, respectively. The sixteen "black counties" showed increases which ranged from 202 in Pender to 2,855 in Halifax. However, 78 white counties registered gains from 49 in Clay to 3,118 in Wake. Only six of the sixteen "black counties" registered increases of more than 1,000,[48] while eleven white counties registered more than 1,000.[49] The "black counties" cast 18,543 votes in 1892 and 33,900 in 1896. There is no doubt that the liberality of the election law of 1895 played a part in this Negro Republican increase of 15,357. While this increase in the "black counties" swelled the Republican victory in 1896, it was not necessary for a Fusion victory, because, "victory over the Democrats had been accomplished in 1894 before the new election law had been passed."[50] The increase also showed that the pro-Dockery influence had been nullified, even if the pro-Dockery faction had not been brought back into the group. Dr. James E. Shepard, a pro-Dockery man, stated that they (the disaffected group) did not vote for Russell and urged as many Negroes as they could contact not to do so.[51] The Republican vote leaped from 372 to 1,469 and 347 to 1,571, respectively, in Chatham and Nash, two of the three counties which had been Populist in 1892. The total Republican vote in 1896 was only 19,761 more than that polled in 1888, when

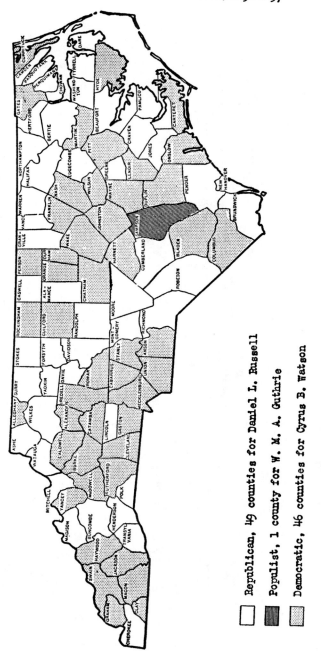

GUBERNATORIAL ELECTION, 1896
(*North Carolina Manual*, 1913, 1005-6)

☐ Republican, 49 counties for Daniel L. Russell

▨ Populist, 1 county for W. M. A. Guthrie

▦ Democratic, 46 counties for Cyrus B. Watson

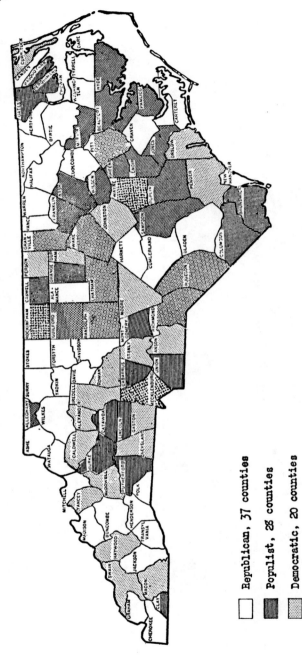

Fusion State Election to the North Carolina House of Representatives, 1896
(*Caucasian*, January 14, 1897)

Republican, 37 counties

Populist, 28 counties

Democratic, 20 counties

Republican-Democratic Fusion, 1 county

Republican-Populist Fusion, 7 counties

Populist-Democratic Fusion, 3 counties

there was no third party in the field and Negroes voted under the intricate fraudulent Democratic election law, and was not much greater than that which that party polled in each election after the Civil War.

The Democratic party showed gains in 1896 as compared with 1892 in 71 counties, maintained the *status quo* in one (Union), and showed decreases in 24.[52] The gains ranged from six in Pamlico to 699 in Wake. The losses ranged from four in Montgomery to 5,378 in Rockingham; however, no loss was more than 480 with the exception of Halifax (1,331) and Rockingham. Twenty-one of the 24 counties in which the party lost in votes were white counties.[53] Aside from the Republican increase in the three "black counties," it is to be noted that in 20 of the 21 white counties the decrease in Democratic vote was accompanied by an increase in the Republican vote. Of the Populist counties of Chatham, Nash, and Sampson in the 1892 election, only Sampson remained in the Populist column in 1896, while the other two went Democratic. The total gain for the Democratic party since 1892 was 9,747, but this gain could not offset the Republican gain of 57,103. Democratic losses in 15 counties were accompanied by substantial Republican increases.[54] Twelve of the 15 were white counties.[55]

It is difficult to estimate the Populist showing in the election of 1896. The party had polled 47,840 in 1892 and polled 16,697 less than that in 1896,[56] yet it was claimed in 1894 that the party had increased to 70,000.[57] By individual counties, the party decreased in votes in 64 counties. In 15 of the 64, the loss ranged from 299 to 2,261.[58] It gained votes in 15 counties, and the gains ranged from four to 343.[59] It was evident that the small gains did not offset the huge losses.

Three factors were involved in the decline of the Populist vote in 1896: first, some Populists returned to the Democratic fold because of the fear created by Democratic propaganda of Negro rule; second, Guthrie advised fusion with the Democrats; and, third, some supported the total Republican ticket, as fusion had been effected in part. The word "some" is used advisedly because contrary to the first two factors wherein the expected Populist decline should have shown Democratic increases, the reverse was true in 23 counties.[60] These 23, of which only Caswell, Northampton, Vance, and Warren were "black counties," showed Populist decreases, Democratic decreases, and substantial Republican increases. The size of the Republican vote in 1896 was due in part to new voters, the majority of whom were Negroes.[61]

A Republican governor presided over the General Assembly of 1897 for the first time since 1876. Governor Daniel L. Russell was accompanied into office by the entire Fusion ticket.[62] The House of Representatives had a roll call of 54 Republicans, 39 Populists, 26 Democrats, and a lone Silverite.[63] Among the 54 Republicans were three Negroes.[64] The Senate was composed of 25 Populists, 18 Republicans, and 7 Democrats.[65] There were two Negro

Republican senators.[66] A. F. Hileman, Populist, was chosen speaker of the House; and C. A. Reynolds, Republican, presided over the Senate. The Fusionists were represented in the United States House of Representatives by five Populists, three Republicans, and one Democrat.[67]

Governor Russell delivered his inaugural address on January 12. Respecting the problem of local government, which had racial implications, he said:

Our present county government law gives expression to the popular will and representation to minorities. Unfortunately the conflicts of national politics in this country extended to the management of local municipalities. Party lines are drawn in the strife of party men for party rewards. This General Assembly will be called on to deal with the management of towns and cities. There should be no attempt to avoid the necessity of protecting the tax-payers of these municipalities against the danger of mis-rule by propertyless and ignorant elements.[68]

His inaugural address embodied two other points which had no presumable racial implications, but showed the stature of the man in the face of the opposition of his enemies. All previous Democratic legislatures in the late 1880's and early 1890's had faced the great struggle over legislative appropriations for the University of North Carolina. The background of the struggle of private (church-supported) versus public (state-supported) colleges is too long a story to relate here.[69] In the midst of Methodist-Baptist pressure on the legislatures to withhold money from the University, and the bitter rancor created among the closest friends of the University, Governor Russell did not fail to take a stand firmly in support of the school. He admonished the legislature to hear the complaints from denominational colleges with the deference due their authors and to make them feel that the state rejoiced in their growing prosperity and power, "But, the University is a part of the State, and must be preserved."[70]

The Fusion party had hoped to do something about the North Carolina Railroad lease and had made use of this "unholy" transaction in the campaign of 1896. Governor Carr had endorsed the lease in August, 1895, an endorsement for which the Populists assigned two reasons: first, he had waited for the Fusion legislature of 1895 to adjourn, thereby indicating that he feared to air the transaction in the legislature; second, knowing that he could not succeed himself in the gubernatorial chair, he made one last effort to do the "corporation" Democrats' bidding thereby muddying the waters for the next legislature.[71] Carr explained in his farewell address that he favored the lease, that it was done by the State Board of Directors with his full concurrence and endorsed by the stockholders without a dissenting vote. He held further that the Board had the legal power through express Supreme Court decisions to lease the property, and he denied that the lease was made either hastily or secretly unless "that be called haste and secrecy which is not done in a court house or published in the public press before consummation."[72]

To the Fusionists this explanation did not explain! Russell's intentions to do something about the lease appeared to be sincere. His inaugural address in 1897 expressed these sentiments:

The State has a large and what ought to be a controlling interest in the North Carolina Railroad. An attempt has been made to pass from the State its interest in the great property for what is believed to be an inadequate consideration. The lease of ninety-nine years of all the rights, franchises and property, real and personal and mixed, of this railroad company to a foreign or non-resident corporation was made without the sanction of the Legislature or of the people of the State. . . . It was made without application to the Legislature. It was made without due discussion or submission to the people of the State, all of whom were interested, because the railroad is their property. It was made six years before the existing lease expired. . . . If this foreign corporation is not compelled to pay for this property a sum commensurate with their needs and its values to them, the fault will be with this General Assembly.[73]

The General Assembly of 1897 could not attack the North Carolina Railroad lease until it had accomplished the pressing task of electing a United States senator. Jeter C. Pritchard, who had completed Vance's unexpired term, sought re-election in his own right in 1897. The Republicans held the Populists to their promise of 1894 when the Fusionists had agreed to elect one Populist senator and one Republican senator. The Republican convention of 1896 had endorsed Pritchard for re-election. The executive committees of both parties had endorsed Pritchard in the September agreement of 1896; however, since that time feeling against him had grown in the Populist ranks. Marion Butler was the spearhead of this opposition; and the Republicans reminded the Populists, prior to the opening of the legislature, that Butler had been accorded the long senatorial term in 1895 only on the ground of acceding to the nomination of Pritchard in 1897.[74] The political air was tense on this question when the legislature of 1897 opened. Butler urged Populist representatives not to support Pritchard. Why had Butler and Pritchard, the architects of state Fusion, broken with each other? There can be only speculation as to causes until Butler's personal papers are open to the public; however, it is known that, irrespective of how much they agreed on state policies, they were distinctly apart in the United States Senate. Republicans and Populists were diametrically opposed on national policies.

Harry Skinner, Populist representative in the United States Congress in 1897, was chairman of the Populist State Committee. Skinner held that the Populist pledge of 1894 to support Pritchard was binding and that loyal party members in the legislature should support Pritchard.[75] The situation resulted in a lasting political break between Butler and Skinner, and it was aired to the public.[76] Those Populist members who believed as Skinner did were referred to as "bolters." The regular Populist caucus nominated Cyrus Thompson as its choice.[77] The election of United States senator took place on January 20, and Pritchard won by a plurality vote of twenty-four in the Senate and sixty-four in the House over his opponents—Rufus Doughton (Democrat), who polled seven in the Senate and twenty-four in the House; and Cyrus Thompson, who secured seventeen in the Senate and twenty-six in the House.[78]

Pritchard's election had shaken Fusion to its foundation. Partisanship continued to rear its head in the Assembly every step of the way. The "regular" Populists, followers of Butler, were at sea when the time came to support Fusion measures. The "bolters," followers of Skinner, pursued the path of cooperation with the Republicans. The minority Democrats continued to delay and bungle legislation.

The Assembly of 1897 sought to repeal all measures of 1895 which had proven to be boomerangs, to implement those which had loopholes, to make more generous appropriations for education, to curb railroad influence in state politics, and to alter municipal charters. The preceding legislature had enacted an Assignment Act which prohibited giving preferences to creditors who would execute sales, assignments, mortgages, or deeds in trust to secure any debt, obligation, note, or bond. The apparent purpose of the law was to prevent preferences only in case of assignments for benefit of creditors, but the Democrats charged that it was "equivalent to a stoppage of business, that in effect it was held to extend much further, and that banks, associations, and others were afraid to lend money on mortgages."[79] They also held that the act had been passed in an unconstitutional manner, and the question was presented to the Supreme Court in an application for an injunction to prevent the secretary of state from publishing it. The Supreme Court divided in its opinion with a three-two decision which favored the Fusion law.[80] The court held that it had not the power to go back of the record of the legislature which showed ratification of the act and that the remedy, if any were needed, was with the legislative branch of the state government.[81] Because of the rancor created by the Assignment Act and the divided court's interpretation of the same, the Fusionists repealed it in 1897.[82]

Irrespective of the intentions of Governor Russell and the Populists to direct stringent blows at the railroad interests, only three pieces of legislation emerged designed to curb railroad influence in the state. The Democratic legislatures had been complacent on the issuance of free passes to Democratic officials, but the Fusionists enacted a law which expressly forbade it.[83] Too, the Democrats had kept on the law books for many years a Fellow-Servant Act. This act made it well nigh impossible for anyone to collect damages for accidents incurred while in the employment of the railroad. The abolition of this pro-railroad act wiped out the technical loopholes which railroad lawyers had used in cases involving suits against the railroads.[84] Daniels, who favored its abolition and fought for that end through his press, said that this "ancient" act was abolished in an easy manner in 1897 because the railroad lawyers were so busy opposing interference with the lease and reduction of rates that they paid no attention to the repeal of the act.[85] The last blow directed at the railroads was an enactment for the better protection of the traveling public whereby all railroad and steamship companies were held liable in damages for any and all injuries to baggage or freight for which they had collected a fee.[86]

The election law of 1895 had occasioned much Democratic comment. The Fusionists held that the law was fair and just, while the Democrats held that it was anything but pure and that it even imposed the franchise upon Negroes who were not constitutionally qualified to exercise it. The Assembly of 1897 amended the election law with the result that the process of "challenging" became more intricate. This action was taken partly because the Democrats had relied upon challenging names on the registrars' books to decrease the opposition's numbers and cause general confusion. Furthermore, the selection of judges and registrars of election was removed from the hands of the state party chairmen and placed in the hands of the clerk of the court in each county.[87] County government was so amended that it provided for additional county commissioners and made the positions subject to popular election rather than legislative appointment.[88] Stormy opposition was encountered when the legislature altered and amended city charters for the purpose of granting a greater degree of local control.[89] The legislature gave added financial support to public education through increased local taxation.[90]

While this same legislature faced implications of the Negro problem in the election law, county government, and municipal charters, it also ran into a racial snag over the question of cadavers. The white medical colleges wanted a legislative enactment granting to them certain bodies for the promotion of medical science. An act was passed which created a board to procure and distribute the bodies, and ordered all officers, agents, and servants at public institutions to notify the board of any dead bodies which required burial by the state. Of course, if any kin claimed the body, proved the kinship, and paid the burial expense, then the medical colleges could not secure the body.[91] Shaw University, a Negro school located at Raleigh, had as one of its divisions the Leonard School of Medicine and naturally wanted to enjoy the privileges of this act. Because the act did not specify that Negro bodies would go to Shaw University, the Democratic press maintained that the Fusionists were not satisfied with fraternizing with Negroes in life, but had decreed that social equality must be maintained even in death.[92]

In the main, the legislature closed with the feeling that it had consolidated some of its gains, in spite of tremendous Democratic opposition outside the legislature.

NOTES TO CHAPTER FOUR

1. J. D. Hicks, *The Populist Revolt, A History of the Farmers' Alliance and the People's Party*, 354-55, 363-66.
2. Josephus Daniels, *Editor in Politics*, 167.
3. *Congressional Record, Fifty-fourth Congress, First Session*, XXVIII, 607 (Pritchard's speech).
4. Hamilton, *History of North Carolina Since 1860*, 255.
5. *Caucasian*, May 21, 1896.
6. *The Union Republican*, March 26, 1896.
7. *News and Observer*, May 16, 1896.
8. Craven, Cumberland, Edgecombe, Franklin, Mecklenburg, Perquimans, Union, Wake, Wilkes, and Wilson.
9. *News and Observer*, May 16, 1896.
10. *Caucasian*, May 21, 1896.
11. *The Union Republican*, June 25, 1896.
12. *News and Observer*, May 15, 1896.
13. Josephus Daniels, *Editor in Politics*, 153.
14. Weaver, The Gubernatorial Election of 1896 (Unpublished M.A. Thesis), 50.
15. *News and Observer*, May 16, 1896.
16. *Caucasian*, May 21, 1896.
17. *News and Observer*, May 16, 1896; and *Caucasian*, May 21, 1896.
18. *Caucasian*, April 12, 1896; *Progressive Farmer*, April 21, 1896.
19. *The Union Republican*, April 23, 1896.
20. Florence E. Smith, Populism And Its Influence in North Carolina (Unpublished Ph.D. dissertation), 142.
21. *News and Observer*, May 20, 1896.
22. *Ibid.*, July 2, 3, 1896.
23. *Ibid.*, July 3, 1896.
24. *Ibid.*
25. *Caucasian*, July 2, 1896.
26. *Public Documents*, 1897, Appended Abstract of the Election of 1896.
27. *News and Observer*, June 28, 1896.
Also *Caucasian*, July 2, 1896; *Progressive Farmer*, June 30, 1896; no *Democratic Handbook* of 1896 available at Duke University Library, University of North Carolina Library, State Archives, or the Library of Congress.
28. Delap, "The Populist Party in North Carolina," 62.
29. *Public Documents*, 1897, Document No. 34, Abstract of Votes for State Officers 1896.
30. *Progressive Farmer*, August 18, 1896.
Also *Caucasian*, August 20, 1896.
31. *The Union Republican*, August 20, 1896.
32. *Caucasian*, August 20, 1896.
33. *News and Observer*, May 16, 1896.

34. *Ibid.*, October 30, 1896.

35. Interview with Judge Armond W. Scott, Washington, D. C., October 27, 1945.

36. J. G. Kerner to Daniel L. Russell, July 17, 1896, Daniel Russell Papers, University of North Carolina Library.

37. Richmond Pearson to Daniel L. Russell, July 22, 1896, Daniel Russell Papers, University of North Carolina Library.

38. *News and Observer*, July 31, 1896, August 12, 1896.

39. *Caucasian*, September 10, 1896.
Also *News and Observer*, September 11, 1896.

40. *Caucasian*, October 29, 1896.

41. Weaver, *op. cit.*, 71, 73.

42. *Elizabeth City North Carolinian*, July 23, 1896.

43. J. R. Henderson (Wilkesboro, North Carolina) to Daniel L. Russell, May 21, 1896, Daniel Russell Papers, University of North Carolina Library.

44. "An Address To The Populist Party of North Carolina," campaign pamphlets, University of North Carolina Library.

45. See maps, 57, 58.

46. *North Carolina Manual*, 1913, 1006.

47. *Ibid.*, 1005-6.

48. Craven, Edgecombe, Halifax, New Hanover, Northampton, and Richmond.

49. Alamance, Buncombe, Chatham, Cumberland, Forsyth, Franklin, Mecklenburg, Nash, Pitt, Robeson, and Wake.

50. Weaver, *op. cit.*, 81.

51. Interview with Dr. James E. Shepard, President of The North Carolina College for Negroes, Durham, North Carolina, June 22, 1944.

52. Alleghany, Bertie, Carteret, Columbus, Cumberland, Currituck, Davidson, Forsyth, Gates, Green, Halifax, Johnston, Martin, Mitchell, Montgomery, New Hanover, Onslow, Polk, Robeson, Rockingham, Sampson, Union, Wilson, and Yadkin.

53. Bertie, Halifax, and New Hanover were "black counties."

54. Alleghany, Bertie, Carteret, Columbus, Cumberland, Currituck, Forsyth, Halifax, Mitchell, New Hanover, Polk, Robeson, Union, Wilson, and Yadkin.

55. Bertie, Halifax, and New Hanover were the "black counties."

56. *North Carolina Manual*, 1913, 1005-6.

57. *Appleton's Annual Cyclopedia*, New Series, XIX (1894), 553.

58. Losses of 299, 309, 335, 404, 511, 568, 583, 585, 599, 635, 705, 911, 923, 1,029, and 2,261 in Person, Durham, Caswell, Brunswick, Hyde, Vance, Wayne, Franklin, Northampton, Warren, Rockingham, Cumberland, Pitt, Chatham, and Wake counties, respectively.

59. Gains of 4, 7, 27, 49, 51, 54, 57, 77, 83, 130, 137, 165, 215, 220, and 343 in Alleghany, Chowan, Carbarrus, Nash, Duplin, Pender, McDowell, Mecklenburg, Columbus, Stanly, Union, Robeson, Bertie, Hertford, and Anson counties, respectively.

60. Brunswick, Carteret, Caswell, Chatham, Cumberland, Davidson, Davie, Durham, Forsyth, Franklin, Hyde, Jones, Lenoir, Lincoln, Moore, Northampton, Orange, Pitt, Randolph, Rockingham, Vance, Wake, and Warren.

61. Weaver, *op. cit.*, 78.

62. *Public Documents*, 1897, Document No. 34, Abstract of votes for State Officers, 1896. *Supra*, 54.

63. *House Journal*, 1897, 3-11.

64. W. H. Crews, Granville County; John T. Howe, New Hanover County; and James Young, Wake County.

65. *Senate Journal,* 1897, 7-10.

Party affiliations for both House and Senate found in *Turner's North Carolina Almanac* (1897), 56-57; further checked by *News and Observer,* January 19, 1897; and Hamilton, *History of North Carolina Since 1860,* 452.

66. W. B. Henderson, Eleventh District, and W. Lee Person, Fifth District.

67. *Biographical Directory of the American Congress 1774-1927,* 452.

Party affiliations secured from biographical sketches.

68. *Public Documents,* 1897, Document A, 12-13.

69. Luther Gobbel, *Church-State Relations in North Carolina Since 1776,* 132-71; also Josephus Daniels, *Editor in Politics,* 102-11, 227, 230-33, 318-24.

70. *Public Documents,* 1897, Document A, 15.

71. *Progressive Farmer,* August 20, 1895.

72. *Public Documents,* 1897, Document No. 1, 18-20.

73. *Ibid.,* Document A, 8-9.

74. *The Union Republican,* December 24, 1896.

75. *News and Observer,* January 8, 1897.

76. *Caucasian,* February 4, 1897.

77. *News and Observer,* January 16, 1897.

78. *House Journal,* 1897, 106.

79. *Appleton's Annual Cyclopedia,* New Series, XX (1895), 556.

80. *Carr* v. *Coke,* North Carolina Reports, XVI, 224-70.

81. *Ibid.,* 234, 240.

82. *Public Laws,* 1897, Chap. 14, 68.

83. *Ibid.,* Chap. 206, 347.

84. *Private Laws,* 1897, Chap. 56, 83.

85. Josephus Daniels, *Editor in Politics,* 220-21.

86. *Public Laws,* 1897, Chap. 46, 95.

87. *Ibid.,* Chap. 185, 311-19; *Infra,* Chap. V.

88. *Ibid.,* Chap. 366, 549.

89. *Infra,* Chap. IX, 124-35.

90. *Public Laws,* 1897, Chap. 127, 180; Chap. 421, 605-7.

91. *Ibid.,* Chap. 203, 344.

92. *News and Observer,* March 4, 1897.

CHAPTER FIVE

FUSION ELECTION LAW

THE DEMOCRATS CONDEMNED the Fusion election law of 1895 on the grounds that it was designed to permit a large number of Negroes to support the Republican ticket, and that Governor Russell had been elected in 1896 by the votes of 120,000 Negroes. The Fusion election law must be interpreted against the background of the preceding Democratic election law to see if it differed, and, if so, to what extent. It is only through a comparative study of both laws that the political implications inherent in each can be properly estimated.

The Civil War and Reconstruction left in North Carolina, as in the entire South, the enfranchised Negro. The Bourbon Democrats in this state were aware of the Negro's allegiance to the Republican party. While the Democrats considered the Republican party as an "alien" seed transplanted to new soil, the Negro saw it as the party of liberation. The problem in North Carolina after 1876 was how to restrict and nullify the Negro vote, and do so within the framework of legality. The Southern states resorted to one or more of four specific methods to negate the political influence of the Negro: centralization of election machinery, payment of taxes before voting, intricate and complex election laws, and express educational qualifications for voting.[1]

The North Carolina Negro, entitled to manhood suffrage by the North Carolina Constitution of 1868 and the Fifteenth Amendment to the Constitution of the United States, was controlled in the exercise of suffrage by centralization of election machinery and state election laws. These laws were strikingly different in the periods of Democratic ascendancy, 1876-94; Fusion control, 1895-98; and Democratic supremacy in 1899.

The election law of 1877 was enacted by a Democratic legislature.[2] It required that all state officers be elected every four years and members of the General Assembly, Congress, and certain county officials every two years. The Tuesday after the first Monday in November of an election year was election day. The regulation of all elections was placed under the complete jurisdiction of the Board of Justices of the Peace in each county which selected, one month prior to election day, the registrars anad judges for each precinct and had the power to alter old and create new places of election.[3] In 1879, the elective functions of the Board of Justices of the Peace were transferred to county commissioners who were still appointed by the justices of the peace who were in turn appointed by the legislature.[4] The General Assembly was Democratic from 1876 to 1895; hence a Democratic legislature

67

chose a preponderant majority of Democratic county commissioners who in turn chose mainly Democratic registrars in their counties. Thus the dominant party in the legislature enacted a law which controlled election machinery through centralization. Effective Democratic control from the center to the outer periphery offered little opportunity for political opponents to get a hand in election procedure. The same Board of Justices of the Peace (later county commissioners) appointed four judges of election, and two of the appointees were required to be of a different political party, where possible, from the registrars.[5] What determined "where possible" was left to the intent and purposes of the Democratic Board of Justices of the Peace. The 1889 alteration stipulated that if a selected judge could not attend, then the one chosen in his place would not have to be of the same political party as the judge first selected.[6] There was positively no guarantee of party representation at the polls except Democratic party representation. If in some precints "where possible" Democratic commissioners chose Republican judges, there was no guarantee that "the chosen judges would be of sufficient intelligence and partisan zeal to defend their party's interest."[7]

The registrars revised the existing registration books without the necessity of a new registration. If they chose to omit certain names, a sufficient number of omitted persons might supplicate the Board of Justices of the Peace to demand a new registration,[8] but whether a Democratic board would grant a new registration if the cry for one came from opponents of the Democratic party is a matter of conjecture. The important point is that the task fell upon the elector to prove that his name belonged on the books. The applicant's affiliation with an opposing party would be unlikely to induce Democratic registration officials to act in his favor in areas where the anti-Democratic voters equaled or nearly equaled the Democratic. If the applicant were a Negro, his race served as a double deterrent. The law further stated that the elector must register and vote in the precinct in which he was a bona fide resident, or show certificate of removal from the last county, township, or precinct in which he voted.[9] A bona fide resident was one who had lived in the state twelve months and in the county ninety days prior to election.[10] This section was designed to deny the vote to many Negroes who migrated frequently. Too, many Negroes were not careful in saving their certificates of removal, if indeed they bothered or were able to secure them from their former registrars. A registrar could request of any applicant to prove his identity, or age and residence, by the testimony of at least one elector under oath.[11] This provision would debar many Negroes who, from size, height, and appearance, were visibly over twenty-one but had no birth certificate, physician, or midwife to corroborate their age claims. Twelve years later, 1889, the Democratic law inserted specifically that "no registration shall be valid unless it specifies as near as may be the age, occupation, place of birth and place of residence of an elector as well as township or county from whence the elector removed (if removed) and full name by which the voter is known.[12] The meaning of the phrase "as near as may be" in relation to the applicant's age was left to the registrar. He was omniscient and omnipotent. Many Negroes were inclined to designate their places of residence by the colloquial names of certain areas, such as "Coon's Hollow," "Chittlin Switch," "Across the Railroad Tracks," "Sampson's Creek," or "Marse Ned's Plantation." But these places of residence were not correct in the sense of true mailing address. In these cases, the registrar could and would merely write the responses, knowing that such answers would invalidate the Negroes' registrations. The issue of a full name came into play as some Negroes had initials and nicknames. A response as "W. T. Majette" or "Puddin Jones" might debar him. A conscientious registrar could help matters by going beyond the letter of the law and clarifying it to the applicant, but little could be hoped for at the hands of a Democratic registrar when the innovation was deliberately aimed to check voting by Negroes who attempted to support the Republican ticket.

The Democratic election procedure required that the books be opened for registration for five Saturdays preceding the Tuesday of election. Any citizen could examine the books on the fifth Saturday, the Monday preceding election, and on election day and demand the registrar to mark "challenged" by an objected name and the judges of election to hear the challenges.[13] In an area where 250 Negro names might be challenged, one can see the utter farce of trying to hear cases on Monday, much less on Tuesday. Not all the judges who heard the cases were of a different political party from the registrars. A "challenged" person might clear himself by proving his identity, his continued residence in the precinct, securing the sworn testimony of one other elector, and by taking an oath himself.[14] If a "challenged" person cleared himself through the above steps, the judges could refuse to permit such a person to vote, if they were satisfied from record evidence or their own knowledge or other legal testimony that he was not a legal voter.[15] In 1889, the law extended the period of registration from five to six Saturdays and, thereby, allowed one week between the challenge and the clearing of the challenge.[16] This extension of time gave a challenged elector ample opportunity to marshal evidence in his behalf. If the Negroes had safely leaped the hurdles of registration, and been challenged and cleared, they found a further barrier in that all ballots had to be handed to the judges who placed them in the ballot boxes.[17] The judges sat high above the electors' heads, and their sheer honesty determined whether the ballot was put in the box of the elector's choice. The ballots, after being counted, were turned over to the register of deeds in each county. The Democrats themselves admitted that they used fraud at times and that "in some sections, over-run by Negroes, improper methods may here and there have been resorted to."[18]

The Democratic election law of 1876-77 created county canvassers. One man was selected from each precinct by judges of election to serve as county canvasser. He took a return of his precinct vote to the county canvassers' meeting which convened on the second day after election. The county canvassers opened and re-counted the precinct returns in the presence of the sheriff and others who chose to attend. The returns of the county canvassers were sent to the State Board of Canvassers who in turn announced the true count.[19] Whether the Democratic State and County Boards of Canvassers manipulated votes for Democratic victories is a matter of speculation, but the possibility of manipulation was present because canvassing boards were allowed, in cases of disputed elections, to decide by a majority vote the true count—a decision left to their minds and to their consciences. It is questionable whether the election law of 1876-77 conferred judicial powers upon the canvassers. They did exercise it, and MacLeod believes that the Democratic legislature of 1877 which enacted the election law intended it to be that way,[20] although it was not timely so to state.[21] In 1883, the Democratic legislature specifically directed the canvassers "to judicially determine" the returns.[22] MacLeod's examination of Supreme Court cases affecting election procedures shows that the Democratic Supreme Court considered the conferring of judicial power upon canvassing boards as unwise.[23] The canvassers could affect election returns.

If the Negro could escape the numerous snares in the intricate election laws, deliberately laid by Democratic legislators and election officials, he might cast his vote and have it counted as cast. The basic consideration in the election laws from 1876 to 1894 was the perpetuation of Democratic control, "monolithic solidarity" of a single party, to prevent unwary Negroes from 1876 to 1894 and Populists from 1892 to 1894 from voting.[24] An analyst of North Carolina's Democratic election law stated that nothing could be said in its defense.[25]

The Fusionists, having won the election of 1894, repealed *in toto* the Democratic election laws and passed their own on March 8, 1895.[26] The number of state officers to be elected every four years, the number of county officers to be elected every two years, and the time of election remained as they had been under the Democratic law. The law defined a political party as a political organization whose candidate for governor received as many as thirty thousand votes in the last general election (1892),[27] thus giving to the Populist party official standing. The clerk of the superior court had the power to establish, alter, or create separate places of voting.[28] Two factors stood out relative to the clerk and his functions: first, his position in county

DEMOCRATIC ELECTION LAWS FROM 1877 TO 1894: CENTRALIZATION

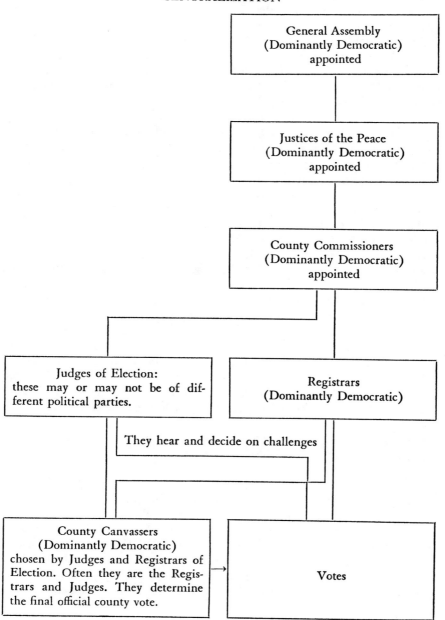

General Assembly
(Dominantly Democratic)
appointed

Justices of the Peace
(Dominantly Democratic)
appointed

County Commissioners
(Dominantly Democratic)
appointed

Judges of Election:
these may or may not be of different political parties.

Registrars
(Dominantly Democratic)

They hear and decide on challenges

County Canvassers
(Dominantly Democratic)
chosen by Judges and Registrars of Election. Often they are the Registrars and Judges. They determine the final official county vote.

Votes

government was dependent upon popular election and not legislative appointment; and, second, he was required to have a voting place for every 350 electors, the first instance in the history of election laws in North Carolina which required a ratio of voting places to voters in accordance with the density of populated areas.

The Fusionists realized that the selection of judges and registrars of election was a determinant in conducting an honest election. The appointment of judges and registrars was handled by the clerk of the superior court. He appointed one elector from each political party in each precinct as registrar and one as judge, only upon written recommendation from or approval by the chairman of the state executive committee of each party in the state.[29] Each precinct board of election then had one Republican, one Populist, and one Democrat as registrars and the same ratio as judges. To the most casual observer, here was an intent at impartiality. The very fact that the chairman of the state executive committee of each party had the power to recommend registrars and judges showed that the Fusionists desired to escape the criticism that they were as partisan as the Democrats. The distinguishing difference at the outset between the Democratic and Fusion election laws was that under the former the justices of the peace (later county commissioners) which set up election machinery were appointed by a partisan legislature, while under the latter the clerk of the superior court was popularly elected and served as an agent of the chairman of each state executive committee.

Of the three registrars appointed in each precinct, one was chosen by them as chairman to preside over their deliberations.[30] Democratic opposition charged that the arrangement was unfair since representation of three parties at the polls meant in reality the representation of two parties because the Republicans and the Populists had fused and were one. In reality, the Republicans and Populists were each attempting to secure an election law which would guarantee representation to each party on the election boards irrespective of whether fusion did or did not occur in subsequent elections.

The Fusionists retained the Democratic feature of the 1889 law which required a period of six consecutive Saturdays for the total process of registration. The books were opened during the first four Saturdays for registering names, while the fifth Saturday was reserved for inspecting the books and challenging the names. The law stated that no challenge could be made after the specified Saturday for such, except in case of voters who had become twenty-one years of age since the books were closed. The Saturday before election Tuesday was reserved only for clearing challenges.

The Fusionists, realizing that many of the intricate provisions of the Democratic law applied to the Negro and Populist voters, adopted a clear and simple provision for registration:

Every registration may specify as near as may, the age and residence of the elector, as well as the township or county from whence he removed . . . but no registration shall be invalidated because of a failure to specify age and residence, etc., unless it shows that upon the registrar properly questioning the elector, he declined to answer the questions pertaining to these matters.[31]

The law further specified that no name could be arbitrarily crossed from the books in so far as the entry of name, age, residence, and date of registration was presumptive evidence of the regularity of registration and the right of such a person to vote.[32] There was no doubt that the liberality of these sections safeguarded Negroes and whites who might not have been able to prove their basic qualification.

The 1895 law made a clear break with the past by providing that ballots could be on paper of any color, and such ballots could have thereon a party device.[33] The Democrats had required white paper, and therefore charged that the Fusionists permitted different colors of paper in order that the ignorant voter could identify his party ticket by color.[34] Irrespective of the Democratic assertion that the party used no device for its ignorant voters, there is this information from the titular leader of the party to the Democratic chairman of Wake County:

I forwarded to you yesterday a communication enclosing general tickets *pinned* together, and suggesting that you have the entire democratic tickets, to be voted by an elector, so *pinned* before sent to the several precincts, in order that each elector should be certain to get every ticket.

Upon reflection I think it best *not to pin* them, as even so small a thing as a *pin hole* in a ticket may be construed to be a "device," and thus cause the ticket to be thrown out.

Have them put together and put around each set of tickets a *small rubber* band in a way to hold them securely. I suggest this change by way of precaution, in order that we will avoid all possible danger. The rubbers will cost but little more, if any, than pins.[35]

While the elector continued to hand his ballot to the judges to be placed in the ballot boxes, there was less opportunity for doing away with ballots. A judge from each political party presided over the ballot boxes.[36] Ballots found in the wrong boxes were not the fault of the voters but of the judges of election, and the Fusionists required that they be counted. The ballots, after being properly counted in the presence of the Republican, Populist, and Democratic registrars, judges of election, and candidates for office, were sealed and placed in the custody of the clerk of the superior court. The clerk gave a signed receipt for them, sent a copy of the abstract to the register of deeds, one to the secretary of state, published one in voting precincts, and kept a copy.[37] Such provisions for careful preservation had never been made before.

The Fusion law, in order to prevent Populists and Negroes, mainly the latter, from being kept from the polls on registration and election day, stipulated that all electors were privileged from arrest on those days except for treason, felony, or breach of the peace committed on that day.[38] In order to combat the fear that Democratic employers might try physical intimidation or economic pressure on their white and Negro tenants and employees, the Fusion law fined heavily any person who by force or violence broke up or stayed an election by assaulting the election officials; any person who aimed at influencing the election by treating with meat or drink on election day or any previous day; any person who discharged from employment, withdrew patronage from, injured, threatened, oppressed, or intimidated a voter because he might or might not have voted a particular ticket; any person who gave or promised to give money, property, or reward to a voter to be elected; and any person who gave away or sold intoxicating liquors at any place within five miles of the polling place within twelve hours before or after an election.[39] The Fusionists sought to cut the ties of economic inducement which might influence voting.

For the first time in the state's history, candidates for public offices were required to file an itemized record of campaign expenses and contributions with the secretary of state or forfeit office,[40] and the judges of the Supreme and superior courts had general supervisory powers over the final interpretation of the processes involved in election procedure.[41] If the sincere desire for an honest election is to be judged by the punitive consequences for violating the law, then the Fusionists were in earnest. Their election machinery included representation of all parties.[42]

The Fusion parties won the election of 1896 and the subsequent legislature amended the 1895 election law.[43] The important changes involved the organization of the Board of Election, procedures in challenging, interpretation of the Supreme Court's power, and deletion of the 1895 provision relative to a candidate's campaign expenses. There were also minor changes and additions.

The 1897 law removed the power af appointment of judges and registrars (board) of election from the chairman of the state executive committee of each party and placed it in the hands of the county board of election which consisted of the clerk of the superior court, register of deeds, and chairman of the county commissioners of the respective counties.[44] This appeared to the Democrats as partisan strategy because in Fusionist counties all three officers would be Fusionists. The law, however, still compelled the board to appoint a representative from each party as judge and registrar. Three democratic features stand out even in this change: first, the requirement of having each political party represented on the precinct board was still a *sine qua non;* second, the three members of the county board (clerk, register of

THE FUSION ELECTION LAW OF 1895

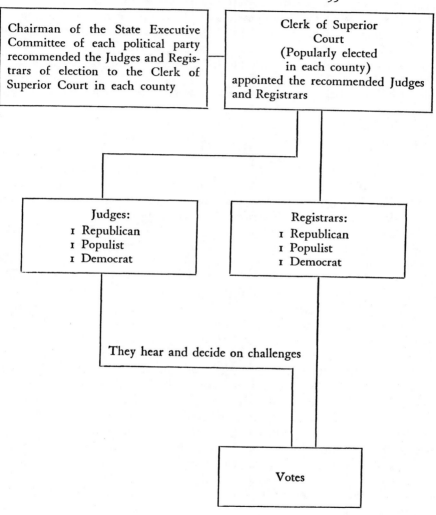

Chairman of the State Executive Committee of each political party recommended the Judges and Registrars of election to the Clerk of Superior Court in each county

Clerk of Superior Court (Popularly elected in each county) appointed the recommended Judges and Registrars

Judges:
1 Republican
1 Populist
1 Democrat

Registrars:
1 Republican
1 Populist
1 Democrat

They hear and decide on challenges

Votes

deeds, chairman of county commissioners) were popularly elected; and, third, it placed control of activities into the hands of the county. The elimination of correspondence between county clerk and state chairmen, also, relieved the latter of much labor. It should be noted, too, that these state chairmen or county party chairmen were not left out of the picture, for the 1897 change specified that the Supreme Court had the power, upon complaint of the chairman of either political party or upon the substantiated complaint of ten good citizens, to remove any registrar or election official appointed by the county board and substitute qualified persons of the same political faith.[45]

The Democratic party had, no doubt, made flagrant abuse of the simple method of challenging, and the Fusionists decided to make the process more difficult. Contrary to the practice of having voters say to the registrar "I object to so and so's name," and the registrar marking "challenged" by it, the Fusion change required any person objecting to a name on the registration book to state by means of an affidavit the specific cause of challenge and pay twenty-five cents. The fee was refunded by the county commissioners in each case wherein the challenge was sustained.[46] At the time of the trial, any protesting voters could cross-examine the challenged voter. The Democrats criticized the fee and contended that the law made no provision for paying the challenger for the expenses and trouble involved in securing the witnesses to prove the allegations.[47] The fact that any person could cross-examine the "challenged" voter at the time of the trial was an evidence of fairness. The Democrats also bitterly opposed the use of an affidavit or an oath to be taken in challenging. But there should have been no opposition to an affidavit since it contained specific causes rather than general charges and clarified the case when it reached the judges of election.

The courts had been granted supervisory power over elections, and the change specified their powers more clearly. In cases of alleged conflict of decision among precinct boards or county boards of election or party chairmen over the interpretation of the election law, the Supreme Court was required to proceed without delay, and to the exclusion of all other business, to hear, try, determine the question, and render such decision as should reconcile conflicting decisions of the judges and so determine the law.[48] The courts, also, had supervisory control over the county boards of 1897 which appointed the election officials. The Fusionists were determined that the courts be the haven of refuge for conflicting opinions on the interpretation of the election law.

Whereas the law of 1895 placed all state and federal candidates for office on one ticket, the 1897 change provided an individual ballot for each slate, and each party was required to file with the secretary of state its list of candidates and its party device.[49] The ballot could in 1897 be partly written and partly printed, but an elector was permitted to erase a printed name from the party list and insert another name.[50] The Fusionists required that a list of all candidates be filed before an election with the secretary of state. The Democrats condemned this requirement as a "violation of the right of free people of North Carolina to vote for whom they pleased, without regard to whether the party they voted for had been nominated by a partisan convention or committee."[51] The Democrats added further that, when the right to write any name in place of one erased was given, it was the object of the Fusionists to force the Negro to vote the Republican ticket.[52] Voting places were required to be open and clear to all alike, and ballot boxes were not to be concealed from public observation.

While the former Fusion law provided for the safekeeping of ballots and ballot boxes, the 1897 change provided the same for registration books and all election materials. The Fusionists intended to have every bit of election material available in the event contested elections arose; such materials the Democrats had never carefully preserved.

The Fusionists had declared a man immune from arrest while attending registration or election, except for certain crimes, and the Democrats countercharged in the campaign of 1896 that a man could do anything and go "Scot" free all day on registration day. The parties in power felt that, since the registration books were opened beginning with the sixth Saturday preceding election, the local police authorities need not wait until registration or election day to arrest a man; hence, they further specified that an elector could not be arrested from the day of the opening of the registration books until after the election for failure to list his property or poll, and any police agent so arresting would be fined and imprisoned.[53]

To insure greater freedom to vote, the Fusionists attempted to eliminate economic pressure and barriers from tenant farmers, sharecroppers, city workers, white and black, whose white Democratic employers might compel them to work on registration or election day, by providing that an elector was entitled to absent himself from service and employment for sufficient time to go and return from registration and voting. If an employer failed to designate a proper time, and the employee absented himself for such, the former could impose no penalty on the latter.[54] While the Fusionists inaugurated many advanced and democratic reforms, they took one backward step in 1897 by repealing the requirement which specified that candidates file itemized statements of finances received and expended for campaign purposes.[55] Irrespective of this change, the Fusionists continued to give representation to all parties at the polls.[56]

As was to be expected, the Democrats saw nothing good in the Fusion election law, and their campaign literature alleged that the liberality of the law was to encourage Negro voting and consequently Negro office-holding.[57]

THE FUSION ELECTION LAW OF 1897

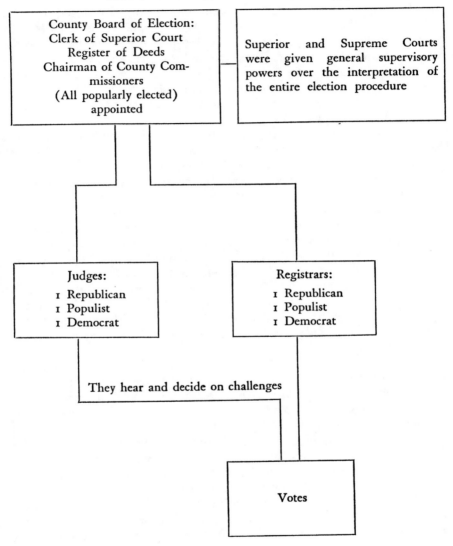

County Board of Election:
Clerk of Superior Court
Register of Deeds
Chairman of County Com-
missioners
(All popularly elected)
appointed

Superior and Supreme Courts were given general supervisory powers over the interpretation of the entire election procedure

Judges:

1 Republican
1 Populist
1 Democrat

Registrars:

1 Republican
1 Populist
1 Democrat

They hear and decide on challenges

Votes

They made the law an issue in the campaign of 1898. Recent historians have appraised differently the election law. Hicks claims that the Fusion legislature worked out a drastic election law to prevent corruption at the polls, and the law worked reasonably well.[58] Smith held that the long and detailed election law did not differ fundamentally from the Democratic ones it replaced.[59] Mabry interpreted the Fusion election law as a reaction against the more intricate Democratic election law designed by the Democrats to disfranchise Negroes, but which had been used more recently against white Populists and Republicans, and concluded that which of the two election laws came nearer serving the ends of justice is a matter of opinion.[60] Delap, the first writer in North Carolina to see Populism in a truer perspective, stated that the important and lasting laws passed by the Populists were few in number, but the laws providing for a revision in the election laws, local self-government, and a better system of public schools are the best outward testimonies of their work.[61] Weaver, the only writer who apparently has analyzed significant provisions of the law, in comparison with the Democratic law, not only affirmed that the new law worked reasonably well, but also that under it the non-Democratic voters of the state had an opportunity to show their full strength for the first time since the Democrats had overthrown Republican rule in the state.[62] Hamilton, a severe critic of the Fusion period, insisted that the new election law was worse in many respects than the old one which it replaced and that one provision, representation of each party at the polls, was criticized in principle by the Democrats with utter unfairness but with considerable justice in the particular case.[63] While the Democratic accusation and pro-Democratic historians have held that the law was designed to encourage Negro voting, Turner and Bridges took an extreme opposing view. They alleged that it was designed to keep Negroes *from* voting the Democratic ticket, an allegation ludicrous in the light of the tense racial antagonism of the 1890's. These authors recorded that the occasion for the change in the election law was the fact that in all eastern counties, and in Edgecombe in particular, many Negroes had evinced a desire to vote the Democratic ticket but were afraid because of ostracism and violence or expulsion from church. They further contended that under the old law Negroes enjoyed the privacy of voting and were not intimidated; but under the new law secrecy could not be had, thereby causing Negroes to be betrayed in their manner of voting.[64]

In appraising the Fusion election law, the comments range from "good," "worked reasonably well," "no better than the one it displaced," "worse than the one it displaced," "encouraged the Negro to vote the Republican ticket," to "prevented him from voting the Democratic ticket." In reality, the Fusionists effected a less discriminatory election law.

The sixteen "black counties" cast 15,357 more votes in 1896 under the

Fusion election law than in 1892 under the Democratic law.[65] Whereas Buncombe, Davidson, Forsyth, Guilford, Surry, and Watauga, white western counties, showed Democratic pluralities of 400, 100, 600, 300, 300, and 100, respectively, in the election of 1892, they showed under the Fusion election law in the election of 1896, anti-Democratic pluralities of 400, 500, 1,100, 100, 300, and 130, respectively. The increase in votes in 1896, in the black as well as white counties, was caused in part by the liberality of the Fusion election law. The Republican-Populist generalization that the Democratic party manipulated votes in the above counties in the election of 1892 cannot be proved because many potential voters may not have been interested in voting, but the large anti-Democratic victory in 1896 suggests strongly election crookedness in 1892.

Two interpretations of the Democratic election law rendered by the Supreme Court of North Carolina shed light upon the ethical factors which could arise in the functions and duties of Democratic election officials. These two interpretations, at the same time, place the Fusionist objectives in bold relief. In 1890, Travis N. Harris ran against George M. Scarborough for the office of register of deeds in Montgomery County and was defeated. Harris learned that some ballots cast for him had been thrown out and instituted proceedings against Scarborough for the position. The special term of the Superior Court in Montgomery County favored Scarborough, and Harris appealed to the Supreme Court. It was revealed that the registrar had thrown out some ballots because the electors had failed to designate either place of birth, place of residence, or name of township from whence removed. The question hinged around whether the registrar had performed his duty in seeking direct and explicit answers to these omissions or had accepted the indefinite answers knowing that the registration would be invalidated. The court refused to examine the procedure of the registrar, relied upon the assumption that he had performed his duty, and rendered the opinion that the rejected ballots were invalid.[66] The court held to the letter of the law and exonerated the registrar irrespective of the fact that the electors had given wrong township names unknowingly, that the registrar had not tried to aid them in more accurate specifications, and that the electors had not tried to register and vote in any other township.[67] The court, in interpreting the election law, placed the burden of proof upon the elector rather than upon the registrar. One of the five judges who dissented, Walter Clark, pleaded for a more liberal interpretation of the requirements placed upon the elector and a more liberal spirit on the part of the registrar in seeking responses to registration.

In the election of 1894, J. H. Quinn ran against T. D. Lattimore for the office of clerk of the Superior Court of Cleveland County and was defeated. Quinn entered a suit against Lattimore on several grounds, chief among which were that electors voting for Lattimore voted in townships in which they did not reside, and electors were registered irregularly by persons who had the registration books in their possession and acted for the registrar. The Supreme Court, composed of three Republicans, one Populist, and one Democrat, reasoned unanimously that the votes of qualified electors living near the indefinite dividing line of two townships must be counted in the township where they had carried on civil and political pursuits, since they registered and voted in good faith, paid taxes, and sent their children to school in the township in which they did not actually reside.[68] The Fusion election law of 1895 was more in harmony with the Supreme Court's interpretation (*Quinn* v. *Lattimore*) of what an election law should do, in that it placed the responsibility for accurate registration upon the registrar rather than the elector unless the elector was guilty of fraud by deliberately choosing to answer evasively.

The Fusionists guaranteed representation to each party at the polls, made liberal provisions to encourage registration and voting, made punitive consequence for violation heavy, provided means for safeguarding ballots, and gave to the courts of the state general supervisory powers over election procedures. Their election law was not pure in the sense of the Australian ballot, but such a ballot was not in use anywhere in the South at the time. The liberality attributed to their law does not come from the fact that the Republican or Populist parties were "Negro-loving" parties, but from the fact that each party wanted to safeguard its own status at the polls. The fairness in the election law was the result of necessity and may or may not have generated from an ideal of purity. The Fusion election laws of 1895 and 1897 were enacted before the election years of 1896 and 1898, at times when the Republicans and Populists had not agreed to fuse. Any attempt on the part of Democrats and historians to show that these laws were designed as pieces of political chicanery to perpetuate Fusion is an attempt to read into the laws a situation which had not materialized at the time of the enactments. Democratic condemnation, however, was predicted on the assumption that the "lion and the lamb had decided to lie down together" henceforth and forever.

NOTES TO CHAPTER FIVE

1. Stephen Weeks, "The History of Negro Suffrage in the South," *Political Science Quarterly*, IX (1894), 692.

2. *Public Laws*, 1876-77, Chap. 275, 516-44.

3. *Ibid.*, 516-17.

4. *Public Laws*, 1879, Chap. 152, 286-88.

5. *Public Laws*, 1876-77, Chap. 275, 519.

6. *Public Laws*, 1889, Chap. 287, 289-91.

7. John B. MacLeod, The Development of North Carolina Election Laws, 1865-1894 (Unpublished M.A. thesis, University of North Carolina, 1946), 56.

8. *Public Laws*, 1876-77, Chap. 275, 517-18.

9. *Ibid.*, 518, 521.

10. *Ibid.*, 520.

11. *Ibid.*, 521-22.

12. *Public Laws*, 1889, Chap. 287, 289-91.

13. *Public Laws*, 1876-77, Chap. 275, 522.

14. *Ibid.*, 519.

15. *Ibid.*, 522-23.

16. *Public Laws*, 1889, Chap. 287, 289-91.

17. *Public Laws*, 1876-77, Chap. 275, 523.

18. *Democratic Handbook*, 1898, 91.

19. *Public Laws*, 1876-77, Chap. 275, 524-26.

20. MacLeod, *op. cit.*, 86.

21. The Democratic election law of 1876-77 "was passed eight days after President Hayes took office. The Democrats in North Carolina and elsewhere had been denouncing the recent partisan canvass made by the Republican State canvassing boards in Florida and Louisiana as the mammoth fraud of the age. Except for the exercise of judicial power by these boards, the Democratic candidate would have become President."—*Ibid.*

22. *Code of 1883*, Section 2694.

23. MacLeod, *op. cit.*, 77-102.

24. See chart, 71.

25. Weeks, *op. cit.*, 691, 693.

26. *Public Laws*, 1895, Chap. 159, 211-36.

27. *Ibid.*, 211.

28. *Ibid.*, 211-12.

29. *Ibid.*, 212-15.

30. *Ibid.*, 215.

31. *Ibid.*, 216.

32. *Ibid.*, 217.

33. *Ibid.*, 218.

34. *History of the General Assembly of 1895*, 37.

35. Furnifold M. Simmons to E. Chambers Smith, October 12, 1892, Edward Chambers Smith Papers, 1892-1916, Duke University Manuscript Collection.

36. *Public Laws*, 1895, Chap. 159, 218.

37. *Ibid.*, 218-20.

38. *Ibid.*, 235.

39. *Ibid.*, 226-31.

40. *Ibid.*, 235-36.

41. *Ibid.*, 215.

42. See chart, 75.

43. *Public Laws*, 1897, Chap. 185, 311-19.

44. *Ibid.*, 311-14.

45. *Ibid.*, 313-14.

46. *Ibid.*, 314-15.

47. *Democratic Handbook*, 1898, 87.

48. *Public Laws*, 1897, Chap. 185, 313.

49. *Ibid.*, 315-16.

50. *Ibid.*, 316.

51. *Democratic Handbook*, 1898, 90.

52. *Ibid.*

53. *Public Laws*, 1897, Chap. 185, 316.

54. *Ibid.*, 317.

55. *Ibid.*, 319.

56. See chart, 78.

57. *Democratic Handbook*, 1898, 42-43, 144-45.

58. Hicks, *The Populist Revolt*, 378.

59. Florence E. Smith, Populism and Its Influence in North Carolina (Unpublished Ph.D. dissertation), 127.

60. Mabry, "The Negro in North Carolina Politics Since Reconstruction," 37.

61. Delap, "The Populist Party in North Carolina," 74.

62. Weaver, The Gubernatorial Election of 1896 (Unpublished M.A. thesis), 33.

63. Hamilton, *History of North Carolina Since 1860*, 248, 267.

64. Joseph K. Turner and John Bridges, *History of Edgecombe County*, 309.

65. *Supra*, Chap. II, 15, 17-18.

66. *Harris v. Scarborough, North Carolina Reports*, CX, 232-44.

67. *Ibid.*, 243.

68. *Quinn v. Lattimore, North Carolina Reports*, CXX, 426-39.

CHAPTER SIX

NEGRO OFFICE-HOLDING: FEDERAL

IT WAS INEVITABLE that Fusion victories in 1894 and 1896 would bring the Negro more actively into politics. Irrespective of how little the Populists cared to see the race advance politically, necessity forced them to join with the Republicans in playing for Negro support.[1] Negro office-holding was nothing new to North Carolina for there had been Negroes in the state legislature intermittently since Reconstruction. Henry Plummer Cheatham, Negro, Vance County, had represented the Second Congressional District in the United States Congress from 1889 to 1893. He was a candidate for the same position in the election of 1892 and lost to Frederick Woodward, his Democratic opponent. The fact that he lost to Woodward by a small majority, and in a district composed largely of "black counties" where even the Democrats admitted that votes were often suppressed, prompted him to contest the latter's seat in the opening session of Congress, 1893.[2] He was unsuccessful in this contested election case. Ardent anti-Negro politicians spoke highly of Cheatham: "At least one Negro Congressman won the confidence of the people of both races—Henry P. Cheatham."[3] With the overthrow of the Democrats in 1894, the Republicans were bound to cast some political crumbs from the party's table to the Negroes who supported the ticket.

The Fusion victory of 1896 sent one Negro, George H. White, to the United States House of Representatives. While White represented the Second Congressional District, the remaining eight districts sent white representatives. White served two terms, 1897 to 1901, having been elected to the fifty-fifth and fifty-sixth Congresses. He was no novice in politics in 1896, nor was he ignorant. He had served as a member of the state House of Representatives in 1880 and of the state Senate in 1884; as solicitor and prosecuting attorney for the Second Judicial District in the state from 1886 to 1894, and as a delegate to the Republican national convention at St. Louis in 1896. To this political experience were added his academic training and experience as a graduate of Howard University, practising lawyer, and principal of the Colored State Normal School of North Carolina in Oxford.[4]

White's election in 1896 and 1898 deserves special analysis. He represented a district composed of nine counties, of which five were "black." While he was a staunch Republican and Negroes in the Second District recognized him as their titular leader, it is not amiss to say that white voters helped him to win. The Democratic press conceded him a 3,900 majority over Woodward, his Democratic opponent in 1896, before the official figures were proclaimed.[5] The guess was fairly accurate in the light of the results.[6]

An examination of the official declarations of the vote in the Second District for 1896 and 1898 will best show the comparative strength of White and his opponents.[7] Bertie, Edgecombe, Halifax, Northampton, and Warren were considered "black counties" because Negroes made up more than 50 per cent of the population. While Democratic propaganda termed this district the "black" district because of these counties, the potential voting strength

GEORGE W. WHITE, NEGRO, UNITED STATES HOUSE OF REPRESENTATIVES, 1896, 1898
SECOND CONGRESSIONAL DISTRICT VOTE 1896*

COUNTIES	GEORGE WHITE REPUBLICAN	FREDERICK WOODWARD DEMOCRAT	D. S. MOSES POPULIST	MACON DAIL	JAMES MEWBORNE
Bertie	2,199	1,440	216	—	—
Edgecombe	2,750	1,766	370	—	—
Greene	995	1,020	202	1	—
Halifax	3,955	2,056	205	—	—
Lenoir	1,401	1,652	291	—	3
Northampton	2,302	1,757	144	—	—
Warren	2,155	1,120	61	—	—
Wayne	2,159	2,811	438	—	—
Wilson	1,422	1,746	811	—	—
Totals	19,338	15,368	2,738	1	3

*Comparative Vote for Governor and Members of Congress 1892–1896, North Carolina, 10.

SECOND CONGRESSIONAL DISTRICT VOTE 1898†

COUNTIES	GEORGE WHITE REPUBLICAN	WM. FOUNTAIN DEMOCRAT	JAMES B. LLOYD POPULIST	SCATTERING
Bertie	1,871	1,151	375	94
Edgecombe	2,449	2,462	87	—
Greene	1,093	1,207	134	—
Halifax	2,626	1,162	78	95
Lenoir	1,465	1,679	279	2
Northampton	2,137	1,767	93	327
Warren	2,236	927	278	—
Wayne	2,102	2,444	534	—
Wilson	1,582	2,148	589	—
Totals	17,561	14,947	2,447	518

†Comparative Vote for Governor, 1900, and for Members of Congress, 1898 and 1900, North Carolina, 6. (Campaign pamphlets, University of North Carolina Library).

of the races was nearly equal. Negroes of voting age exceeded whites of voting age by 128.[8] The number of votes which White received in Bertie, Northampton, and Warren counties approximately totalled the number of Negro males of voting age in each county. His returns from Edgecombe and Halifax counties were large enough to offset the votes of his chief Democratic opponent (chart, 85). The Democratic candidate, Frederick Woodward, did not receive the potential white support in any of the nine counties. His failure to do so cannot be ascribed to the split in the white ranks by the presence of the Populist party, because the sum of the Democratic opposition plus the Populist vote did not total the number of white males of voting age. White garnered more votes for his Congressional election in 1896 in Bertie and Edgecombe counties and as many votes in Halifax, Northampton, and Warren counties as did the Republican gubernatorial candidate, Daniel L. Russell.[9] White lost Greene County (white) by twenty-five votes.

In 1898, White won again by a 2,612 majority over William Fountain, his chief Democratic opponent. He lost Edgecombe by a close margin yet carried the other four "black counties." Wayne County, white, went Democratic again, but the Democratic candidate of 1898 polled fewer votes in this county than in 1896; and, while White lost Wayne in both elections, he suffered no appreciable decline there in either election. The most surprising element in White's second victory was his re-election in the face of the withering fire of the "white supremacy" campaign of 1898 which was attended by intense racial intolerance. A Democratic paper actually stated that it could not understand how White won with a majority of 2,600.[10]

As a congressman from North Carolina for four years, White from time to time displayed partisanship, race consciousness, and nonpartisanship. His partisanship demonstrated itself in support of the Dingley tariff (a Republican measure).[11] His race consciousness came to the front in his defense of the Federal Anti-Lynching Bill which he proposed[12] and about which he expressed the deep concern that "there are more outrages against colored women by white men than there are by colored men against white women, as evidenced by the great numbers of mulattoes in the Southland."[13] His proposal urged that persons guilty of mob violence be guilty of treason against the United States and be tried for the same. White desired to place the victims of lynch-law under the protection of the federal government. He was primarily responsible for transferring $100,000 unclaimed by Negro soldiers to the establishment of a home for aged Negroes in Washington, D. C. He was anxious for the United States government to appropriate one million dollars to reimburse depositors who had lost their savings through the failure of the Freedman's Saving and Trust Company. He felt that, inasmuch as the company had been mismanaged after 1870 and failed, owing to no fault of the ex-slave depositors, Congress owed to the people their savings.[14] In this position, he was supported by a North Carolina Democratic legislature which admonished its representatives and senators as follows:

We are informed that there is [sic] three millions of dollars ($3,000,000) in the United States treasury belonging to the colored people of the United States in the nature of unclaimed pensions and bounties; therefore, we request each representative and senator in congress to favor the passage of a bill already introduced or to introduce an equitable bill to pay the colored people back the money they lost through the failure of the Freedman's Saving and Trust Company.[15]

He wanted Congress to reduce Southern representation in proportion to the number of Negro votes suppressed, a principle embraced in the Fourteenth Amendment. Some think that he became "a bitter, uncompromising assailant of everything that resembled or could be distorted into racial discrimination. No matter what the topic under discussion might be, White, like Cato of Rome, could always bring it around to a discussion of Negro rights."[16] His nonpartisanship exemplified itself when benefits were to be derived from the national government for the state of North Carolina such as the establishment of a federal building in Durham.[17]

White was more disliked in North Carolina than any previous Negro congressman. The comparison was often made in the 1890's between him and Henry Plummer Cheatham who served earlier. The difference between the two seemed to have been a matter of temperament and personality. Cheatham apparently knew how to manipulate his politics in such a way as not to incur the wrath of the white people of the state, and White seemed to have rubbed them in the wrong direction.[18] It may have been that Cheatham's mannerisms were more pleasing because he was a congressman at the time the Democrats were in the saddle, and White was a congressman at a time when the Democrats were out of power in the state and when the Negro was the chief target of their attack. White was given to making disparaging remarks to his adversaries.

On the eve of the election of 1898, White was involved in a circus brawl which had dire repercussions on race relations. Seemingly he attended a circus in Tarboro and sat with the white people. The manager of the circus ordered him to move. He refused. The Democratic press claimed that he felt himself better than the other Negroes and that Fusion had brought about social equality. James B. Lloyd, a prominent Populist of Edgecombe County, wrote to Marion Butler that the affair was embarrassing to the Populists:

I enclose some affidavits from citizens here, with reference to White's conduct at a circus here on Oct. 8th . . . it is *exceedingly* embarrassing to us, and since White has made himself so obnoxious I have advised Mr. Fountain to notify the County Republican Executive Committee that unless they remove all the Negroes from the ticket we would have nothing to do with the election. . . . I have urged Holton [Republican State Chairman] to come here and take all the Negroes down but he seems indifferent. If we attempt to carry the present burden since White's escapade, it will destroy us.[19]

Upon casually reading this letter one might conclude that the Negro had committed an unpardonable crime in race relations. However, there are certain facts to be kept in mind in reading this letter. First, it was from a Populist county chairman to the state Populist leader. Second, the writer had political grievances against White because both men ran in the Second Congressional District campaign of 1898.[20] At the time of Lloyd's letter, the election had not taken place, and Lloyd's alarming views on his political adversary could easily have been the distorted figment of the imagination of a man wanting to win his race and seizing upon every opportunity possible to belittle his opponent in the closing days of the campaign.

The Democratic papers of the late 1890's satirized White; and, while their leaders detested him, there is a shining example of how one ardent Democrat chose to make use of him. The following letter was received by him when this Democrat wanted and needed political support:

Windsor, N. C., June, 1890

Hon. Geo. H. White, Rocky Mount, N. C.:
My Dear Sir:—I regret that I can not attend the Judicial Convention on account of pressing engagements. Please put in a word to secure my nomination for Judge. While there is not much hope for an election, still the remote possibility of riding the District with you is a great pleasure. Wishing you success,
I am yours very truly,
(Signed)   FRANCIS D. WINSTON[21]

The letter is significant because of the later activities of this Democrat.[22]

Little can be said of White's legislative accomplishments, and for that matter little can be said for the white North Carolina Democratic congressmen of the 1890's, but there is no doubt that he spoke fluently and was not an embarrassment to his constituents when he took the floor—and he often did. One writer has said that "his record in Congress, though not outstanding, seems to have been no discredit to the State."[23] Historians of his native county hold that

White was a man of great ability, and had a reputation of being impartial in his prosecution. He had practised law in Washington City, and also had considerable experience in law in other cities. His greatest weakness was his desire for social equality.[24]

He understood the tempo of the times when he said in his valedictory address in 1901, "This marks, perhaps, the Negroes' temporary exit from the American Congress. The Negro has been maligned."[25] In reality, he was the last of his race elected to Congress until 1930. The congressman under discussion was the only Negro sent by North Carolina to the United States Congress during the Fusion period. His white colleagues in the House of Representatives from his native state totaled eight and in the Senate two. The ratio of one to ten cannot warrant the charge of Negro domination.

There were Negroes in the Fusion period who held offices as a result of federal patronage. The foremost federal appointee in North Carolina was John C. Dancy who served as collector of customs at the port of Wilmington. Dancy served two terms as collector, one under Republican President Harrison, 1889-93, and the other under Republican President McKinley, 1897-1901. He might have held the same position from 1893 to 1897, had the Democratic President Grover Cleveland not given the spoils of victory to his North Carolina supporters.

He began his political career as register of deeds in Edgecombe County in the 1880's. Dancy was neither an ignoramus nor a political novice. He had studied at Howard University, had served as a clerk in the Treasury Department, established a printing office at Salisbury, and edited the *African Methodist Episcopal Zion Quarterly Review*.[26]

Dancy was regarded as a magnificent speaker. The student body of Wofford College, South Carolina, after a public address there in the 1890's, presented him with a walking cane with a gold head. "Cotton Ed" Smith made the presentation to him. Dancy was a high-ranking member of the Odd Fellows and the Masons.

Dancy's salary as collector of customs was approximately $4,000 per year, $1,000 more than the annual salary of the Democratic Governor Elias Carr; $2,000 more than Charles M. Cook received as secretary of state; $1,000 more than Worth received as state treasurer; and $1,500 more than the Supreme Court judges received.[27] This alone gave economic grounds for the whites of Wilmington and the state to want him removed and for the *News and Observer* to harp continuously on his position.

Every Republican convention in the state found Dancy present and serving often as one of the secretaries. He was, in the opinion of many, a very conservative man on race questions.[28] Booker T. Washington wrote to him on September 21, 1899, "It is pleasing to note that the strong men of the race are committed to rational conservatism as a proper means of solving the great problems now pressing upon us in the South. I feel more and more the necessity of the leaders of the race standing by this position, because in my judgment no other can win."[29]

At the time of the Wilmington race riot of 1898, Dancy and his family fled from Wilmington to Salisbury for a few weeks, after which he returned and continued to serve as collector until 1901. The riot and bitterness of the campaign of 1898 caused him to make many sober reflections in his editorials. Here is an example of his "rational conservatism" after the campaign:

There is no doubt of one thing, and that is that the harsh criticisms of the Negro during the past few years, and the constant parading of all his faults through the newspaper and associate press dispatches, has so influenced public opinion in the State that we have lost much in public esteem. . . . What ever we may do in high walks of life seems to count but little, as compared with the startling accounts of depravity. We must ask a suspension of hastily formed judgments as to the general drift of the race. We need to study statistics and without prejudice prove to an unfriendly world that our cause is not nearly so bad as it has been led to believe. Let it be shown then in spite of a vast amount of crime charged against us that there is not one criminal in a thousand of the race, and that the most of these are for petty offenses, not equaling in the aggregate the value of the single theft of another man of the superior race, and that nine-hundred and ninety-nine of the race are moving upward against the one who persists in the downward road. . . . There is no good reason for the storm of abuse and malignity which has in the past few years been heaped upon the Negro. He has done scarcely nothing to deserve it.[30]

While Dancy rendered unto God the things that were God's, through his conspicuous service in the African Methodist Zion church, he found time to render unto Caesar the things that were Caesar's. He realized that North Carolina was changing from an agricultural to an industrial state in the 1890's and he intended to reap some of the fruits of industry. He was a partner in the Coleman Manufacturing Company along with W. C. Coleman and others. The company's charter of incorporation in 1897 prescribed a capital stock of fifty thousand dollars and the powers to spin, weave, manufacture, finish, and sell warps, yarns, cloth, prints, and fabrics made from cotton and wool; buy and sell wood, iron, steel, tin, and other metal products; to make, manufacture, buy, and sell brick, pipe, and tile; and to mine, quarry, cut, shape, and sell all kinds of rock and stone.[31] Dancy said in reference to this economic undertaking:

. . . . the mill is finally in operation, running on full time with its fair quota of operatives. This is the first genuine cotton mill yet built and controlled by colored men in the history of the country. It stands two miles from Concord, North Carolina, in the midst of a plot of about 140 acres of fertile soil. Five residences are already set up, while the directors have let control for five more. There is no good reason why there should not be a splendid town there governed by ourselves in the near future.[32]

Some of the Negro leaders of the 1890's were attempting to enter the competitive textile field. A more comprehensive picture of Dancy's and Coleman's economic venture is revealed by an authority on the period in these words:

There was a cotton mill, not only operated, but owned and managed, by Negroes. . . . The project was received with enthusiasm and every influence in the race was enlisted. Ministers recommended the enterprise from the pulpits; mass meetings making a strong appeal to race consciousness were held over the whole South, while the Negro newspapers urged subscriptions as a duty to the race. . . . About $50,000 was subscribed, and the company was organized in 1897. Encouraged by the ready response, the capital stock was increased to $100,000, and subscriptions were sought from whites also. Those who responded were millmen, who were willing to risk a few dollars on the trial of the experiment, and a few philanthropists.[33]

A white Republican paper praised the Negro economic experiment and encouraged people of all races to buy stock.[34]

There is no doubt that Dancy's solution to the Negro problem had economic security as its cornerstone. He admonished Negro groups:

We cannot all be professional men, nor a majority of us. The larger percent must enter trades, mercantile and commercial life. Our fortunes must come through these channels. Talk may be the other way, but real results must come this way. Money and capital may be of secondary importance as viewed by some, but they are really of first importance to a race noted for its poverty and dependence on others. The moment we are independent in a financial way, our word for it, that moment we are largely independent in every other way.[35]

He was discriminating; and, contrary to the assumption that Negroes loved and never found any fault with the Republican party, there is this statement of his:

The Negro feels relieved after the severe tension [the year of the disfranchisement amendment, 1900] to which he has been subjected for many months. He feels that his friends are still in possession of the National Government [Republicans]. They have not done as much for him in the way of positive legislation as he has led himself to believe to hope; but he would like to see the question of the franchise and the amendments to the Constitution settled definitely once and for all, and the tampering with his manhood rights cease. . . . He therefore looks to the powers that be to insure him against further encroachments upon his franchise and thus permanently fix his status in the nation.[36]

Dancy was wary of state Republican leaders. He followed Senator Pritchard until after the Disfranchisement Amendment. When Pritchard declared himself in favor of a "lily white" Republican party in his address at the Republican state convention in Greesboro in 1901, Dancy broke with him.

The tension of the election of 1898, the Wilmington race riot, and the election of 1900, centering around the race issue, caused Dancy to be removed to Washington, D. C., as recorder of deeds. He served in such capacity from 1901 to 1910, and thus ended the political career of the collector of customs at the port of Wilmington.[37] This lone solitary position did not restrain the Democrats from using his name and position to substantiate their cry of Negro domination.

Dr. James E. Shepard of Durham served in two positions, through federal patronage, during the Fusion period. He was selected by Henry P. Cheatham, former congressman and recorder of deeds in Washington, D. C., for the position of comparer of deeds in Cheatham's office in 1898. He was recalled to Raleigh in early 1899 as deputy collector of the United States Department of Internal Revenue in his state, a position he held until 1905.[38]

Dr. Shepard, born in 1875, reached the legal age of manhood during the Fusion victory election of 1896, in which he cast his first vote. He attended the Republican state convention in 1896 and distinguished himself as an intelligent leader.[39] He was ably prepared by intelligence and training to understand fully the issues at stake during the Fusion period, having graduated from Shaw University and the department of pharmacy at the same institution at the age of nineteen. He studied theology between 1894 and 1898, thinking that he might follow in the footsteps of his illustrious father, Dr. Augustus Shepard.[40] Employment as a federal officeholder delayed his theological career, and when his term of office expired, he entered the field of education.[41] He was the first and only Negro to serve as deputy collector of internal revenue in his state.[42] As testimony to his political acumen, his demeanor as a Negro officeholder, and the integrity manifested in his political career, he, alone, escaped the Democratic abuse leveled at Negro officeholders.

It is difficult to ascertain accurately federal patronage in terms of postmasterships awarded to Negroes. A Democratic source cited the number as being between fifteen and twenty-five.[43] Since the citation comes from a campaign pamphlet with emphasis on Negro domination, the number may or may not be correct. There were "some" and they were in densely Negro-populated areas. Mention is often made of S. H. Vick, Negro postmaster of Wilson, who was hounded out of office by the incessant cry of the Democrats after the campaign of 1898. A few excerpts from his letters to John C. Dancy best describe the tension and strain under which he tried to maintain the position:

I sent my application for reappointment to Senator Pritchard. He made no acknowledgment of it. I did not wish to file one with the department except through him, as it would seem to ignore him. Since matters seem to be changing somewhat, do you think it advisable to file application directly to the department?[44]

The Republican whites of Wilson, after the party had gone "lily white" in 1902, eager to remove this Negro postmaster, filed charges against him. He wrote Dancy:

From newspaper comments I learn that my case will be taken up and settled next week. I have answered every charge presented against me. The charges were false from beginning to end. I need not tell you that because I am sure you know the same. . . . I am sure you could do me much good just now if you could by some means interview the President in my behalf.[45]

As evidence of the fact that Vick's former Republican friends did not abate their efforts to remove him is his letter near the close of 1903:

The fight made against me is a very low one indeed. The charge of disloyalty is one, I never dreamed that Republicans would bring against me. If anything I have been too loyal—often blindly following the dictates of the party leaders. I notice that the article in the Washington *Post* does you and me both an injustice. I am not sure of the author of the article. A gentleman came to me some time ago and wanted my photo for the Washington *Post*. I did not have one convenient, but told him he could secure my cut from the *Colored American*. I suppose he is the author of the article. Gain an audience with the President and put in a word as to my fidelity to the party. Have never voted other than Republican ticket in my life.[46]

It would help this study to know the exact number of Negroes who held postmasterships in North Carolina.[47] After the Republican victory of 1896, this revelation was made by a white Republican of Charlotte to Governor-elect Russell: "The vote you got in this county came almost entirely from the colored people. We have got very few white Republicans. There are two positions to come up in the Post Office. I suggest that you recommend one to a white and one to a colored."[48] Had the rewards of political patronage been commensurate with the voting strength of the Negroes in some localities, there would have been no question of dividing the offices between white and colored.

Not only was the number of offices held by Negroes incommensurate with their voting strength or their population ratio, but the economic return from many post office positions was too inconsiderable to become the basis of opposition. There were instances wherein the positions paid less than ten dollars per month. Walter A. Clark, associate justice of the state Supreme Court, wrote to United States Senator Marion Butler, Populist, in support of a man who he thought would fill a post office position: "The P. O. pays,

I suppose, between $50 & $100 a year. The appointment of Mr. Brock will probably prevent that of some incompetent negro, for no other white man but the R. R. agent can afford to take it."[49] The average white man would hardly have been interested economically in a position which paid between fifty and one hundred dollars per year. It may be concluded that Democratic opposition to Negro postmasters was not based on economic jealousy. It was based on the fact that a Negro held the position. The number of federal Negro officeholders, in actuality, was small. Negro office-holding as an act in itself provided fuel for the ousted Democrats to raise the cry of Negro domination.

NOTES TO CHAPTER SIX

1. Mabry, "The Negro in North Carolina Politics Since Reconstruction," 36.
2. *Biographical Directory of the American Congress,* 441, 805.
3. Josephus Daniels, *Tar Heel Editor,* 176.
4. *Biographical Directory of the American Congress,* 1690.
5. *News and Observer,* November 6, 1896.
6. See table, 85. Second Congressional District Vote, 1896.
7. See table, 85.
8. Voting Population over twenty-one years of age: United States Department of Commerce, Bureau of Census, Twelfth Census, 1900, I, Part I (1900), Table 92, 992-93.

	Negro	White
Bertie	2,204	2,137
Edgecombe	3,493	2,498
Greene	1,185	1,502
Halifax	4,394	2,855
Lenoir	1,697	2,593
Northampton	2,470	2,181
Warren	2,441	1,393
Wayne	2,785	4,159
Wilson	2,066	3,290
	22,735	22,608

9. *North Carolina Manual,* 1913, 1005-6.
10. *News and Observer,* November 10, 1898.
11. *Congressional Record,* Fifty-fifth Congress, First Session, XXXII, Part 1, 550-51.
12. *Ibid.,* Fifty-sixth Congress, First Session, XXXIII, Part 1, 1021; Part 2, 2151-54, 2894.
13. *Ibid.,* Part 1, 1365, 1507, 2151-54.
14. *Ibid.,* 1637.
15. *Public Laws and Resolutions,* 1899, 965.
16. Samuel D. Smith, *The Negro in Congress 1870-1901,* 125-26.
17. *Congressional Record,* Fifty-fifth Congress, Third Session, 2895-96.
18. Josephus Daniels, *Tar Heel Editor,* 176-77.
Samuel D. Smith, *op. cit.,* 131.

19. James B. Lloyd to Marion Butler, October 8, 1898, Marion Butler Papers (Shorter Collection), University of North Carolina Library.

20. *Supra,* chart, 85.

21. *Peoples Party Handbook* 1898, 25; cited also in Turner and Bridges, *History of Edgecombe County,* 312.

22. The writer of this letter was one of the leading Democrats of the 1899 legislature and was the man who introduced the "Winston Bill" which finally, after much shaping up, became the Disfranchisement Amendment of 1900. His anti-Negro activities in 1899 were a far cry from the "pleasure" it would give him to associate with a Negro candidate in 1890.

23. Mabry, "The Negro in North Carolina Politics Since Reconstruction," 40.

24. Turner and Bridges, *op. cit.,* 287.

25. *Congressional Record,* Fifty-sixth Congress, Third Session, XXXIV, Part 2, 1638.

26. Many of the leading Negroes of the Fusion Period were stalwart workers in the African Methodist Episcopal Church and in fraternal societies. Rivera, a contemporary, admits that in the Star of Zion Lodge, the members devoted more than half the meeting to the discussion of political issues; Interview, July 20, 1944.

27. *Turner's North Carolina Almanac,* XI, No. 11 (1896), 30-33.

28. Josephus Daniels, *Editor in Politics,* 309, 312.

29. Private Correspondence of John Dancy.

30. *African Methodist Episcopal Zion Quarterly* (December, 1898), 60-61.

31. *Private Laws,* 1897, Chap. 28, 47-49.

32. *African Methodist Episcopal Zion Quarterly* (December, 1900), 321.

33. Thompson, *From the Cotton Field to the Cotton Mill, A Study of the Industrial Transition in North Carolina,* 253, 254-55, 256.

34. *The Union Republican,* February 27, 1897.

35. *African Methodist Episcopal Zion Quarterly* (March, 1900), 104.

36. *Ibid.* (December, 1900), 52-53.

37. Private Papers and Correspondence of John Dancy were used in this analysis through the courtesy of his son, John Dancy, Jr., Director of the Urban League, 606 East Vernor, Detroit, Michigan.

38. *Who's Who in America,* XXIII (1944-1945), 1921.

39. *Supra,* Chap. IV, 50.

40. Dr. Augustus Shepard was a graduate of Shaw University, founder of the Orphanage Asylum for Negroes in Oxford, N. C., Missionary of the American Bible Institute of Philadelphia for North Carolina, and preacher.

Thomas O. Fuller, *Twenty Years in Public Life, 1890-1910,* 193.

41. Founder and president of North Carolina College for Negroes, Durham, N. C.—*Who's Who in America,* XXIII (1944-1945), 1921.

42. Interview with Dr. James E. Shepard, President of North Carolina College for Negroes, Durham, N. C., September 8, 1945.

43. Simmons' Letter to Jeter C. Pritchard, Republican United States Senator, Oct. 30, 1898, Appendix, 234-36.

44. S. H. Vick to John C. Dancy, Recorder of Deeds, Washington, D. C., November 13, 1902, John Dancy Private Correspondence, in possession of John Dancy, Jr., 606 E. Vernor, Detroit, Michigan.

45. *Ibid.,* January 17, 1903.

46. *Ibid.,* November 5, 1903.

47. The United States Post Office Department did not have the time during the Second World War to permit the use of the files. See letter in Appendix, 237.

48. John S. Leary to Daniel L. Russell, December 9, 1896, Daniel Russell Papers, University of North Carolina Library.

49. Judge Walter Clark to Senator Marion Butler, December 19, 1899, Private Papers of Marion Butler, University of North Carolina Library, through the courtesy of Dr. Hugh T. Lefler.

CHAPTER SEVEN

NEGRO OFFICE-HOLDING: STATE

THE DECISION of the Populists and the Republicans to fuse in 1894 set in motion the formation of county tickets for the state legislature which had some Negroes on them. James Hunter Young, of Wake County, and William H. Crews, of Granville County, Negroes, were elected to the House of Representatives in 1895.[1]

James Young was easily the outstanding Negro in the state legislature during the Fusion period, and no Negro received more unfriendly comments from the Democratic press than Young. His election from Wake, a white county, in 1894 and 1896 along with two whites is recognition of his position in the party as one of the architects of Fusion. Zebulon Vance Walser, speaker of the House of Representatives in 1895, acknowledged Young's ability by appointing him to the following important committees: Judiciary, Privileges and Election, Finance, Special Election Law, Institutions for the Blind, Education, Printing, Colonial Records, and chairman of the committee to fill the vacancies in the Board of Trustees at the state-supported Negro college, the Agricultural and Mechanical College, Greensboro.[2] The legislative session of 1897 accorded him the same appointments in addition to a place on Election Law, County Government, and Insane Asylum committees.[3] Young's position on such committees as Election Law, County Government, Finance, and Judiciary was noteworthy because around the results of these four committees hangs the crux of Fusion politics.

To say that he was ignorant, an allegation frequently made of Negro officeholders, is to judge him erroneously. His influence among his constituents and his way of getting things done were not those of an ignorant man. He was astute enough to pave his way into politics by owning and editing his own paper, The Gazette,[4] and by securing for himself the position of grand master of the Masons of North Carolina. Both positions allowed him to secure political supporters and keep them informed. His influence in helping to map the fusion strategy of 1894 and in maneuvering the nomination of Russell over Dockery in the Republican state convention of 1896[5] gave him prominence in the party. A political enemy thus appraised him, ". . . . outside of Butler, Pritchard, and Holton, hardly any man had so much influence as Jim Young. He was a very bright mulatto and was reputed to be a son of a prominent white man in Vance County. I guess that was true. His political astuteness was attributed by the Democrats to his white blood."[6]

Young was born in Henderson, North Carolina, October 26, 1858. He attended the public schools of Henderson, entered Shaw University in 1874, graduated in 1877. He was employed in the office of collector of internal revenue for the Fourth District in Raleigh.[7] His white father is reputed to have placed him in that position.[8] Young served as chief clerk and cashier in that department from 1879 to 1885 and handled nearly a million dollars each year. President Cleveland removed him. He served as chief clerk in the office of register of deeds in Wake County, 1887-89. In July, 1889, he was appointed, upon recommendation of former Congressman Cheatham, special inspector of customs, a position which he held until 1893, when he was again removed by Cleveland. Young might have served as collector of customs for the port of Wilmington in 1891, but Democratic Senator Ransom of North Carolina manifested such pronounced opposition before the Senate Committee on Commerce that he failed to get the position. He was a delegate to every state convention of the Republican party from 1880, alternate at large in 1884 to the Republican national convention, and a delegate from the Sixth Congressional District to the Republican national convention of 1892. In June, 1893, he assumed editorial charge of *The Gazette*. In 1894, he was the unanimous choice of the Republican and Populist county conventions on the legislative ticket from Wake County.[9]

His ingenuity in legislative proposals is amply demonstrated in the *House Journals* of 1895 and 1897. He was particularly interested in the development of the deaf, dumb, and blind institutions. Some of his proposals[10] which resulted in public enactments for the benefit of the Raleigh school were an appropriation of $34,500 for new buildings for the white division, $11,500 for the colored, $10,000 for equipment for both, the use of the proceeds from the sale of some unsuitable land for the purchase of a garden, and the procuring of one white and one Negro physician.[11]

Young was interested in education in general and the education of Negroes in particular. He favored increased taxation for the support of public education, longer school terms, and higher pay for teachers.[12] He proposed that the seven Negro normal schools in the state receive direct state aid.[13] The legislature of 1897 appropriated $4,000 annually to their support.[14] He asked that the Agricultural and Mechanical College for Negroes receive its pro rata share of the land scrip fund;[15] and, while the Greensboro school did not receive consideration in this direction, it was granted $5,000.[16]

One of Young's chief proposals was to amend the charter of the city of Raleigh,[17] a bill which evoked much Democratic opposition in the legislature and press.[18] The charter was finally revised in terms of the Fusion interpretation of municipal government. To enhance the beauty of Raleigh, he secured an enactment to have the streets around Capitol Square paved.[19] He unsuccessfully urged the Fusionists to live up to their campaign pledge of 1894 and 1896 for the establishment of a reform school for youthful criminals.[20]

Young held the personal confidence of Governor Daniel L. Russell and was appointed by him as chief fertilizer inspector for the state in 1897 and a colonel of the Negro regiment which volunteered for the Spanish-American War in 1898. Neither he nor his regiment left the continental United States during the entire war. The Democratic press stated that he was inefficient as an officer[21] and based its allegation upon the fact that he returned from Florida to North Carolina for political reasons in the midst of the campaign of 1898. Young's appointment to command over a solid Negro regiment caused condemnation to be heaped upon Governor Russell's head.

Each gubernatorial appointment Young received fired the Democrats' wrath, but the one which caused state-wide consternation was the appointment to the Board of Directors for the Deaf, Dumb, and Blind Institutions in 1897.[22] His appointment was well deserved because no legislator of the Fusion period offered as many proposals and effected such beneficent legislation for the development of the physical plant, efficiency of the staff, and health of the students as had James H. Young. Insofar as the institute had a colored division, it was not amiss for a Negro director to be the inspector for that division. The Democrats greeted his appointment with an outburst of prejudice. He was cartooned in the heat of the "white supremacy" campaign of 1898 inspecting the living quarters of white women of the institution. This was deliberately firing the flames of racial antipathy in a section of the country where Negro men were never in the presence of white women except in menial tasks. The sinister innuendo was that helpless blind white girls were at the mercy of a ravenous beast. The cartoon was predicated upon the possibilities inherent in the duties of a director and not upon what actually happened, but the Democrats set forth the "possibility" as a fact. In reality, Young was prudent enough never to visit these living quarters.[23] His appointment was presented in the "white supremacy" campaign as follows:

Jim Young is not officially known as chairman of the board, but practically he is the chairman of the whole outfit. There is not an official in any of these institutions who does not know that Jim Young is the head of the directorate and that Tonnoffski is merely Jim's agent to do his bidding. In official circles, the name of Tonnoffski appears as chairman; in the practical operation of the board, Jim Young is as complete a boss as Quay in Pennsylvania and Platt in New York are bosses of the Republican party. . . . While it takes four men to control the board, one man—and he the negro politician, Jim Young—is its dictator. . . . He cracks the whip, and his three automatons make the motions as he directs. . . . How do you like such white slavery to a negro master in Raleigh? . . . Jim Young is a hard man to satisfy.[24]

The Populist party attempted to counteract Democratic propaganda through their explanation:

The cartoons, with the comments under them, attempt to leave the impression that the negro man is chairman of and controls the Board of Trustees of the State Institution for the Blind, and that in the capacity of "boss" and member of the Board he goes officially alone through the private apartments of the Institution on visits of inspection. All this is intended to fool the people—to deceive them—to make them believe what is pictured actually occurs, and is intended to make the public believe that such proceedings are sanctioned by the present anti-Democratic administration. Well, a meaner, baser, more contemptible falsehood and slander on white women was never spawned by the low-born, sneaking, cowardly defamer who invented it and circulated it. No negro has ever been chairman of the Board of Trustees of the Institution, and there was no negro member of the Board when these cartoons were sent out. But this makes no difference to the Democratic machine and its minions. An organized liar will not stop lying simply because it cannot FIND something to lie about. It will invent something.[25]

A new building for the institution was erected following an appropriation by the legislature of 1897. On the cornerstone were inscribed the names of the Board of Directors. So angry were the whites of Raleigh because a Negro's name was there, that a mob, in the midst of the heated campaign of 1898, tore away the cornerstone. The Democratic legislature of 1899 was in accord with the state of feeling of the mob and proposed in early January of that same year a bill providing for the permanent removal of the name of James H. Young.[26] Twelve Republicans in the House voted against it.[27] Only two of the four Negroes in the House professed enough party and race loyalty to oppose a resolution aimed at bringing into disrepute their fellow member. They were J. Y. Eaton, of Vance County, and W. C. Coates, of Northampton County. The vote of J. H. Wright is not recorded, but the vote of Isaac Smith was recorded in the Democratic list.[28] In other words, Smith, Negro, had voted with the Democrats for the removal.[29] The resultant act showed the anti-Negro spirit of the legislature, for it specifically ordered that the inscription of the cornerstone of the new buildings be changed so that it would show only the date of the founding of the institution, the date of erection of the new buildings, and the names of the principal and the architect.[30] Obviously, the name of Young was omitted. A white Republican paper stated, "There is no reason why James Young's name should not be on the cornerstone, and to say that his name being there has disgraced the State is nothing more than a corrupt form of political rot."[31]

Two men who fought this Negro with all their influence as men, Democrats, and printers were Josephus Daniels[32] and Needham Broughton.[33] If one wished to ascribe personal motives to these men in their hatred for the legislator, one would have to go back to the election of 1896 and the legislative activities of 1897. Young was appointed to the Committee on Public Printing by the legislature of 1897.[34] Previous to 1895 and 1897, the Democratic legislatures had let the contracts for public printing to P. M. Hale, Captain S. A. Ashe, and Josephus Daniels, all Democrats. Daniels had been official state printer for seven years prior to 1893. The work was usually done by the printing houses of Raleigh, which houses turned over to the state printer 15 per cent of the money received. The Fusion legislature of 1895 proposed to let the public printing to the lowest bidder irrespective of political party affiliation. The printing job of 1895 was let to M. I. and J. C. Stewart Brothers of Winston, North Carolina. The Fusion legislature of 1897 provided for the public printing to be done under the supervision and management of the Council of State which prescribed the rules and regulations.[35] By this very action, the Fusionists had repealed the 1895 law which required that printing contracts go to the lowest bidder.[36] When the time came in 1897 to let the printing contract, Daniels entered a bid for his press, which the Council of State ignored. Whether the *News and Observer* sincerely wanted and intended to get the contract is a matter of conjecture. The press owners later stated that they never suspected that they would get it, but that they intended to prove to the people of the state that their bid was lowest and that the Fusionists cared nothing for economy or the taxpayer.[37] It is hard to ascertain how much "sour-grape rationalization" may have been in this. It was equally felt that Young's influence on the Council of State, of which he was a member, manifested itself in denying to Daniels or Broughton the printing contract. This was natural in view of Daniels' vicious criticisms of the Fusionists. The printing job of 1897 was assigned again to M. I. and J. C. Stewart.

In the election of 1896, the Wake County Democrats pitted Broughton against Young. Young was declared the victor. The Democrats were not satisfied. Immediately after the election returns were announced, J. C. Marcom, a justice of the peace, applied to D. H. Young, clerk of the superior court, to open the ballot boxes for a recount. D. H. Young refused; and Marcom made application to Justice Clark, of the Supreme Court, for a ruling to show cause why the clerk should not grant the application. Justice Clark rendered the interpretation that the clerk was right in refusing to grant a recount to a justice of the peace as the election law specified that the clerk must be ordered by a judge of the superior or supreme courts to grant a recount. Clark then ordered the clerk to open the boxes for a recount, on December 30, 1896, in the clerk's office before the contestant, contestee, and those who chose to attend. Clark let it be known that the General Assembly was the final judge of accepting or rejecting its own members in contested elections.[38] No further appeal was taken in the case, and the Democrats proceeded to marshal their forces to get the case settled by the House in January and February of 1897.

The case was brought before the House on January 14 and was referred to the Committee on Privileges and Elections.[39] On January 27, it was scheduled to be heard the next week. The delay in hearing the case caused the Democratic press to charge that the Fusionists feared a fair trial, that a Negro was kept in the House of Representatives by fraud, and that the Republicans with the minority Populists were shielding him.[40] The Democrats in the House, during the latter part of the month, presented "Broughton's Memorial" to the General Assembly. The memorial stated that the Wake County vote for Broughton and Young was 4,720 and 4,738, respectively; that the clerk of the superior court had recounted and still maintained a victory for Young, but that the clerk had erred by refusing to count ballots found in the wrong box and by refusing to count ballots with names pasted on; and that the real count for Broughton and Young was 4,731 and 4,710, respectively.[41] The House, seemingly, took no action on the memorial, and on February 5 refused a second time to review the contested case.[42] On February 25, Young was seated by a vote of 61 versus 33.[43] The Democratic cry went forth that "The Negro is on top. Jim Young must be kept in at all cost." [44]

The Broughton versus Young contested election case takes on added significance when it is reflected that Broughton was very influential in religious circles. There is no evidence in the 1890's that he had political aspirations. He was editor of a Baptist paper and had been for some years, yet he suddenly appeared in the election of 1896 as a candidate against Young. It was charged that Broughton was drafted by the Democrats in 1896 as the only possible candidate who might defeat Young and that his religious connections were his chief political asset.[45] The Democrats themselves commended Broughton "As a good citizen, a kind man, an honor to his race and people," who had "hosts of friends all over the State. Against his inclinations, his friends and neighbors in Wake persuaded him to stand for the Legislature. He yielded to their solicitations." [46]

The second Negro in the 1895 legislature was William H. Crews of Granville County. He was re-elected in 1897. Crews was born October 11, 1844, a few miles from the city of Oxford. He was taken from his mother at the age of two years and reared by a white family whose name he bore. He stated that he was unaware of the system of slavery until he was twelve years old. He attended the public and private schools of Oxford and served as deputy sheriff and constable in Granville County for twelve years, member of the Oxford School Committee, a justice of the peace, and for four terms as a member of the legislature of North Carolina—all before the Fusion period. His biographers state that Crews ran for public office for twenty-three years in Granville County without being defeated. He was elected to the legislature in 1894 by a majority of eleven.[47] Crews was by no means as important a personage as James Young, yet his Republican confreres respected his presence in the Assembly. He was appointed on the Public Buildings and Grounds and the Propositions and Grievances committees.[48] In 1897, he served on the same committees in addition to those on Judiciary and Health, and the committee to select trustees for a colored school to be established later.[49]

His first activity in the legislature of 1895 gave the Democrats a weapon with which to harass the Fusionists throughout the rest of their administration, the "Fred Douglass Affair."[50] The repercussions of this episode may have abated his ardor for more active participation, because he took the floor few times thereafter. He introduced, in 1895, a bill for a normal school in Oxford for the preparation of Negro teachers.[51] The measure was defeated. In 1897, a similar bill was introduced, and the Fusionists enacted a provisional law which created a North Carolina Industrial and Training School for Colored Teachers. The enactment further provided for a school term of thirty weeks, $5,000 for its maintenance, and tuition free to those who intended to teach in the state.[52] The Fusionists made clear their objectives: first, to give colored men and women such education and training as would fit them for their work as professional teachers; and, second, to provide such industrial and liberal education and advanced methods of instruction as would render more efficient the colored schools of North Carolina.[53] The legislature did not designate any location, and it was plainly evident that Crews could have it located in Oxford if he chose. The most important proviso in the law was that the school had to be located at some place where the citizens would furnish the necessary buildings or money sufficient to erect them.[54] Crews was appointed a member of the board of trustees to select teachers for the "possible" school.[55] The school was never established.

North Carolina had preserved a custom of making women prisoners work on the public roads. William H. Crews introduced a bill in the legislature of 1897 to prohibit the working of women on chain gangs on the streets or public roads.[56] The resultant law abolished this custom throughout the state.[57]

While the study on office-holding should concern itself with legislative achievements, there were numerous bills proposed by Negroes which were defeated. Some of them reveal the stress and strain of race relations of the period as well as the mental attitudes of the proponents. Crews desired the Fusionists to aid financially the colored widows whose husbands were wounded while serving as soldiers in the Confederate Army.[58] The proposal itself was stupid in the light of the facts of history and the spirit of the time. No slave served in the Confederate Army with the status of a soldier. The spirit of the 1890's, when North Carolina found it difficult to pay pensions to Confederate veterans, made it foolish to insert the Negro issue in the pension question. He felt that, if the Fusionist party was as pro-Negro as some of its speakers had led his race to believe, such a law was possible. The legislature rejected it.[59]

Emancipation day is a day of celebration for Negroes throughout the South. It is the custom among North Carolina Negroes to observe January 1. Crews asked permission to use the General Assembly Hall for the celebration in 1898.[60] He was denied it. It became evident to the Negro legislators that the Republicans and Populists were not agreed on privileges to be granted to Negroes.[61]

The Fusion triumph of 1896 added a third Negro to the House of Representatives, John T. Howe, of New Hanover County, and placed two Negroes in the Senate. Howe represented a county which had 13,935 Negroes—58.0 per cent of the total county population.[62] Wilmington was the center of New Hanover, and politics was always rife in that city and county in the 1890's because the Populists supporting the Negro Republicans could always out-vote the Democrats. Howe used his excellent opportunity to build up his Negro political supporters as traveling agent for the Wilmington *Record,* a Negro newspaper edited by Alex Manley. He served in the 1897 legislature on the committees on Claims, Fish Industries, and Federal Relations.[63] While he supported proposals for better schools and more appropriations for them, he asserted little, if any, direct pressure on broad state measures and was seemingly content to let his one contribution be an amended charter for the municipal government of Wilmington, which created a larger number of wards to secure more effective participation of Republican voters.[64]

The Senate of 1897 contained William L. Person and W. B. Henderson. Person had been a candidate from the Fifth Senatorial District of Edgecombe County in 1894 and lost to W. P. Mercer, Democrat, by a narrow margin. He always felt that the Democratic election law had cheated him out of his victory.[65] He marshalled his supporters carefully in 1896 and, under the Fusion election law, won his seat in the Senate.[66] The president of the Senate appointed him to the committees of Privileges and Election, Claims, and the Institution for the Deaf, Dumb and Blind.[67]

Person in the Senate was not as powerful as his friend Young in the House, but they teamed up on several measures which each labored for in his respective chamber. The similarity between Person's Senate bills and Young's House bills indicates that they sought to increase the public school fund, increase the efficiency of public school teachers and their pay, prevent discrimination in making jury lists, establish and maintain an insurance department, and permit the trustees of the Deaf, Dumb and Blind Institution to employ two more physicians.[68] No outstanding enactment of 1897 stands as a monument to Person's legislative initiative. Minor concessions accorded him by his Senate confreres resulted in the incorporating of certain Negro lodges, banking concerns in Edgecombe County, and the Pickford Sanitarium for the treatment of consumptive Negroes.

Person's race consciousness came to the front two days after the opening of the General Assembly when he undertook to secure an effective anti-lynching law.[69] North Carolina had on its statute books a law to protect persons confined to jail under the charge of crime until they could be fairly tried by a jury of good and lawful men in open court and prescribed a fine of $500 and imprisonment from two to fifteen years for persons who seized prisoners from jails through violence.[70] Person felt that too many variables were left unspecified. The Democratic law was applicable only after the culprit was apprehended by the police. Especially was it singular in its omission of any punitive consequences to members of mobs who seized the culprit before he reached the jail. Person wanted an anti-lynch law which would deter mobs from wreaking vengeance on accused persons before the proper police authorities had been notified of the accusation. His first proposal was lost in the Judiciary Committee. This did not deter him from trying several times, with different wordings for each bill, such as recovering damages from lynchings, protecting the lives of prisoners or accused persons, or suppressing mob violence [71]—all to no avail. His race consciousness continued to manifest itself in the proposals designed to prevent discrimination in passenger accommodations,[72] to prevent discrimination in making jury lists,[73] and to prevent cohabitation between the races.[74] None of these bills, Negroid in inference, was enacted into law.

Many of Person's legislative proposals, though defeated, were more nearly calculated to place his state on a higher socio-economic level than those proposed by any other state senator of his time. Such a measure as the one to prevent the hiring of convicts in competition with free labor[75] was an intelligent step toward advancing the wages of labor. Measures to compel corporations that employed labor by the week to pay their employees every Saturday rather than on the first and fifteenth of the month,[76] and to pay expenses for physical harm suffered by employees while engaged in their work,[77] were indicative of a mind which was sociologically and economically attuned to the real problems of the working man. A measure calculated to lessen the expenses of maintaining prisoners demonstrated economy.[78]

The Eleventh Senatorial District of Warren and Vance counties elected W. B. Henderson to the senate in 1896. While he served on the committees of Penal Institutions, Public Roads, Insane Asylum, and Claims,[79] his legislative initiative and activities in the senate were meager. He gave support to educational measures designed for the entire state.[80] His four proposed measures for the entire session pertained to fences, live stock, register of deeds, and a dispensary for Vance County.[81] In 1898 Governor Russell appointed him chief fertilizer inspector of the state to succeed James Young,[82] the position made vacant by the latter's appointment as a colonel in the Spanish-American War.

The legislature of 1899 was overwhelmingly Democratic,[83] yet four Negroes won seats in the House of Representatives and one in the Senate. The most loquacious Negro in the 1899 legislature was Isaac Smith, representative from Craven, a "black county." When it was learned in the early fall of 1898 that Smith was the candidate from his county, the Democratic press began to besmirch his reputation in these words,

. . . . the black banker from Craven has reason to be a little hilarious over this latest turn of kaleidiscope. A native of Jones County, taught school. He lives in grand style, runs a bank all his own, and has a criminal record of forgery and perjury.[84]

The chief task of the legislature was to frame a suffrage amendment designed to curb the Negro vote, and Smith bent every effort possible toward preventing its passage. His method of opposition aroused the ire of his Republican friends, white and colored. He sought through begging, cajoling, and appeasing to quell the wrath of the infuriated Democrats of 1899. He voted with them on measures designed to cripple Negro activity in politics and to curb the activity of his own party, the Republican. He supported the Democrats' removal of the name of James Young from the cornerstone of the new buildings in Raleigh in spite of the fact that Republican Snipes (white) had warned that the party ought to stick together. Smith stated when voting on the measure, "I desire that the two races stay separate, therefore I vote 'aye' (applause)."[85] So delighted were the Democrats at this schism in the Republican party that they circulated an article entitled "Isaac Smith Goes A-Snipe Hunting."[86]

The Republicans of the House, early in the legislature, January 7, expelled Smith from the caucus meeting "because of his alleged friendly words and acts approving Democratic policies as against Republican policies."[87] It was also reported, prior to his expulsion, that he refused to support Republican caucus nominees, voted for the Democratic speaker of the House, and told the Democrats that if they would give the colored voter one more chance they would get their share of colored votes. He would guarantee this.[88] Republican Petree of Stokes County introduced the resolution of expulsion:

Whereas it appears from the recent acts, speeches, utterances, and votes of Isaac H. Smith, Representative from Craven county, that the said Smith is not in true sympathy and accord with the Republican party and its principles, therefore resolved (1) that the said Isaac H. Smith is hereby excluded from participating with the Republican members in their caucus, (2) that the Republican party will in no way be responsible for the acts, speeches, and votes of Isaac H. Smith.[89]

The proof that Smith had lost caste even with his Negro legislators is attested by the fact that four of them were present at the time the resolution of expulsion passed unanimously.[90] The Democratic press, gleeful over Smith's pro-Democratic views, stated that "Smith was expelled because he favored good government."[91] Smith showed his anger at being expelled from the party caucus by trying to clear himself before the House. He asked permission to explain the resolution expelling him from the caucus,[92] to explain the allegation printed in the *News and Observer*,[93] and to explain the statement published in the *Star of Zion* (Negro fraternal paper) charging that he had betrayed his trust.[94] Smith stated that he was a loyal supporter of the party, adding, "I spent more money during the last campaign than any Republican in the State."[95] Smith sought to incur the sympathy of the Democratic House though this blanket appeal, "I am here as part and parcel of this grand body, and I am from a county where you find the homes and graves of good, honorable, virtuous men. An attack on one member of this body is an attack on the whole General Assembly. An unwarranted attack has been made on me by a caucus of people calling themselves Republicans. This malicious and unjust action, they have published to the world. They have read me out of my own party, and declared that I no longer take part in its councils. The very men who have done this charged in the campaign that the Democrats would disfranchise the negro. And yet before the Democrats have had even a chance to disfranchise anybody these very fellows go out and disfranchise the only negro in this Legislature who has acted on the true interest of his race. They have denounced the only man of them who has done what he has a right to do under the Constitution—vote as he thinks just and proper."[96] Humorously the Democratic legislature enjoyed his explanation.

Smith was governed by a race philosophy of his own. His education was meager, but he had accumulated some wealth in real estate and banking. He operated a bank in New Bern, was a partner in the Coleman Manufacturing Company of Concord, was a high-ranking officer in the Masonic Order, and was popular in Craven County. He had gained local reputation through one of the acquired techniques of Negro survival—agreeing with the leading whites on measures involving Negroes and individually getting ahead himself with their smiling benediction that "Smith is a good Negro." To his Negro Republican friends, he was a typical "Uncle Tom." In reality Smith stood between an unfriendly Republican party and an unfriendly Democratic party. While appeasing the Democrats, he was treated as harshly by the Democratic press as was James Young, the ardent anti-Democratic leader.

The majority of Smith's proposals were Negroid in inference and stood no chance of passage in a Democratic legislature which regarded its victory in 1898 as a mandate to curb Negro influence in politics. Smith wanted Craven, a "black county," transferred from the Third to the Second Congressional District.[97] The Second Congressional District already had five "black counties" and four "white counties"[98] and one more "black county" would give full assurance of victory to any Negro candidate. His attempts to secure equality of pay for witnesses in court irrespective of color, one Negro trustee for each colored institution, and compulsory education for children between six and eleven years old for Craven County[99] were indicative of the degree of his race consciousness. His accomplishment was the lone resolution requesting North Carolina congressmen to favor passage of a law returning to Negroes money they lost by the failure of the Freedman's Saving and Trust Company chartered by Congress.[100] Smith left the legislature of 1899 "begging his white friends not to charge to Negroes the mistakes and misrule of Governor Russell."[101]

James Youman Eaton, another legislator, was born in Louisburg in 1866 of recently emancipated slaves. His childhood days were not fraught with abject poverty because his parents were thrifty and enterprising, having accumulated seven hundred acres of land by the middle of the 1870's. Eaton attended the local public schools of Louisburg and graduated with the Bachelor of Laws degree from Shaw University in 1894. He began the practice of law in Henderson immediately thereafter, a practice which he pursued for twenty-five years. His participation in politics was rewarded by his election, in 1896, as county attorney of Vance County by the Board of County Commissioners, and by election as representative to the General Assembly of North Carolina in 1899.[102]

In the legislature of 1899, Eaton served on a subcommittee of the joint Committee of Institutions for the Insane and his special task was to inspect the Negro hospital at Goldsboro.[103] He took the floor four times to offer bills in the interest of abolishing the second week of the May term of Vance Superior Court, to provide Supreme Court Reports for Vance County, to regulate the appointment of guards over convicts, and to reimburse two Negro school teachers.[104] Only the first and last measures passed.[105] Eaton's proposals were related specifically to Vance County and were not Negroid in nature. Whether to attribute this to his realization of the sensitivity of the Democratic legislature which had just ridden to power on the "white supremacy" cry, or to his broadness in being able to serve his biracial constituency of Vance County, is hard to ascertain. Only once did he ask to present a petition of the colored citizens in which they pleaded for a guarantee of equality in length of school term for both races.[106] The petition was turned over to the Committee on Education and there died. Eaton voted with the minority Republicans against removing the name of James Hunter Young from the cornerstone of the new buildings at the Deaf, Dumb and Blind Institution at Raleigh.

The "black county" of Northampton sent W. C. Coates to the House of Representatives in 1899. Coates made no attempts at significant legislation. He was content to secure for Northampton an increase in the number of commissioners,[107] a proposal which was in conformity with the Democratic practice in 1899 of legislative appointment of commissioners rather than popular election in a county predominantly black.[108] Upon his request,[109] the legislature incorporated Rich Square Academy in Northampton County.[110] Coates demonstrated his party and race loyalty by voting with the Republicans against the removal of James Young's name from the cornerstone.

J. H. Wright represented Warren, another "black county," in 1899. He attempted to stay the hand of a Democratic legislature bent on making county government officials appointive rather than elective by asking that the Fusion system of county government be amplified rather than repealed.[111] He lost.

The last Negro to serve in the North Carolina Senate was Thomas O. Fuller, elected to the 1899 legislature from the Eleventh District, Warren and Vance counties. Fuller was born October 25, 1867, in the town of Franklinton, North Carolina. He attended a private school at five, entered Normal School of Franklinton at fifteen, graduated from Shaw University, Raleigh, at twenty-two, received the Master of Arts degree from the same school at twenty-five, and was senator in the North Carolina General Assembly at thirty-one. Between 1890 and 1894, he secured the organization of the Girls' Training School of Franklinton by special legislative act;[112] and, from 1895 to 1898, he served as principal of Shiloh Institute in Warrenton, North Carolina. He was drawn into the vortex of politics in 1898 against any desire on his part. In relating how he was chosen as senatorial candidate from the Eleventh District of Warren and Vance counties, two "black counties," he stated that Charles A. Cooke, an eminent white lawyer, won the nomination over W. H. Warwick, the colored principal of Reedy Creek Institute at Littleton, North Carolina; that later in the campaign, Cooke was nominated for criminal court judge, leaving a vacancy in the senatorial nomination; and that the joint executive committee of the Republican Committee of the two counties in a meeting in Manson, North Carolina, literally begged him to accept the nomination.[113] He said that he received all the votes cast for senator in his district except forty-two, which were divided among three independent white candidates.[114]

In view of the tense repercussions of the "white supremacy" campaign of 1898, Fuller advised, when the election was over, that the people let unnecessary agitation cease and shun anarchy, intimidation, and riot.[115] On January 4, Fuller entered the Senate. The roll of the Senate was supposed to have been called in alphabetical order. In that case "F" would have been reached early in the roll call; however, he was the last Senator, the fiftieth, to take the oath. When it is remembered that he was the only Negro in the

Senate, and that all "kissed the Bible" upon taking the oath, it can readily be understood why he was the last. Other senators were seated alphabetically, but Fuller was assigned to seat number 50.[116] Extreme partisanship exhibited itself in the failure to appoint this Negro senator on a committee. Charles A. Reynolds, Republican, presided over the Senate, and announced that it would be his policy to appoint on committees only those recommended by the Democratic caucus.[117] The Democratic caucus ignored Republican Fuller.

As testimony to Fuller's legislative initiative, four achievements remain. Two were nonracial and two were racial in scope. A previous Democratic legislature had established a new criminal court for the judicial district which included Warren and Vance counties, taking from the superior court all jurisdiction in criminal cases. The criminal court held sessions in Warren County every six months and was an expense to the county in that it kept in jail for six months prisoners who were not able to secure bond or whose cases were not bailable. Both prisoners and county suffered. In order to clear the jails every three months and expedite the judicial process, Fuller drafted and introduced a bill to give the superior court concurrent criminal jurisdiction in all criminal cases.[118] The bill became a law.[119] The legislator's home town appreciated this law as a measure of economy, adding, "we thank Senator Fuller for the bill, he having introduced it."[120]

The town of Warrenton had an open bar. The temperance forces of the state brought pressure on the Democratic legislature of 1899 to rout whiskey from the state. A white representative in the House offered a resolution to abolish the open barroom and substitute a dispensary to be operated by the county.[121] The bill passed the House and went to the Senate. The Warren County dispensary bill was referred to the Committee on Propositions and Grievances and had failed to leave the committee by a vote of one. Fuller appealed to Republican Senator Franks, of Swain County, to change his vote in favor of the dispensary bill.[122] The appeal was not in vain as the bill emerged from the committee room, took its place on the calendar, and passed.[123] Fuller's resolution to request North Carolina's congressmen to vote for the ratification of the treaty of peace, which was to conclude the Spanish-American War, and to labor for self-government in the newly acquired territory, died at its second reading.[124]

A group of intelligent and energetic Negroes in the state organized a benevolent society titled The North Carolina Mutual and Provident Association and sought an act of incorporation from the legislature of 1899. Senator Fuller introduced the bill to incorporate the organization,[125] and related that its passage in the Senate was an easy matter, but to get it through the House cost him the hardest fight of his legislative career. The bill came at a time, seemingly, when it had been decided to put a check on benevolent insurance and when the Democratic House was not interested in sanctioning any

Negro business enterprise. The organization, however, was incorporated.[126] The second bill with racial inference was instigated by Fuller and resulted in the repeal of an act which prohibited outside labor agents from recruiting Negro labor in the state.[127]

In analyzing the legislative proposals of the ten Negroes from 1895 through 1899, it appears that the measures were largely Negroid in nature. They were the result of the psychosis of race which showed a minority tending toward a racial point of view and then toward a state point of view. The Negro delegates labored under the psychosis of minority limitations and the desire to substantiate gains made by political party advantage. The ennui of perpetual repression and the superiority complexes so demonstrated by the white opponents were ample inducement to herd the Negroes together in thought and action.

Of the ten Negro officeholders, James Young, J. Y. Eaton, T. O. Fuller, and W. L. Person were college graduates. Young was editor and owner of *The Gazette* and grand master of the Negro Masons in the state; J. Y. Eaton was a lawyer; and T. O. Fuller was the possessor of two academic degrees, founder of a school, and principal of two others. Isaac Smith and William Crews attended college and taught school; and Smith became, long before his legislative career, a banker of prominence and real estate dealer. John Howe was business manager of the *Wilmington Record*. The majority of these Negro Republicans had been political officeholders before their election to the General Assembly. A young North Carolina liberal of the present day states that "All Negro legislators were not peanut munching apes," and added the further conviction that

I happen to be a Democrat and a Southerner who thinks the whole story of Reconstruction in the South and particularly the story of the freed Negroes after the war needs to be written with a good deal less old-time Democratic politics and prejudice in it. There were definitely superior men among the Negro leaders after the war. In politics, however, they were black and that was enough.[128]

All of the ten Negro officeholders of the state legislature belonged to one or more of the Negro fraternal organizations of the period—Masons, Knights of Pythias, Knights of Gideon, and Star of Zion. These organizations serve benevolent and political purposes and constitute an unwritten chapter in the history and sociology of Negro life. Prior to 1900, they served as spring boards for Negro political leadership, while at the time preparing him for moral and social leadership in the transitional period between emancipation and 1900.

The ratio of Negro legislators to the total membership of the General Assembly was small. The sixteen "black counties" elected to the 1895 legislature one Negro representative, twenty white representatives, and contributed to the election of eighteen white senators. They elected to the 1897 legislature two Negro representatives, two Negro senators, nineteen white representatives, and contributed to the election of sixteen white senators. They elected to the 1899 legislature four Negro representatives, one Negro senator, seventeen white representatives, and contributed to the election of seventeen white senators.[129] Oddly enough, James H. Young, Negro, who served in the legislative sessions of 1895 and 1897, was from Wake County which had a white population of 53 per cent.[130] If the "black counties" had sent their "possible" quota to the House of Representatives, there would have been twenty-one Negroes in 1895, 1897, and 1899 instead of one, two, and four, respectively.[131] The House of Representatives in 1895, 1897, and 1899 had a roll call of two, three, and four Negroes as compared with 118, 117, and 116 whites for the respective years. The Senate had in 1895, 1897, and 1899 no Negroes, two, and one as compared with 50, 48, and 49 whites for the respective years.[132] It is evident, then, that the ten Negroes who went to the General Assembly between 1895 and 1900 did not establish Negro domination.

NOTES TO CHAPTER SEVEN

1. *North Carolina Manual*, 1913, 625, 833.
2. *House Journal*, 1895, 17, 26, 51, 61, 70, 111, 123, 301.
3. *House Journal*, 1897, 21, 24, 25, 61, 81, 174, 198.
4. A few copies are preserved at the University of North Carolina Library.
5. *Supra*, Chap. IV, 49-50.
6. Josephus Daniels, *Editor in Politics*, 133-34.
7. Collins and Goodwin, *Biographical Sketches of the General Assembly of North Carolina, 1895* (Duke University Library Pamphlet Collection), 52.
8. Interview with Attorney James Young Carter, grandson of James Hunter Young and Professor of Law at North Carolina College for Negroes, Durham, North Carolina, September 8, 1945.
9. Collins and Goodwin, *op. cit.*, 52-53.
10. *House Journal*, 1897, 91, 147, 243, 252, 401.
11. *Public Laws*, 1897, Chap. 152, 209; Chap. 207, 348; Chap. 197, 337; Chap. 321, 492; and *Public Documents*, 1899, Nos. 12, 32.
12. *House Journal*, 1895, 140.
13. *House Journal*, 1897, 365, 731.
14. *Public Laws*, 1897, Chap. 443, 631; Chap. 465, 649.
15. *House Journal*, 1897, 590.
16. *Public Laws*, 1897, Chap. 486, 662.
17. *House Journal*, 1897, 658.
18. *Infra*, Chap. IX, Negro Office-holding: Municipal.
19. *House Journal*, 1897, 489; *Public Laws*, 1897, 755.
20. *House Journal*, 1897, 237.
21. *News and Observer*, October 5, 1898.
22. The Governor's Appointments and Commissions (North Carolina Historical Commission, Raleigh, North Carolina), 105.

23. Interview with Mrs. Martha Ray, daughter of James H. Young and contemporary, Winston-Salem, North Carolina, June 17, 1944.

24. *News and Observer*, August 11, 1898.
This same article, word for word, is found in the *Democratic Handbook*, 1898, 147-48.

25. *People's Party Handbook*, 1898, 9.

26. *Senate Journal*, 1899, 17.

27. *House Journal*, 1899, 92-94.

28. *Ibid.*, 94.

29. Isaac Smith was read out of the Republican party for this and similar acts of appeasement of the Democrats; *Supra*, 106-7; *Infra*, 180.

30. *Public Laws*, 1899, Chap. 60, 196.

31. *The Union Republican*, January 12, 1899.

32. Josephus Daniels, Editor of the Raleigh *News and Observer*.

33. Needham Broughton, Editor of *The Biblical Recorder*, part-owner of Edwards and Broughton Printing Company.

34. *House Journal*, 1897, 174.

35. *Public Laws*, 1897, Chap. 464, 649.

36. *Public Laws*, 1895, Chap. 20, 44-45.

37. *News and Observer*, March 17, 1897.

38. *N. B. Broughton v. James H. Young*, North Carolina Reports, CXIX, 915-17.

39. *House Journal*, 1897, 62.

40. *News and Observer*, January 23, 1897.

41. *Ibid.*, January 30, 1897.

42. *House Journal*, 1897, 344-45.

43. *Ibid.*, 906-7.

44. *News and Observer*, February 26, 1897.

45. Interview with Mrs. Martha Ray, daughter of James H. Young and contemporary, Winston-Salem, North Carolina, June 17, 1944.

46. *Democratic Handbook* 1898, 82.

47. *Biographical Sketches of the General Assembly of North Carolina*, 1895, 36.

48. *House Journal*, 1895, 123, 124.

49. *House Journal*, 1897, 40, 61, 108, 137, 1101.

50. *Supra*, Chap. III, 41-43.

51. *House Journal*, 1895, 254.

52. *Public Laws*, 1897, Chap. 255, 433-36.

53. *Ibid.*, 433.

54. *Ibid.*, 436.

55. *Ibid.*, 436.

56. *House Journal*, 1897, 316.

57. *Public Laws*, 1897, Chap. 270, 453.

58. *House Journal*, 1895, 390.

59. The only action taken by the legislature of 1895 or the 1897 legislature with regard to ex-slaves was to amend Rule 13, Section 1281, of *The Code* so as to allow the grandchildren of certain ex-slaves to inherit and become distributees of their estates.—*Public Laws*, 1897, Chap. 153, 210.

60. *House Journal*, 1897, 293.

61. The use of the Hall, during the same session, was granted to a white woman, Miss Hellen Morris Lewis, to address a group of whites on Woman Suffrage.—*House Journal*, 1897, 232-33.

62. United States Bureau of Census, *Negro Population in the United States, 1790–1915,* 784.

63. *House Journal,* 1897, 61, 81, 96, 151.

64. *Private Laws,* 1897, Chap. 150, 282; see *Infra,* Chap. IX.

65. Turner and Bridges, *History of Edgecombe County,* 308-9.

66. *News and Observer,* November 19, 1896.

67. *Senate Journal,* 1897, 14, 16, 21.

68. *Ibid.,* 128, 150, 157, 175, 237, 258, 306, 356, 420, 443, 479, 489.

69. *Ibid.,* 23.

70. *Public Laws,* 1893, Chap. 461, 440-41.

71. *Senate Journal,* 1897, 101, 306.

72. *Ibid.,* 157.

73. *Ibid.,* 420.

74. *Ibid.,* 356.

75. *Ibid.,* 237.

76. *Ibid.,* 258.

77. *Ibid.,* 462.

78. *Ibid.,* 443.

79. *Ibid.,* 14, 15, 16.

80. *Ibid.,* 444.

81. *Ibid.,* 23, 75, 109, 107.

82. *Charlotte Observer,* May 31, 1898.

83. *Infra,* Chaps. XII, XIII.

84. *News and Observer,* September 18, 1898.

85. *Ibid.,* January 14, 1899.

86. *Ibid.,* January 23, 1899.

87. Josephus Daniels, *Editor in Politics,* 329; *The Union Republican,* January 10, 1899.

88. *The Union Republican,* January 19, 1899; *News and Observer,* January 10, 1899.

89. *Ibid.*

90. *Ibid.*

91. *News and Observer,* January 12, 1899.

92. *House Journal,* 1899, 45.

93. *Ibid.,* 100.

94. *Ibid.,* 356.

95. *The Union Republican,* January 10, 1899.

96. *News and Observer,* January 10, 1899.

97. *House Journal,* 1899, 475.

98. *Supra,* Chap. VI.

99. *House Journal,* 1899, 68, 83, 201, 553.

100. *Ibid.,* 135.

101. Josephus Daniels, *Editor in Politics,* 329.

102. A. B. Caldwell (ed.), *History of American Negro,* North Carolina Edition, IV, 129-32.

103. *Public Laws,* 1899, 970.

104. *House Journal,* 1899, 68, 114, 285, 374.

105. *Public Laws,* 1899, Chap. 644, 840; Legislative Papers and Bills, January 24, 1899.

106. *House Journal,* 1899, 158.

107. *Ibid.,* 114.

108. *Public Laws,* 1899, Chap. 346, 477.

109. *House Journal*, 1899, 477.
110. *Private Laws*, 1899, Chap. 265, 781-82.
111. *House Journal*, 1899, 68.
112. *Private Laws*, 1895, Chap. 18, 28-29.
113. Thomas O. Fuller, *Twenty Years in Public Life, 1890-1910*, 37-38.
114. Thomas O. Fuller, *A Pictorial History of the American Negro*, 272.
115. Fuller, "An Address To The Colored People Of The Eleventh Senatorial District of North Carolina," *Twenty Years Of Public Life, 1890-1910*, 40-43.
116. *Ibid.*, 49.
117. *The Union Republican*, January 5, 1899.
118. *Senate Journal*, 1899, 379.
119. *Public Laws*, 1899, Chap. 436, 573.
120. *Warrenton Record*, March 19, 1899.
121. *House Journal*, 1899, 357, 622, 924.
122. Thomas O. Fuller to Henry P. Cheatham, 1899 (citing from a letter, Fuller, *Twenty Years of Public Life, 1890-1910*, 52).
123. *Public Laws*, 1899, Chap. 483, 622-28.
124. *The Union Republican*, January 26, 1899.
125. *Senate Journal*, 1899, 508, 527, 538.
126. *Private Laws*, 1899, Chap. 156, 375-76.
Original charter included John Merrick, Dr. A. M. Moore, Dr. James E. Shepard, W. G. Pearson, D. T. Watson, T. O. Fuller, E. A. Johnson, and N. C. Bruce. The corporation is known in 1950 as The North Carolina Mutual Life Insurance Company, the largest Negro insurance company in the world.
127. *Infra*, Chap. XII, 190-91.
128. Jonathan Daniels, *Tar Heels: A Portrait of North Carolina*, 126.
129. The "black counties" (italicized in this citation) contributed to the election of eighteen white senators in 1895, sixteen in 1897, and seventeen in 1899. The number of senators alloted those districts in which the "black counties" are located and the number of representatives allotted the same counties are herein stated:

DISTRICTS

First	Fifth	Eleventh
Second	Eighth	Seventeenth
Third	Ninth	Eighteenth
Fourth	Tenth	Twenty-third

COUNTIES	SENATORS	REPRESENTATIVES
Currituck, Camden, *Pasquotank, Hertford,* Gates, *Chowan,* Perquimans.	2	1, 1, 1
Tyrrell, *Washington,* Martin, Dare, Beaufort, Hyde, Pamlico.	2	1
Northampton, Bertie.	1	1, 1
Halifax	1	2
Edgecombe	1	2
Craven, Jones, Carteret, Lenoir, Greene, Onslow.	2	1
Duplin, Wayne, *Pender.*	2	1
New Hanover, Brunswick.	1	2
Warren, Vance.	1	1, 1
Granville, Person.	1	2

Caswell, Alamance, Orange, Durham.	2	1
Richmond, Montgomery, Anson, Union.	2	2
	18	21

Senatorial districting: Chap. 421 *Public Laws,* 1891, 495-96.
                Supplemented Act to Public Laws, 1891, Chap. 368.

130. United States Bureau of Census, *Negro Population in the United States, 1790-1915,* 784-85.

131. See maps 17 and 208 for "black counties"; see Negro population for 1890, 1900, in Table I, Appendix; see number of white representatives sent to the North Carolina legislature in 1895, 1897, 1899, in *House Journal,* 1895, 1897, 1899; *cf.* the number of Negro representatives from the "black counties" (see below, footnote 132) with the number of white representatives from the same counties for the years 1895, 1897, 1899, (*Supra,* 111-12).

132. The Negro roll call totalled nine in the House of Representatives and three in the Senate during the Fusion period. It must be noted that two members who served in the House in 1895 also served in 1897.

HOUSE OF REPRESENTATIVES	SENATE
1895 1. James H. Young*	
2. William H. Crews, Jr.	
1897 James H. Young*	8. W. Lee Person
William H. Crews, Jr.	9. W. B. Henderson
3. John T. Howe	
1899 4. J. Y. Eaton	10. Thomas O. Fuller
5. W. C. Coates	
6. Isaac Smith	
7. J. H. Wright	

*Wake county ("white county").
North Carolina Manual, 1913, 500-843; *House Journal,* 1895, 1897, 1899; 2-4, 3-5, 4-6.

CHAPTER EIGHT

NEGRO OFFICE-HOLDING: COUNTY

COUNTY GOVERNMENT IN NORTH CAROLINA has undergone several significant changes from the beginning of statehood to the present. Before 1868, county government rested on a basis of strong centralization. The county court was the instrument of control. The justices of the peace were the most important officers, for they comprised the county court. Their powers were both administrative and judicial. They chose one among their number as chairman, and any three constituted a sufficient number to transact county business. They received their positions through recommendation by the General Assembly and appointment by the governor to hold office during good behavior.[1] It is unquestionably true that the political flavor of the General Assembly was bound to be reflected in the appointments. One of the most thorough students of county government in this state held that "since the members came from different sections of the county it was a representative body but it was not a democratic body in that members were not directly dependent upon popular vote."[2]

The Civil War and Reconstruction brought to the state a new type of county government, commonly known as the County Commission Plan.[3] The Republicans composed of Yankees and Negroes and native North Carolinians, chiefly of the lowest economic and social classes, instituted the plan in the Constitution of 1868. The commission plan provided for a board of five county commissioners elected by the popular vote of the county. The administrative powers, duties, and finances were in the hands of the commissioners. Such county officers as treasurer, surveyor, register of deeds, clerk of the superior court, sheriff, and coroner were subjected to popular election and served for a term of two years. This Reconstruction constitution introduced a new device known as the township unit. This meant a redivision of the county into township units based on population for purposes of local government and local taxation. The township unit was presided over by a board of trustees comprising a clerk (who was treasurer) and two justices of the peace popularly elected for two-year terms. The board of trustees handled taxes, finances, and local projects within their confines; but were held to strict accountability by the county commissioners. There was no doubt that significant changes had occurred under the commissioner plan; and these changes were, that the administration of county affairs was transferred from the justices of the peace to county commissioners; townships were created as separate administrative units; county and township officers were made elective by popular vote; justices of the peace were reduced to petty magistrates with minor duties in connection with the township; and the judicial powers of the old county court were distributed among the justices of the peace, the superior court, and the clerk of that court.[4] Furthermore, in a system of county government based on popular election, some Negroes in the "black counties" were elected to office. The commission plan was an adaptation of the Pennsylvania plan of county government to North Carolina, and the state was by attitude and historical heritage opposed to it from the beginning. The fact that Yankees and recently enfranchised Negroes supported the plan, and that popular election meant democracy as well as the possibility of Negroes holding office, added to its unpopularity in North Carolina and hastened its overthrow. The confusion during Reconstruction never gave the plan a good opportunity to demonstrate its merits; however, the Republicans had attempted to give to the people a plan which "in theory was a democratic system, directly dependent upon the popular will, [and] subject to short terms of service."[5]

The Constitutional Amendment of 1876 gave to the legislature the power to handle county government. The Democratic legislature of 1877, partly inspired by the removal of federal troops from the South, enacted a Democratic system of county government for North Carolina.[6] This system, which held sway from 1877 to 1895, reverted once more to centralized control of county government by restoring justices of the peace, appointed by the Democratic Assembly, as the most important officers. Popular election of all county officers, except register of deeds and surveyor, was abolished. The Democratic set-up retained the board of county commissioners, disrobed of their power, and subjected their election to the justices of the peace. The justices of the peace, once more, possessed completely all administrative and judicial powers. Lest the retained board of county commissioners might not understand their duties, the Democratic law specifically stated that commissioners could not levy taxes, purchase property, borrow money, alter or create new townships, or remove county buildings unless so ordered by the justices of the peace. In reality, the Democrats had resorted to centralized control through legislative appointment thereby guaranteeing perpetuation of Democratic control over "black counties" and white Republicans. Local self-government was abolished not only for "black" and Republican but also for "white" Democratic counties.

The repeal of the commissioner plan of government based on popular election was a sore spot with the Republicans and some liberal Democrats from 1876 to 1894. Both Republicans and Populists had endorsed the restoration of local self-government in their party platforms of 1894. Fusion victory brought forth Fusion county government. The county government act of 1895 made county commissioners supreme in administrative authority and relegated the justices of the peace to positions of minor importance. Three commissioners were elected biennially for each county by popular vote.[7] Other county officers, such as clerk of the superior court, clerk of the inferior court, sheriff, coroner, treasurer, register of deeds, surveyor, and constable, were likewise popularly elected.

The Fusionists were aware that they were experimenting with a system which had not been practiced for twenty years in the state. They sought cautiously to make county commissioners responsible to public opinion between election years. Also they arranged for representation of the minority party by providing that whenever five electors, supported by a petition of two hundred electors, made affidavits before the clerk of the superior court, immediately after the election that they felt that three commissioners could not properly manage the business of the county, the judge of that district was to appoint two honest and discreet citizens of a different political party from the majority of the commissioners and thus secure a board of five. Too, wherever two more commissioners had been added, the board could pay out no money and incur no debt, except with the concurrence of as many as four of the five commissioners.[8] Never had the Democrats made provisions for the representation of an opposing political party in county government. Never before in the history of North Carolina had county commissioners been made so responsible to public opinion. The retained justices of the peace were shorn of their power. The Fusion legislature followed for expediency's sake, since 1895 was not an election year, the Democratic practice of legislative appointment for three justices of the peace for each township and one for every thousand inhabitants in each town and city; however, beginning with the election of 1896 and every two years thereafter, they were to be elected by popular vote.[9] Thus the Fusionists had carried out their campaign pledge—restoration of local self-government. This achievement was an aid to their victory in 1896.

The Fusion legislature of 1897, realizing that it had been under the hail of Democratic fire in the campaign of 1896, made further changes in the 1895 system. Where formerly five electors could appeal upon affidavits to the clerk of the superior court that they felt that county administration would be improperly managed by three commissioners, the 1897 change required that twelve electors must petition the clerk, and they must prove to the judge of the district that they had carefully examined the administration of the county and had found that the board of commissioners had unlawfully and wilfully mismanaged the business affairs. If the judge, after a complete hearing, was satisfied that the charges were true, then he might add two men of the opposing party to the three popularly elected commissioners.[10]

The flexibility of the Fusion provisions for securing two additional commissioners served two purposes. If the Populists feared domination in county government by their Republican copartners, then there was an instrument for redressing grievances. Moreover, the Democrats could use it to add Democrats to the board, provided they could prove mismanagement. Never had the Democrats been so generous with opposing parties from 1876 to 1894.

In analyzing the merits of Fusion county government, there are varying opinions. Florence Smith feels that the system was bad, but it was the attempt of the [righteous] Populists to redeem their campaign pledge, and they proceeded on the theory of the democratic ideal.[11] She ascribes no such high motives to the Republicans, though it is an historical fact that the Fusion system was largely the reproduction of the Reconstruction plan instituted by the Republican party in North Carolina. Another writer considers the Fusion set-up as "a great step forward in local self government."[12] The leading student of county government in this state, in 1928, analyzed the commissioner plan, though not in connection with his treatment of the Fusion period, as one in which "popular government is furthered by simplicity and directness. The commissioner plan compares favorably with other types of county government in general use. It fits the South better than a system in which the township figures prominently. . . . So long, however, as its functions remain primarily administrative, a board of three or five members is superior to a larger one."[13]

Any system of county government based upon popular election and predicated upon fair election laws would bring some Negroes to county office in some of the sixteen "black counties." It is impossible to secure county records of office-holding for the ninety-six counties of the Fusion period, or even for the sixteen "black counties." The Democratic press is the chief source. Democratic opposition to Fusion county government is expressed in the feeling that

The Republican party then, as now, was weighed down by the Negro, and to appease him, counties and towns, were turned over to him to pillage and plunder. The credit of the counties and towns, like the credit of the State, was destroyed. Negro magistrates and Negro officials then, as now, went through the farce of administering the law.[14]

The Fusionists were quick to reply that the Democrats had exaggerated the number of Negro officeholders, and that the Democrats themselves had appointed or elected Negroes as notaries public, county commissioners, aldermen, school committeemen, policemen, road overseers, and deputy sheriffs at various times between 1876 and 1894.[15] The Democrats declared that their Negro appointments had been few and were in sections to accommodate the local constituency. Democratic denunciation was based on the race question. The Democrats made no attempts to appraise the merits or the idealism of the system. So inseparably did they link it with the race question that the virtues were submerged in a sea of emotionalism.

In the last days of the "white supremacy" campaign of 1898, state Democratic Chairman Simmons set forth the strongest charge of Negro domination in a letter[16] to Jeter C. Pritchard, Republican United States senator from North Carolina, in which he stated that there were Negro officeholders in Bertie, Caswell, Craven, Edgecombe, Granville, Halifax, New Hanover, and Warren counties; that Negro candidates were running for office in 1898 in Craven, Granville, Halifax, Pasquotank, Warren counties; and, that already there were more than three hundred Negro magistrates in eastern North Carolina. County positions herein ascribed to Negroes constituted magistrate (justice of the peace), register of deeds, deputy register of deeds, coroner, constable, deputy sheriff, treasurer, and county commissioner. Be it noted that this Democratic campaign document appeared before the election of 1898 and cited Negro candidates for office as well as Negro officeholders. There is to be observed the difference between "running" and "winning." In 1900, the *News and Observer* summarized the Negro officeholders in the heavily populated Negro counties in this way: in Craven, Negroes held the positions of register of deeds, deputy register, deputy sheriff (3), coroner, county commissioner, and magistrate (27); New Hanover County elected a register of deeds, constable, and deputy sheriff, and in 1895 had forty magistrates appointed by the legislature; Warren County not only had four or five federally appointed postmasters but elected a register of deeds and a commissioner; and Bertie, Edgecombe, Halifax, Granville, and Caswell counties had sixteen, thirty-one, twenty-nine, seventeen, and seven Negro magistrates, respectively.[17]

Apparently the Democratic charge of Negro domination was based upon the fact that some Negroes held minor positions in eight "black counties" of the east. What of the other eight "black counties" which elected white Republicans to county positions? And what of the other eighty "white counties"?

An analysis of county officers showed that the largest number of Negroes were magistrates (justices of the peace). When it is reflected that the Fusion county government law stripped the justices of the peace of most of their power and importance in county affairs, leaving them with the main function of trying cases with less than $200 involved, it seems clear that the Negro magistrates in a few Negro counties did not bring Negro domination to North Carolina or its counties. The appointment of Negroes to the lowly office of magistrate was the reward for faithful and substantial contribution to the victorious party.

Craven and Warren counties were reputed to have elected one Negro commissioner each during the Fusion period. While the office of commissioner was the highest in a county, each county had by law three to five commissioners, and one Negro commissioner in Craven or Warren could not control his board.

Craven, New Hanover, Vance, and Warren counties each had a Negro register of deeds and there were in some eastern counties deputy registers of deeds. The register of deeds and the deputy register were minor county officers without power to formulate policies. It was the register's job "to record all instruments delivered to him for registration after the same have been probated by the clerk of the superior court, . . . [and] issue marriage license."[18] The register of deeds was empowered to appoint deputies who might perform any of the duties of the office but for whose acts the register himself was responsible.[19] The Negro deputy registers were in most cases appointed by and subordinate to white registers. While four counties had Negro registers of deeds, ninety-two counties in the state did not, nor did twelve of the sixteen "black counties" elect Negroes as registers of deeds.

Scant materials on Negro registers of deeds reveal that Thomas S. Eaton served Vance County with honesty and integrity for ten years, 1888-98. Eaton was a man of high educational attainment, even surpassing the standards of his time for such a position. He was a graduate of Boydton Institute (Boydton, Virginia) and Shaw University (Raleigh, North Carolina). He was the brother of James Y. Eaton who served in the North Carolina legislature in 1899. The position of register of deeds was more honorary than remunerative. No fixed salary accompanied the position, and Eaton gained his livelihood and affluence through the acquisition of real estate.[20] A Southern newspaper commented at the time of his death, "He was one of the oldest and most respected citizens of Vance county . . . a man who was trustworthy, believed in upright living . . . a wise counsellor and a safe leader."[21] Eaton's position as register of deeds was not the result of Fusion politics. His election in 1888 was effected under Democratic domination,—the position being one of the two left to popular election by the laws of 1876-77.[22] He never accepted his party's stand on Fusion. The race tension in the campaign of 1898 convinced him that he should not seek re-election.

It is of little concern whether the Democratic charge that there was one Negro coroner is true; it has been adequately stated that "a county surveyor and a coroner are elected for two years, but these offices are not of very great importance."[23] The sheriff of a county was the process officer of the superior court and tax collector of the county. It was charged that there were Negro deputy sheriffs in a few "black counties." It may be reasonable to assume that they officiated primarily in arresting violators in Negro districts.

But the Democratic press emphasized Negro domination in the east. The Fusion county government law provided for eleven to thirteen county officers including the three to five commissioners, clerk of superior court, clerk of inferior court, sheriff, coroner, treasurer, register of deeds, surveyor, and constable. If Negroes had dominated even in the sixteen "black counties," they must have held at least a majority (more than one hundred) of the thirteen positions. However, so far as can be learned, the Negroes supplied two county commissioners, a few registers of deeds, one treasurer, one coroner, a few deputy registers of deeds and deputy sheriffs, and a quantity of magistrates.

The Democrats sought to produce a startling effect by using the alleged total of one thousand Negro officeholders rather than a tabulation by offices. Moreover, it was possible to achieve a total of impressive size only by including magistrates or justices of the peace.

NOTES TO CHAPTER EIGHT

1. A. C. McIntosh, "The County Government System of North Carolina," *County Government and County Affairs in North Carolina,* The North Carolina Club Year Book, 1917-1918 (1919), 20-22.

2. Paul W. Wager, *County Government and Administration in North Carolina,* 57.

3. *Public Laws: Special Session,* 1868, Chap. 2, 22-34; further implemented by *Public Laws,* 1868-1869, Chap. 14, 56-57; Chap. 259, 606-7.

4. Wager, *op. cit.,* 18-19.
A. C. McIntosh, "County Government in North Carolina," *National Municipal Review,* XIV (1925), 96-103, stresses that only judicial powers were left to justices of the peace.

5. McIntosh, "County Government in North Carolina," 96.

6. *Public Laws,* 1876-77, Chap. 141, 226-29.

7. *Public Laws,* 1895, Chap. 135, 185-87; also *The Code,* Vol. I, Chap. 17.

8. *Public Laws,* 1895, Chap. 135, 185.

9. *Public Laws,* 1895, Chap. 157, 209-10.

10. *Public Laws,* 1897, Chap. 320, 491-92.

11. Florence E. Smith, Populism and Its Influence in North Carolina (Unpublished Ph.D. dissertation), 128-29.

12. Delap, "The Populist Party in North Carolina," 58.

13. Wager, *op. cit.,* 91-92.

14. *Democratic Handbook,* 1898, 31.

15. *People's Party Handbook,* 1898, 16-25.

16. See Letter in Appendix, 234-36.

17. *News and Observer,* January 28, 1900.

18. Wager, *op. cit.,* 381-82, 384.

19. *Ibid.,* 386.

20. Interview with Mrs. Thomas S. Eaton, wife of the deceased, February 24, 1949.

21. *Norfolk Journal and Guide,* July 14, 1934.

22. *Public Laws,* 1876-77, Chap. 141, 226-29.

23. McIntosh, "County Government in North Carolina," 101.

CHAPTER NINE

NEGRO OFFICE-HOLDING: MUNICIPAL

NEGROES ENTERED THE PICTURE of office-holding in municipal as well as in county government. Towns and cities in North Carolina received their individual charters of incorporation from the General Assembly. These private charters prescribed the governmental machinery for administration, offices, finances, elections, and city welfare. From 1876 to 1894, the Democratic feature of centralization provided for the appointment of major city officials by the state legislature or by city aldermen. When the Fusionists took over the reins of government in 1895 and extended the system of popular election to state and county officers, it was expected that they would be the same to municipal government.

North Carolina was predominantly a rural state. In 1900, only 17.9 per cent of its 1,893,810 people lived in incorporated places.[1] North Carolina cities were comparatively few and small in size. According to the census reports of 1890 and 1900, there were twenty-eight cities which had a population of 2,500 or more.[2] These towns and cities may be classified into three groups in relation to the ratio of their Negro population. The first group consisted of eight in which Negroes were more than 50 per cent of the population.[3] The second group consisted of four in which the Negro and white populations were approximately equal.[4] The third group consisted of sixteen in which the whites were more than 50 per cent of the population.[5]

The Democrats charged that the Fusionists altered the charters of towns and cities in North Carolina in order to turn them over to Negro rule.[6] An examination of the charter changes reveals that of the first group wherein the Negroes were in the majority, the Fusionists amended two and altered four charters of the eight towns and cities; that in the second group wherein there was a parity in racial constituency, they amended three and altered one; and in the third group wherein the whites exceeded the Negroes by a goodly number, they amended one and altered six of the sixteen. The story involving the amending and altering of city charters cannot be told so simply because the Democratic allegation of turning towns and cities over to Negro rule stands or falls not on the number of charters amended and altered but upon the precise alterations prescribed in each Fusion charter and the number of Negroes who held offices under the amended charters.

An examination of the charter changes made in the first group wherein Negroes exceeded whites in numbers reveals that the city of Edenton was among the first to undergo Fusion revision. The Democrats, in amending

Edenton's charter in 1891, provided for six wards. The first and second wards by joint ballot elected two councilmen, and so did the third and fourth and the fifth and sixth. The six councilmen elected a mayor from the city at large.[7] The Fusionists reduced the number of wards to four, each elected one councilman, and permitted the four councilmen to elect a mayor from the city at large.[8] Obviously, the Fusion system of electing a mayor was the same undemocratic system as used by the Democrats.

New Bern's Negro population was approximately three thousand more than its white population in 1890 and 1900. The city charter of 1879 vested power in eight councilmen—five elected by five wards and three chosen by

POPULATION OF PLACES HAVING 2,500 OR MORE, 1890, 1900
NORTH CAROLINA

PLACES	1890*		1900†	
	WHITE	NEGRO	WHITE	NEGRO
Asheville	6,668	3,567	9,970	4,724
Charlotte	6,417	5,134	10,938	7,151
Concord	2,957	1,382	6,121	1,789
Durham	3,626	1,859	4,437	2,241
Elizabeth City	1,760	1,490	3,181	3,164
Fayetteville	2,249	1,973	2,449	2,221
Goldsboro	2,296	1,720	3,356	2,520
Greensboro	2,088	1,227	5,948	4,086
Henderson	1,514	2,677	1,552	2,194
New Bern	2,572	5,271	3,208	5,878
Oxford	1,450	1,457	—	—
Raleigh	6,327	6,348	7,921	5,721
Reidsville	1,570	1,399	2,050	1,206
Salem	2,395	316	3,154	488
Salisbury	2,427	1,991	3,866	2,408
Washington	1,671	1,874	2,290	2,550
Wilmington	8,731	11,324	10,556	10,407
Winston	3,331	4,686	4,963	5,043
Burlington	—	—	3,235	450
Edenton	—	—	954	2,090
Greenville	—	—	3,502	1,108
Hickory	—	—	1,093	1,472
High Point	—	—	1,837	698
Kinston	—	—	3,235	1,528
Mt. Airy	—	—	1,989	691
Rocky Mount	—	—	1,428	1,505
Statesville	—	—	2,368	773
Wilson	—	—	2,394	1,131

*1890: United States Department of Commerce, *Bureau of Census, Eleventh Census,* 1890, Vol. 1, Part 1, From Table 19, p. 473.

†1900: United States Department of Commerce, *Bureau of Census, Twelfth Census,* 1900, Vol. 1, Part 1, From Table 23, p. 633.

the elected five. The councilmen chose the mayor.[9] The Fusionists left the
five wards to elect one councilman each, abolished the three extra councilmen, and continued the election of the mayor by the five councilmen, a Democratic feature. The councilmen appointed all other city officials,[10] another
Democratic feature. In 1897, the Fusionists redistricted the city into six wards
and each ward elected one councilman, and the governor appointed five.
The eleven councilmen continued to select the mayor from the city at large.[11]
New Bern was thus governed by a partly elected and a partly appointed board
of councilmen. It is known that one Negro was elected as councilman.
There were also some Negro magistrates in New Bern, some Negro police
to arrest Negroes, and since the Fusionists controlled the government of the
city, it became a chief target of Democratic attack. The fact that New Bern
was the home of one of the most powerful Democrats of the period, Furnifold M. Simmons, may have given added weight to Democratic denunciation.

The city of Raleigh, under the Democratic regime, had five wards which
elected biennially seventeen aldermen who in turn elected a mayor from
the city at large, passed and executed all ordinances, and appointed all city
officials.[12] The Fusionists reduced the wards to four, and each elected three
aldermen. Such offices as mayor, city clerk, tax collector, and police were
elected by popular vote biennially.[13]

The Fusionists' charter had stormy sailing in the legislature because many
Populists feared that Negroes would be elected to the board through the
newly arranged wards, and the Populists did not favor Negro office-holding.
Raleigh, the capital city, was constantly in the limelight, and the *News and
Observer* kept up a rapid fire on the Raleigh bill. Before the bill had left
the committee room, the charge was made that

The amended charter gives us four wards and the first ward is Democratic and
the three others are Republican—thus turning Raleigh over to Negroes and their
allies. The three Republican wards proposed have each a majority of colored
voters which means nothing more or less than that a majority of the aldermen
may be negroes. Are the Populists willing to turn the capital of their State over
to the control of negroes?[14]

When the bill came before the House on February 19 for a hearing, the
press under the headline, "TO NEGROIZE RALEIGH," reported that

Jim Young's Bill gives 955 negroes full control of Raleigh. The Republican plan
is to let the 2nd ward have 5 aldermen, 4th ward have 4, 1st ward have 4, 3rd
ward have 1, and the 5th have 3. This division would give 2 negro wards nine
out of seventeen aldermen.[15]

But the bill did not come through as the Democrats prophesied, and they contended that the modification was due to their protests as well to as the Populist attitude.[16] Some of the Republicans were willing to resort to strong centralization in the Raleigh bill. On March 2, Republican Ewart offered a substitute, placing the election of the mayor in the hands of the people and creating, by legislative appointment, a police board of seven members which should elect all other city officers. Mr. Young accepted the substitute, saying that the main thing was the elections of the mayor by the people. Ewart named seven men he thought good: J. C. L. Harris, W. S. Barnes, Joseph E. Pogue, W. F. Debnam, Henry A. Miller, E. S. Cheek, and James H. Young, Negro. Pogue and Miller were Democrats, and an amendment was offered to strike out their names and insert two Fusionists, D. H. Young and John Nichols. This led to a bitter debate, and the amendment was lost.[17] As finally enacted, the charter provided for an elective mayor and four wards electing three aldermen each. Far from resulting in Negro rule for Raleigh, the new system permitted the election of only one Negro, E. A. Johnson,[18] as a city alderman in the Fusion period. Raleigh's Negro and white population were equal in 1890, and there were two thousand more whites than Negroes in 1900. One Negro alderman on a board of twelve white aldermen was not an adequate ratio to justify the cry of Negro domination in that city.

The severe condemnation which the Raleigh charter received by the Democrats was because of several factors. It was the Raleigh Negro, James Young, who introduced the measure to revise the charter. Second, as a result of the Fusion redistricting of Raleigh, a Negro was elected as an alderman. Third, the *News and Observer* was located in Raleigh and was most bitter and uncompromising in its denunciation of the Fusion regime. What the Democrats dreaded was the loss of Raleigh to Fusion control and the possibility of Negro office-holding.

Washington, North Carolina, had more Negroes than whites. The Democratic allegation that changes were made in areas with a preponderance of Negroes to enhance their political power, proved false in this city. Washington was allowed in 1895 and 1897 to continue operation under its Democratic system. The only Fusionist requirement for the city from which Negroes may have gained was to establish graded schools for white and colored children, appropriate funds from a special school tax, and equalize the facilities·between the races.[19]

The municipal election of Wilmington in 1894 was won by a fusion ticket of Democrats and Republicans. The Fusion legislature of 1895, intent upon destroying all Democratic influence, yet doing it within the framework of constitutionality, amended Wilmington's charter by creating a "police board" of five men. The five-man board was appointed by the General Assembly and its function was to serve side by side with the elected Democratic-Republican board of aldermen.[20] So broadly entrenched were the powers of the Police

Board that it appointed, fired, set salaries, and rendered ineffectual the board of aldermen. There was no doubt that the Fusion instrument of a police board was a device aimed at the Democrats. In 1897, the Fusionists abolished the Police Board and provided five wards, each of which elected one alderman, and the governor appointed five aldermen, one from each ward. This partly appointed and partly elected board of aldermen elected a mayor from among its ranks.[21] The city election of March 25, 1897, resulted in the election of three Negro aldermen: Andrew J. Walker, Owen Fennell, and Elijah M. Green, while Governor Russell appointed one, John G. Norwood.[22]

The Democrats held that "the Governor's power of appointment is a direct blow to the theory of self government."[23] They criticized the Fusion Police Board. There was absolutely no difference between it and the Democratic Board of Audit and Finance inaugurated in 1877 in Wilmington. The Democratic set-up for Wilmington provided for the election of aldermen, but above the aldermen stood the Board of Audit and Finance composed of five persons appointed by the Governor, whose duties were to audit and pass upon the validity of all claims and demands against the city, to order the payment of such approved claims from the treasury, to restrain the aldermen from levying taxes unless such rates of assessment had been submitted to and approved by the board, to fix salaries and other compensations of all officers and employees of the city, and to create a sinking fund to pay interest on the debt of the city. The chairman of the Board of Audit and Finance served as commissioner of the sinking fund.[24]

Winston's Democratic charter prescribed three wards, each of which elected one alderman. The three aldermen chose the mayor from the city at large and set his salary. The aldermen were all-powerful in that they chose the mayor, passed and executed all ordinances, appointed all city officers, and chose the judges and registrars of municipal elections.[25] The Fusionists provided for five wards, each of which elected three aldermen. The mayor was chosen through popular election. The Fusionists changed the requirement for ward residence for voters from ninety to thirty days and prescribed dismissal for any police who influenced or delayed a voter. School commissioners were elected by the people instead of by the aldermen.[26] In 1897, the charter was further amended to increase the school tax from seventy-five cents to one dollar, and the corporate limits of the town were extended.[27]

The second group of cities whose charters were amended by the Fusionists consisted of those towns and cities in which the Negroes and whites were approximately equal in numbers. In the town of Elizabeth City, the Democrats had created five wards which elected one commissioner each, and the five commissioners chose the mayor and other city officials from the city at large.[28] The Fusionists enlarged the corporate limits but retained every feature of the Democratic charter with the exception of ward residence;[29]

that requirement was reduced from ninety to thirty days. It was obvious that the Fusionists had refused to adhere to their theory of a popularly elected mayor and popularly elected city officials in Elizabeth City.

Fayetteville was operated under a charter of 1883 wherein the General Assembly chose fifteen commissioners and selected one of that number as chairman.[30] Later legislatures twice renewed the five-year terms of the commissioners.[31] The Fusionists made no changes in Fayetteville's undemocratic system of government, and the only power granted it was that to purchase an electric plant.[32]

The city of Oxford, like Fayetteville, was allowed to continue operation under its undemocratic Democratic set-up.

Rocky Mount enjoyed a Democratic charter which created four wards, each ward electing one commissioner. The four commissioners in turn elected the mayor from the city at large.[33] The Fusionists redistricted the city into five wards which elected one commissioner each, but the mayor was popularly elected by the city.[34]

The third group of towns and cities whose charters were amended by the Fusionists consisted of those in which whites exceeded Negroes by large majorities. The Democrats granted Asheville the annual election of a mayor and five aldermen from the city at large.[35] They had rarely allowed the popular election of mayor in the eastern cities. The Fusionists prescribed new corporate limits, and the wardless city was divided into four wards, each electing one alderman. To the four aldermen were added two others who were elected annually from the city at large. The mayor was still elected by the city and he and the board of aldermen passed and executed all city ordinances and appointed other officials.[36] Two years later, the Fusionists required all city officials to be elected by a popular vote.[37]

Concord, with a predominant white majority, had four wards which elected two commissioners each and a mayor elected by the city at large.[38] The Fusionists retained the Democratic features but merely redistricted the city.[39] The Democrats made no cry that the town was turned over to Negroes.

Durham as early as 1875 elected commissioners who in turn elected a mayor,[40] but in 1895 the Fusionists democratized Durham's government by providing for the biennial election by the people of a mayor, seven aldermen, chief of police, and tax collector.[41] Later the board of aldermen was empowered to appoint a city clerk, treasurer, fire department, and police.[42] While the Fusionists offered popular election to some of the offices in Durham, the Democrats never accused their enemies of turning the city over to Negroes. Durham's white population was twice its Negro population.

Goldsboro was incorporated as a city in Wayne County in 1881 with five wards.[43] The first and second elected two aldermen each; the third and fifth wards, one each; and the fourth ward, three. The nine aldermen chose a mayor either from their group or outside it, governed the city, and appointed other municipal officeholders. The Fusionists prescribed larger corporate limits; created two wards, the first electing four and the second five aldermen; and provided for the popular election of a mayor who could not be an alderman and who had to preside over the aldermen.[44]

Greenville, under Democratic administration, had three wards which elected two councilmen each, who in turn chose the mayor, treasurer, clerk, and policemen from the city at large.[45] The Fusionists created four wards and permitted the first and third to elect two councilmen each, while the second and fourth elected one each. The councilmen continued to choose the mayor and other important city officials—a Democratic feature.[46] The Democrats considered Greenville as a shining example of a Democratic town which was turned over to Negro rule. The fact that T. J. Jarvis, Democratic former governor and white supremacy advocate, lived in Greenville gave impetus to the Democrats' attack upon the city. Jarvis furnished Furnifold Simmons and Josephus Daniels, Democratic campaign managers in 1898, with every detail he could muster to use against the Fusionists. Jarvis charged that Negroes dictated the policy of the city; insolent Negroes arrested whites flagrantly; Greenville had sunk to the depths of degradation; the first and third wards were so apportioned as to enable Negroes to be of power in a normally Democratic town; and the board of councilmen in 1896—four Negroes and two whites—appointed white Republicans as mayor and chief of police, a Negro clerk, and two Negro policemen.[47]

James W. Perkins, white Republican mayor in question, stated that Jarvis' letter to the News and Observer was a gross exaggeration of affairs as they existed in Greenville; that the Fusionists in redistricting the wards had corrected an old abuse in that the Democrats had permitted two small Democratic wards to have two councilmen each and one large Republican ward to have two; that the Fusionists simply applied the principle of majority rule by creating four wards, letting two small Democratic wards have one councilman each and two large Republican wards have two councilmen each; and that the Democrats had representation on the board of councilmen, as four were Negro Republicans and two were white Democrats. He further added that no Negro policeman had ever arrested a white man, that the duties of Negro police were to keep the street clean, and that "as Mayor, I have expressly ordered Negro policemen not to arrest any white person, but to report any disturbance and the white policemen would make the arrest."[48]

Kinston's white population was twice the size of its Negro population, and the Democrats provided four wards, each electing one commissioner except the second, which had two. The five commissioners chose the mayor outside their ranks.[49] The Fusionists reduced the wards from four to three, still providing for the popular election of five commissioners by letting the first and third wards elect two each. The mayor was elected popularly.[50] The Democrats made no outcry on this action. Mount Airy's charter change was similar to Kinston's in that the mayor and commissioners were elected by popular vote; however, it was specified that the four Fusion wards be so redistricted as to be "nearly equal in voting strength"[51]—a condition rarely found elsewhere.

Neither the Fusionists nor their opponents, the Democrats, had any uniformity in the provisions of city charters. City charters, at the hands of the legislatures, were results of exigencies, emergencies, racial attitudes, traditions, and expediency. During the Fusion regime some cities were allowed to elect their mayors by popular vote, others were to have their mayors chosen by their aldermen (commissioners or councilmen). Some cities were allowed to elect all their aldermen while others could elect a part of their aldermen, and the governor appointed the remainder. Wards were redistricted in some cities, and in others the Democratic allocation was maintained. Some Fusion charters specified only that there should be a certain number of wards and proceeded to lay them off; in others, there was to be a certain number of wards "nearly equal in voting strength." The length of residence required in a ward for a voter was either fifteen days, thirty days, or ninety days. Some aldermen were elected from specific wards, and others, at the same time in the same city, were elected at large. In the application of the Fusion election law to all the cities, there was required at the polls representation of all parties; yet, in Winston, the judges of election were to be simply "men of good character." In some cities the mayor had great authority, in others he was subservient to the board of aldermen; and in some cities there was popular election of officials, in others there was legislative or alderman appointment.

If it is thought that the Fusionists specifically aimed to turn towns and cities over to Negro rule, the resultant charters of six of these towns condemned by the Democrats may be examined. Edenton's mayor was chosen by four councilmen who also appointed all other city officials; New Bern elected a part of its aldermen, while the governor appointed the remainder, and Wilmington likewise; Washington was allowed to remain under its Democratic set-up, with a mayor chosen by councilmen; and Winston and Raleigh had popular elections of mayor, aldermen, and some city officials.

Except in Greenville, the Democrats made no specific mention of charter changes in cities wherein there was parity in racial population or where the whites exceeded the Negroes in numbers. The Fusionists made changes in those areas for party perpetuity, and the Democrats, to denounce them, would have been rebuking what they themselves had done since 1876. They used those towns wherein some Negroes had achieved municipal office and wherein there was Fusion domination for the purpose of emphasizing their cry of Negro domination.

With specific reference to Negro office-holding in municipal government, Raleigh had one Negro alderman, some Negro magistrates, and some Negro police; New Bern had one Negro alderman, some Negro magistrates, and some Negro police; Wilmington had four Negro aldermen, some Negro magistrates, and some Negro police; and Greenville had four Negro aldermen. The legislatures of 1895 and 1897, which amended city charters, were Fusionist, but not Negro. The Populists and white Republicans had no enthusiasm for Negro office-holding. The majority of Negroes helped elect white Republicans to the positions of importance.

The interpretations of various writers on the Fusion period afford ample grounds for reflection on the question of the number of Negro officeholders. Ashe and other older historians of the state reflect the views of Negro domination backed by Simmons and the Democratic politicians. Recent writers have more moderate views on the Negro officeholder. Newsome and Lefler, two of the foremost historians of North Carolina at the present time, state that

As soon as the counties were self-governing again, some Negroes were elected to office in the East. Since most of the Negroes had voted for him, Governor Russell appointed a few to state offices of lesser importance.[52]

The first student in the new school of thought on the Populist period held that

Undoubtedly the part played by the negro in the affairs of politics and government during the Fusion administration has been over emphasized. Partisan papers in order to prejudice the people against these two parties made the negro question really more deplorable than it was . . . the negro had been in politics to some extent ever since the Civil war, and the Populists cannot be blamed with wilfully and deliberately pushing the negro into politics.[53]

Mabry revealed the real situation when he wrote

But more important than the debatable point of the Negroes' qualifications for office was the influence of Negro office-holding on race relations. There can be no denial of the fact that the white people of North Carolina resented having to deal with Negro officials.[54]

It was never so much a question of the number of positions, for that was negligible in terms of the Negro ratio in population, nor of the quality of positions since few held positions of importance, but it was a question of a Negro being in an office and the whites seeing him in that office.

James B. Lloyd, of Edgecombe County, a member of the Populist Executive State Committee, expressed the attitude of many Populists on Negro office-holding. In the atmosphere of the campaign of 1898, he wrote to Butler:

The situation is not entirely satisfactory here in this county as our Populist committee have partially agreed to take one member of the Legislature and allow the Republicans to have two. We could not with honor and consistency, support the gold candidates who would be Negroes, and I am trying to change matters before our convention meets.

We get the Sheriff, Treasurer and two Commissioners, which will be satisfactory, but we could not under any circumstances agree to support any Negro for the Legislature. I suggest that you write Mr. Fountain [Republican] and *urge* him to change the proposition so as not to require any support from us for their Legislature candidates [Negroes].[55]

The Negroes were not duped by the Democratic cry of Negro domination because they knew two things: (1) they did not hold positions commensurate with their voting strength, and (2) their white Republican leaders were not always on the square with them. A glowing example of dissatisfaction within the Negro group was evinced in a mass convention held at Raleigh on November 4, 1897, at which time The Lincoln Republican League was formed. This dissatisfaction is borne out in the following report concerning the convention:

It was called in protest against giving all the offices, save 10, to the 30,000 white Republicans, and it is said this insulted the 120,000 negro voters. Resolutions were adopted calling on all negro Republicans hereafter to vote for no man opposed to giving the negro full recognition; that in the future before any man is nominated negroes should exact a written pledge that he will give half of his clerical force to the colored Republicans; that all nominees shall give a pledge in favor of negro education; and that colored men who are willing to trade them off for office should not be nominated.[56]

In contradistinction to the allegation that Governor Russell handed out positions to Negroes promiscuously is the reply from one of the most prominent Negro politicians of the period to a Negro office-seeker: "I enclose herewith a letter to Senator Pritchard. You would hardly ask me to do more. The Governor has not granted a single request I have made of him since he became Governor."[57] Governor Russell's refusal to honor John Dancy's request may have been motivated by the fact that the latter belonged to the Republican faction which supported Oliver H. Dockery as a possible gubernatorial candidate in 1896 against him.[58] On the other hand, the Governor made few Negro appointments.[59] Irrespective of Democratic assertions,

Governor Russell was conservative and cautious in regard to appointing Negroes to offices.

NOTES TO CHAPTER NINE

1. United States Department of Commerce, *Bureau of Census, Twelfth Census,* I, Part 1 (1900), lxii.

2. See table, 125.

3. Edenton, Henderson, Hickory, New Bern, Raleigh, Washington, Wilmington, and Winston.

4. Elizabeth City, Fayetteville, Oxford, and Rocky Mount.

5. Asheville, Burlington, Charlotte, Concord, Durham, Goldsboro, Greensboro, Greenville, High Point, Kinston, Mount Airy, Reidsville, Salem, Salisbury, Statesville, and Wilson.

6. *Democratic Handbook,* 1898, 47; also *News and Observer,* October 30, 1898.

7. *Private Laws,* 1891, Chap. 82, 838-40.

8. *Private Laws,* 1895, Chap. 35, 48-50.

9. *Private Laws,* 1879, Chap. 42, 608-22.

10. *Private Laws,* 1895, Chap. 152, 198-200.

11. *Private Laws,* 1897, Chap. 149, 280.

12. *Private Laws,* 1891, Chap. 243, 1173-1203.

13. *Private Laws,* 1895, Chap. 263, 412-41.

14. *News and Observer,* February 9, 1895.

15. *Ibid.,* February 22, 1895.

16. Josephus Daniels, *Editor in Politics,* 134.

17. *Charlotte Observer,* March 2, 1895.

18. *Durham Sun,* July 26, 1944.

19. *Private Laws,* 1895, Chap. 177, 277-78.

20. *Ibid.,* Chap. 121, 158-60.

21. *Private Laws,* 1897, Chap. 150, 282.

22. *W. N. Harriss v. Silas P. Wright,* North Carolina Reports, CXXI (1897), 156-63.

23. *Democratic Handbook,* 1898, 47.

24. *Public and Private Laws,* 1876-1877, Chap. 143, 230-37.

25. *Private Laws,* 1891, Chap. 307, 1345-73.

26. *Private Laws,* 1895, Chap. 161, 226-30.

27. *Private Laws,* 1897, Chap. 83, 133-35.

28. *Private Laws,* 1885, Chap. 15, 719-35.

29. *Private Laws,* 1895, Chap. 85, 97-108.

30. *Private Laws,* 1883, Chap. 112, 885-906.

31. *Private Laws,* 1887, Chap. 51, 868-870; also *Private Laws,* 1891, Chap. 270, 1258-63.

32. *Private Laws,* 1897, Chap. 193, 378.

33. *Private Laws,* 1891, Chap. 316, 1388-97.

34. *Private Laws,* 1897, Chap. 148, 278-79.

35. *Private Laws,* 1883, Chap. 111, 853-85.

36. *Private Laws,* 1895, Chap. 352, 588-633.

37. *Private Laws,* 1897, Chap. 163, 319-49.

38. *Private Laws,* 1891, Chap. 233, 1128-30.

39. *Private Laws,* 1895, Chap. 170, 249-50.

40. *Private Laws,* 1874-75, Chap. 110, 603-22.
41. *Private Laws,* 1895, Chap. 204, 327-32.
42. *Private Laws,* 1897, Chap. 110, 201-4.
43. *Private Laws,* 1881, Chap. 50, 751-69.
44. *Private Laws,* 1895, Chap. 330, 542-44.
45. *Private Laws,* 1885, Chap. 85, 964-72.
46. *Private Laws,* 1895, Chap. 86, 108-10.
47. *News and Observer,* August 11, 1898; also *Democratic Handbook,* 1898, 44-45.
48. *The Union Republican,* October 27, 1898.
49. *Private Laws,* 1885, Chap. 33, 786-819.
50. *Private Laws,* 1895, Chap. 75, 90-92.
51. *Ibid.,* Chap. 107, 145-46.
52. Albert Newsome and Hugh T. Lefler, *The Growth of North Carolina,* 371.
53. Delap, "The Populist Party in North Carolina," 72.
54. Mabry, "The Negro in North Carolina Politics Since Reconstruction," 40.
55. James B. Lloyd to Honorable Marion Butler, August 11, 1898, Marion Butler Papers (Shorter Collection), University of North Carolina Library.
56. *Appleton's Annual Cyclopedia,* Third Series, II (1897), 572.
57. John C. Dancy to Professor C. N. Hunter, June 28, 1898, Charles N. Hunter Papers and Scrapbook, 1878-1902, Duke University Library Manuscript Collection.
58. *Supra,* Chap. IV, 50-52.
59. *Public Documents,* 1899, Document No. 1, 23; also *Infra.* Chap. XII, 178.

CHAPTER TEN

THE "WHITE SUPREMACY" CAMPAIGN OF 1898

THE FUSIONISTS, at the close of the legislative session of 1897, were by no means unaware of Democratic opposition within the General Assembly as well as outside. They well remembered the violent sporadic outbursts of the Democratic press and politicians when Fusion county government, Fusion municipal government, and the Fusion election law were inaugurated and Negroes became officeholders. The winter of 1897 passed calmly, but the spring of 1898 found each party mapping its strategy for a campaign which was destined to be the most tense and exciting in North Carolina's history since 1876.

The Populist convention met first on May 17 in Raleigh. The party faced again the question of fusion, and again the party's association with Negro Republicans threatened its unity. The racial attitude of the Populists in 1898 was as distinct as it had been in 1894 and 1896—anti-Negro. They had sublimated their racial feelings in the two previous elections to effect political victory and, consequently, were forced to face the Democratic charge in 1898 that they endorsed Negro rule. The "bolters" who followed Harry Skinner in 1896 came to the convention with the plan for further fusion with the Republican party irrespective of the issue of "Negro rule."[1] The "regulars" who followed Marion Butler felt that the most feasible path would be fusion with the Democrats.[2] A Democratic paper, feeling that Butler's plan might succeed, stated weeks before the Populist convention that "the adroit way in which Senator Butler, North Carolina's sharpest politician, is playing some of the Democratic leaders causes a smile by people who are on the inside."[3] Cyrus Thompson and Hal Ayer thought, as Butler, that Populist-Democratic fusion would be the course. The convention chose to ignore a decision on fusion and proceeded to make its state platform as an independent party, promising to retain local self-government in the counties, the 6 per cent interest law, prohibition of free railroad passes, and a nonpartisan judiciary. It favored a state reformatory for young criminals, election of railroad commissioners by a direct vote of the people, reduction of freight rates, and a just distribution of the burdens of taxation between debtor and creditor. It condemned the Democrats for the ninety-nine-year lease of the North Carolina Railroad and the Republicans for the 1897 change in the election law.[4] As the Populist platform openly condemned the Republicans on the issue of the election law, it was evident that fusion had not been agreed upon for 1898 and that such condemnation could be construed as an indirect bid for Democratic fusion. Aside from the platform, the convention closed under the assumption that each county would draw up its independent ticket. In case a political emergency arose before election time, a conference committee of six prominent Populists was chosen to handle it.

The Democratic convention met on May 26 in Raleigh. Democratic leadership in 1898 was different from that in 1892, 1894, or 1896. Furnifold M. Simmons, again the chairman of the State Executive Committee, was supported by such keen minds and ardent party followers as Charles B. Aycock, Henry G. Connor, Robert B. Glenn, Claude Kitchin, Locke Craig, Cameron Morrison, George Rountree, Francis D. Winston, William R. Allen, Alfred M. Waddell, Josephus Daniels, and others.[5] The convention was aware of the rumor of Populist-Democratic fusion, but the truth was revealed when T. J. Jarvis presented to the convention a letter from the Populist conference committee which suggested that, "If your Convention shall declare its endorsement of the principles and purposes set forth in these resolutions [Populist platform and a joint Congressional ticket], and favor co-operation with the People's Party in the coming campaign to carry the same into effect, your Convention is requested to name a committee to confer with us as to the details of the co-operation."[6] Majority sentiment rejected the Populist offer in these words: "The proposition for fusion submitted by the Populists is hereby respectfully declined; and the Democratic State Executive Committee is hereby instructed to entertain no further proposition for fusion."[7] Josephus Daniels stated in 1944 that he had favored Democratic-Populist fusion on the grounds that the Populists were but dissatisfied Democrats who had strayed from the fold, and the quicker they were brought back, the better.[8] There is reason to doubt his attitude as stated in 1944.[9] It was reported that Daniels, Rufus A. Doughton, and W. W. Kitchin favored making a strong counter-proposition to the Populists in 1898, one which would be so objectionable to the latter that they would reject it. If, as a result of their rejection, political disaster followed, the Democrats could go before the people with the confirmation that they had done all they could to prevent it, and that responsibility for the failure of the white people to control the state would rest on the Populist party.[10]

The convention adopted a platform which denounced the Republican legislatures of 1895 and 1897 and "Negro domination." It favored the prohibition of removing corporation suits or cases from the state to the federal courts, a strong railroad commission with powers to maintain rates which would be fair to the people as well as to the transportation corporations, the prohibition of free railroad passes, the encouragement of outside capital in the state, the improvement of public schools, charity for the unfortunate, and the popular election of United States senators. It pledged the abolition of "Negro domination" and promised "rule by the white men of the State."[11] Each county was instructed to draw up its Democratic ticket.

It was obvious that the Democratic platform had bait for all the white people of the state. The planks denying the federal courts supervision over state corporation suits, the encouragement of outside capital to invest in the state, and consideration for the railroads as well as the people, evidenced broad strategy in seeking the support of the legal profession, mill and factory owners, and the industrialists, irrespective of party affiliation. The planks condemning free railroad passes and favoring a strong railroad commission, improved public schools, and the popular election of United States senators, which were the Populists' demands when they left the Democratic party in 1892, represented a bid for Populist support. A further touch of strategy in platform presentation was that of refraining from condemning the Populists by casting all odium on the Republican legislatures of 1895 and 1897. "White supremacy" was promised to all who were anti-Negro in their racial attitudes.

The Republican convention met last, July 20, in Raleigh. The party made no reference to fusion. It formulated a platform which commended the past administration of the state because the finances had been wisely, economically, and honestly administered; the laws had been ably, fairly, and impartially administered and the rights of life and property secured thereunder; the signs of progress and development in all the material conditions of the state had exhibited the return of prosperity to the people; honest elections and local self-government inaugurated by the Republicans and Populists had pleased the people; and the financial conduct of the affairs of the counties, east and west, had been honest and circumspect as well as economical. It favored an amendment to the state constitution embodying the provision of the present election law which would guarantee to every citizen the right to cast one free ballot and have that ballot count as cast.[12] The Republican platform staked the coming campaign on its past achievement, praised the Populists, and ignored the Democratic allegation of Negro domination.

Three separate parties entered the campaign of 1898. The Democrats, having chosen Negro domination as the burden of their song, organized in early summer a speakers' bureau composed of the most renowned lawyers of the party: former Governor T. J. Jarvis, Charles B. Aycock, Henry G. Connor, Robert B. Glenn, Claude Kitchin, Locke Craig, Cameron Morrison, Alfred M. Waddell, Josephus Daniels (newspaper editor), and others. During August, September, and October, these men traveled throughout the state circulating the cry of Negro domination. Although the Democratic party had attacked the chief vulnerable spot in the Fusion armor, Negro office-holding, it found itself forced to seek the support of several distinct elements in the white population to whom the promise of white supremacy was not enough. The party needed the support of the business and industrial element, the denominational interests, the western counties which had substantial Republican strength, and the rural whites of the state at large; hence, it formulated an approach which varied according to the geographical location, the occupational constituency, and individual groups' desires of the white population. The strategy of the approach was not revealed until after the election of 1898.

The absolute necessity of the vote of the business and industrial interests indicates the phenomenal growth and influence of the group. North Carolina, in the 1890's, was in the throes of tremendous industrial development. The state's invested capital in manufacturing had increased from $13,000,000 in 1880 to $76,500,000 in 1900; the value of manufactured articles from $20,000,-000 to $95,000,000;[13] the number of cotton mills from 49 to 177 and the value of the products from $2,855,800 to $28,000,000;[14] and capital invested in tobacco products from $1,500,000 to $7,000,000 and the value of the tobacco products from $2,300,000 to $13,800,000.[15] The furniture industry for a shorter period, 1890 to 1900, increased from six factories making $159,000 worth of products to 44 factories making $1,500,000 worth.[16] What had really happened in the cotton business was that textile mills had increased fourfold, invested capital twelvefold, value of products elevenfold, and number of workers ninefold from 1880 to 1900. The development in other industrial fields, though not as great as in textiles, had been phenomenal. The railroad interests had secured their unrestricted charters since 1880 and climaxed their greatest achievement in the ninety-nine-year lease of the North Carolina Railroad in 1895.[17] One writer, interested in the social and economic interpretation of the state's history, writes that "the foundations of many private fortunes in North Carolina were laid during the decade 1890-1900."[18]

The industrial magnates and railroad financiers who managed these aggregate capitalistic enterprises were members and beneficiaries of the Democratic party, had secured their corporation charters before the Fusion regime, were interested in the further expansion of industrial opportunities unhampered by state control, and were not primarily interested in a campaign waged on the hypothesis of Negro domination. These business men knew that there was a vocal element in the Democratic party which resented corporation interests, and they also knew that this anti-corporation element, in case of a Democratic victory, could mean state interference in their economic program of industrialization. The State Executive Committee of the Democratic party also knew the feeling of the business group toward the campaign of 1898. Furnifold Simmons, Democratic State Chairman, made former Governor T. J. Jarvis the representative to visit the bankers, railroad interests, and manufacturers of the state to solicit funds from them for the campaign and, in return for their aid, to make the promise to them that "their taxes would not be increased during the biennium."[19] Simmons admitted that from these economic leaders and Democrats of moderate means he obtained all the campaign funds he needed.

The denominational colleges and their supporters eyed jealously the growth of the University of North Carolina, a state-supported institution. The struggle of each legislature in the 1890's to increase the appropriations to the state university met with determined resistance on the part of the legislators who had attended denominational colleges and lobbyists who were churchmen. The Democratic Executive Committee, through Simmons, promised the denominational interests that in return for their support in the election of 1898 a Democratic legislature in 1899 would not increase the biennial appropriation made to the University of North Carolina.[20] This, too, was a secret arrangement.

The party faced the task of convincing white western counties that Negro domination existed in the east. This was a difficult task for two reasons: first, these counties were tolerant on the Negro question because of their history, tradition, and the scarcity of Negro population and, always eyeing the east jealousy, felt that the Democratic cry of "Negro domination" was a means of restoring state control to the easterners; second, there was the rumor astir that should the Democrats win they would follow some Southern states in a pattern of disfranchisement based on educational qualification. The high percentage of illiteracy in the western counties[21] gave good grounds to fear a literacy test for voting. The Democrats resorted to a picture campaign to combat the first difficulty. Simmons said that anti-Democratic feeling was so strong in the west that he received several letters daring him to appear in that section. However, he went. At Wilkesboro, he promised, "I see you people think I am lying. . . . I am going to have photographs made of Negro officials and candidates. I will have the name of each Negro written under his photograph, and I will send you all these photographs."[22] Thus was born the pictorial campaign which carried the Democratic story of "Negro domination" to the western counties.

The rumor that illiterates would be disfranchised gained ground in the summer of 1898. The Populists issued a circular declaring that "the Democratic machine is making a desperate effort to deprive a large number of citizens of their rights and liberties. You are warned if you wish to vote hereafter, to look before you leap," further asking and answering: "Who passed the disfranchisement acts in Mississippi, South Carolina, and Louisiana? The Democrats!"[23] But the Democrats did not intend to let disfranchisement become an issue in the campaign and their campaign speakers denied the rumor. James H. Pou, member of the State Executive Committee, who was reputed to have promised disfranchisement, declared in an affidavit signed October 1, 1898,

I have never said that, if the Democrats regained control of the State, they intended to disfranchise the negroes and illiterate white voters. I have never said anything like this and I know that such is not the intention of the Democratic party . . . and I do not believe, if such comes before the General Assembly, that it would receive a single Democratic vote.[24]

The Democratic press denied the charge of disfranchisement as the most stupid lie of the campaign designed to befool poor, ignorant Negroes.[25] The official organization of the party issued its denial.[26]

The Democratic party used the press in seeking the support of rural whites throughout the state. It relied upon the fact that the majority of inhabitants in east and west were white and that a depiction of "Negro domination" and a promise of "white supremacy" would induce them to vote unqualifiedly a racial rather than a party ticket. Norman E. Jennett, former cartoonist for the *News and Observer,* was brought back to the state to wield his caustic pen in behalf of Democratic propaganda. Josephus Daniels, editor of that paper, got out supplements for the Democratic papers of the state containing Jennett's cartoons, pictures of Negro officeholders, accounts of Negro crime and violence, and all the supposed scandals of Governor Russell's administration with every fact and argument that he thought would serve to influence the white people. A hundred thousand copies of this type of material were sent to names furnished by the county and state Democratic committees.[27]

To understand the emotional background of the campaign, one needs only to observe the propaganda used by the chief Democratic press of the state. The *News and Observer* led in a campaign of prejudice, bitterness, vilification, misrepresentation, and exaggeration to influence the emotions of the whites against the Negro. Articles with sensational titles, cartoons, and pictures were its stock in trade. From the issue of August 2 through that of November 8 the volley poured forth. Articles appeared under these headlines: "Negro Control in Wilmington," "Unbridled Lawlessness on the Streets," "Greenville Negorized," "The Negro in Power in New Hanover," "Flagman Caught Negro Convict," "Tried to Register An Idiot," "Chicken Under His Arm," "Black Radical Convention Wants to Send Delegate to Congress," "Arrested By A Negro: He Was Making No Resistance," "A Negro Insulted the Post Mistress Because He Did Not Get A Letter," "Negroism in Lenior County," "Negro On Train With Big Feet Behind White," "Negroes Have Social Equality," "Is A Race Clash Unavoidable?" and others.[28] The cartoons were no less exciting and calculated to strike terror to unsuspecting whites. James H. Young was depicted at one time at the white Deaf and Blind School, another time inspecting the living quarters of frightened white women, and a third time at the top of a ladder whispering into Governor Russell's ear with the caption below, "The Source of the Governor's Inspiration."[29] George H. White, Negro congressman, was caricatured addressing a Negro audience saying, "Negroes don't have as many jobs as they will have and I invite the issue," while Isaac Smith, candidate for the legislature from Craven County, and Lee Person, state senator from Edgecombe, were shown grinning widely over their possibilities to rule over white people.[30] Other cartoons depicted the following: a large Negro foot with a white man pinned underneath accompanied with the caption "How Long Will This Last?"; a black Negro hit on the head by the arm and sledge of "Honest White Man" with the expression "Get Back. We will Not Stand It"; a Negro accepted for a position for which a white man was turned down; a body submerged at sea with hand sticking above water with "North Carolina" inscribed and the call "White Men To Rescue"; two white girls in their teens swearing as witnesses before a Negro deputy clerk in Wake Superior Court; a burly Negro road overseer of Craven County leaning on a cane, smoking a pipe, and ordering whites to work on the county roads; and a bat with claws representing Negro hands, "Negro rule" written on its wings, and white women and men beneath the bat's claws, all bearing the inscription "The Vampire That Hovers Over North Carolina."[31] White Republicans and Populists were handed similar treatment: Governor Russell was portrayed holding the books of the penitentiary while crowds clamored to see them and the question was asked, "Which Will Win Taxpayers or Tax-eaters?"; a penitentiary big-wig with diamonds sparkling from his tie holding the books and underneath the statement "The 1899 Legislature Will Put The 1898 Man Behind The Bars For Concealing The Books"; Harry Skinner frowning on Negroes in 1892 and hugging them in social equality in 1898; and Hal Ayer with his foot on N. B. Broughton and his arm around James Young showing Ayer's attitude in the Broughton-Young contested election of 1896 with the delineation "Negroes Preferable To Whites."[32]

The Democrats introduced other techniques of propaganda. At the suggestion of Francis D. Winston, there were organized throughout the central and eastern parts of the state "white supremacy" clubs, purely Democratic cliques. They were designed, by their very nomenclature, to appeal psychologically to race loyalty thereby engendering a sense of racial exclusiveness and the patriotic loyalty to supporting the policy of the dominant race. Speeches were made in these clubs "with the deliberate purpose of inflaming the white man's sentiments against the Negro."[33] The Democrats published a party handbook for the campaign. It reiterated the party's platform, compared the Fusion regime of 1895-97 with the Democratic rule of 1876-94 with supposed facts and figures to show how ridiculous the Fusionists had been, exaggerated the number of Negro officeholders, and promised the return of the Democratic election law and municipal and county government.[34]

The Republicans and Populists, in the early summer, fought back separately in the campaign. Fusion had not been effected, but being the parties in office, they were naturally on the defensive. Neither party had an adequate press. Each party's press had only sectional appeal and influence. The Republicans denied the charge of "Negro domination" and warned the voters that a Democratic victory meant disfranchisement.[35] The Populists, while having no enthusiasm for Negro office-holding, contended that the Democrats had set the precedent of appointing Negro justices of the peace from 1876 to 1894 and had no reason to condemn it in 1898.[36] When the Populists realized that their enemies attempted no discussion of political and economic issues, but staked all hope of success on the Negro issue, they were forced to define their stand on "Negro domination." The party declared that

It is a fact so well known as to make it superfluous to repeat it, that wherever the Caucasian race dwells it rules. It is the work of supererogation to declare that it will always rule in this State. The cry of "negro supremacy" and negro domination is as absurd as a discussion of racial amalgamation. No person or organization can more fully appreciate and understand this statement than the editor of the Democratic papers and the Democratic party itself. At no time in its history has the Democratic party feared or apprehended what they are now pretending to cry against.[37]

The Populists exposed a secret circular which Simmons had sent to all Democrats urging them "to persuade your Populist friends that it is their duty to themselves, their families and their neighbors to help us in the supreme struggle . . . see him and talk with him as a friend." The circular was denounced as a snivelling, absurd, ridiculous, boot-licking document which pleaded, whined, and whimpered for Populists to come to the aid of a Democratic machine which had done everything to insult the Populists.[38]

By mid-August, the Populists realized the gravity of their lone stand. The party faced the issue squarely when Dr. Cyrus Thompson, Populist secretary of state, queried, "What course shall we pursue in the campaign? Shall we go in the middle of the road for a straight fight, or shall we cooperate with the Republicans? If we go in the middle of the road, which might be the best course for us to pursue if we could pursue it and live as an organization, the canvass will be made against our candidates by the Democratic party that 'you have no chance for election. Our candidates will be elected or the Republicans will be. You are simply not in it.' . . . The cooperation has been mutually advantageous, and the advantage so far as numbers were concerned has been largely on our side. I think we can fuse with the Republicans."[39]

The heated campaign, in actuality, attracted the Republicans and Populists to each other like iron filings to a magnet. During the close of August, the executive committees of the two parties agreed upon fusion, the same as in 1894; namely, to divide county candidates and jointly support all other bi-party arrangements.

The Republican and Populist newspapers gave evidence in September and October that fusion between their parties had been agreed upon by refraining from attacking each other. They assailed the Democrats on the grounds that Negro office-holding was first instituted by the Democratic party: "We would like to call the attention of our Democratic brethren who are howling negro domination to the House Journal of 1876-77, which shows that the Democratic Legislature of that Session appointed a large number of negro magistrates to try the good white folk all over eastern North Carolina. Before that time no negro was magistrate or justice of the peace. The Democrats set the precedent and the number of negro appointees that year did not equal the number appointed from 1895 to 1897. T. J. Jarvis was president of that Assembly which appointed negroes yet today he's the loud anti-negro man."[40] The Populists undertook to show that the Democrats had printed twelve basic lies on Negro office-holding when that party itself had suffered white women and orphaned white children to be hired out to Negro employers.[41] The Fusion parties warned the voters that disfranchisement was a certainty if the Democrats won.[42]

The Democratic campaign orators harped on the financial mismanagement of state institutions, and especially the affairs of the penitentiary. Claudius Dockery, Republican, delivered to the press of the state a statement on penitentiary expenses, and the Democratic press refused to publish it.[43] The report stated that the Democrats had stated prior to 1895 that the penitentiary was self-supporting yet had secretly allotted hundreds of dollars per biennium to support it, such appropriations never appearing in the public laws; that the Fusionists knowing it was not self-supporting, publicly allotted an appropriation to it and the Democrats howled "misappropriation of funds." Cyrus Thompson, Populist secretary of state, defied any Democrat to meet him in popular debate and argue the Democratic charge of mismanagement of funds in his department. Thompson stated that the Democratic secretaries of state from 1876 to 1894 had not kept a single record of income or disbursement and that there were no standards by which they could compare his written records.[44] J. W. Denmark, prominent Populist of Wayne County, admonished Democratic orator C. B. Aycock to stop extolling Democratic lies on Fusion stealing and examine the auditor's report. Denmark bluntly told Aycock, "We know you are backed by A. B. Andrews, wealthy railroad Democrat as gubernatorial candidate for 1900, but that is no reason to tell lies."[45]

While Josephus Daniels and his *News and Observer* carried on a mud-slinging campaign, the chief Populist spokesman contended in public print, and perhaps with some justification, that Daniels had grown to regard the job of state printer as a piece of party pie; that for seven years he had been given the job of public printer which he sublet to other printing and binding concerns while he would get a 15 per cent bonus merely for subletting; that he had made on public printing alone not less than $2,500 to $3,000 a year for seven years; that now he was angry because the Fusion legislatures did not continue to let him reap a rich profit; and that this anger caused him to vilify the Fusionists in his paper.[46] The Populists declared that the Democrats had not one streak of integrity because they had refused fusion with the Populist party while proclaiming to the public that the Populists would rather see Negro office-holding continue than support the Democratic ticket.[47] In contradistinction to the charge of being Negro-lovers, the Populist party felt that, in the election of 1894 and 1896, the Democrats, when knowing that they were in the minority in certain counties and districts, refused to support Populist candidates, thereby guaranteeing a Negro Republican the privilege of holding office. If the Democrats had wanted the Second Congressional District represented in the United States Congress by a white man, then they would have supported James B. Lloyd, Populist nominee, rather than stand by and see George H. White, Negro, elected to the position, reasoned the Populists. The Populists did not choose to go out one hundred per cent in defense of Negro office-holding for several reasons. First, they opposed it. James B. Lloyd of the Central State Populist Executive Committee wrote Butler in reference to a Negro candidate in Edgecombe County, "I want you to insist on the withdrawal of the negro when the committee meets on October 27th."[48] And later in reference to the Edgecombe County ticket, he wrote, "I have urged the Republicans that we will have nothing to do with the election, if they do not withdraw all the negroes from the ticket. I have all along strenuously opposed any cooperation if negroes were to be on the ticket."[49] Second, fusion had not been effected in July and early August, hence the Populists had no concerted approach to counteract Democratic propaganda aimed directly at their former allies, the Republicans, and indirectly at them. Sentiment continued to prevail in the party for and against fusion of any kind. One Populist wrote Butler, "If we don't fuse with the Republicans, we will be lost as a party,"[50] another wrote, "it would be much better to fuse with the Democrats as their principles are nearer to the Populists than the Republicans,"[51] while still another wrote, "Democrats in Northampton are making desperate efforts to cooperate with the Republicans, I have thought that we should act in such a way in that county as to force such cooperation, it would mean a great deal to us, by forever silencing the Democrats about our cooperation with the Republicans."[52] From Wilmington came the reminder that "to go to either party will mean suicide for us, for as soon as we have lost our identity we are then gone, and it is plain that the more the Republicans gain, the more they will demand and the sooner they are made to know that they are not to swallow and control the People's party, the quicker we see that our life is prolonged."[53] In reporting a Populist campaign meeting, it was stated that a party member "argued for hours that the proper thing for the Populists to do is to return to the Democratic party."[54] A Populist congressman from North Carolina advised, "Republican fusion means partial surrender to the Skinner Populists [opponents of the Butler Populists] and certainly putting them in the lead. A middle-of-the-road fight means to turn the State over to the Republicans. I believe this will force the Democrats to terms if we put up a straight ticket."[55] The same writer, angry because the Democrats had refused fusion with Populists, wrote, "Let's turn the State over to the negroes and radicals and make the Democrats responsible."[56]

On the other hand, some of the Republicans were angry because the Populists were playing a fence-sitting game. A Republican newspaper from the western part of the state had stated prior to the Republican state convention that "we are mighty tired of fighting for principles and see Democrats and Populists get everything in sight. Indeed we ought to stand this year alone and see the Democrats whip the Populists and take everything in sight. That will teach the Populists a lesson."[57] By mid-August, the same paper sought through ridicule to foster fusion: "The Democrats have slapped the Populists in the face and contemptuously refused aid from them. No self-respecting Populist can vote for a Democrat."[58]

The Republican press argued that Josephus Daniels was famous for exaggeration and had no conscience where the truth was involved, that his *News and Observer* carried headlines with the deliberate intention of misleading the public, and that in one county where the Democrats held a rally, Daniels wrote "Tremendous Crowds Attend Democratic Rally" when in reality only eighty-eight men were present.[59] The same paper admonished the voters of western North Carolina that a Democratic victory meant the return of the Democratic election law which meant fraud at the polls. It lambasted the Democratic *Handbook* for denying fraud during the Democratic administration. It asked, "Where did the Democrats get returns from 1876-1894 if they did not steal them?" It reasoned that "western North Carolina is the home of the white man, the Republican Party. Eastern North Carolina is the home of the colored man, the Democratic Party. Two things are sure: either the Negro voted the Democratic ticket or the white man stole his vote. If the Negro voted the Democratic Party, then quit calling the Republican Party the negro party. If you stole his vote, then admit fraud."[60]

The Republican press came to the defense of James Young, Negro, who was caricatured by the *News and Observer*. It stated that Young was never president of the Board of Directors of the White Deaf and Dumb and Blind Institution of Raleigh, nor did he act in a disrespectful way while serving on the board, and that he had resigned in early June, 1898.[61] The indisputable fact is that Young resigned as a director from the board on June 8 to become a major of the Russell Black Battalion of North Carolina Volunteers in the United States Army.[62] Despite his resignation, the *News and Observer* cartooned him during August and September of the campaign as directing the policies of the board for the express purpose of emphasizing Negro office-holding and boosting the necessity of victory for the "white man's" party. The Republicans contended that the Democratic legislature of 1893 had appointed a Negro on the Board of Directors of the same institution and, by setting the precedent, had no basis for denouncing the Fusionists.[63]

Any treatment of the campaign is incomplete without reference to the Manly article. There appeared in the Wilmington *Record*, a Negro newspaper, a commentary written in refutation of the Democratic declaration that as long as Fusion reigned Negro men would increase their "advances" to white women. Alex Manly's paper replied:

We suggest that the whites guard their women more closely, as Mrs. Felton says, thus giving no opportunity for the human fiend, be he white or black. You leave your goods out of doors and then complain because they are taken away. Poor white men are careless in the matter of protecting their women, especially on the farms. They are careless of their conduct toward them and our experience among poor white people in the country teaches us that the women of that race are not any more particular in the matter of clandestine meetings with colored men than the white men with colored women. Meetings of this kind go on for some time until the woman's infatuation or the man's boldness brings attention to them and the man is lynched for rape. Every negro lynched is called 'a Big Burly Black Brute' when in fact many of these who have been thus dealt with had white men for their fathers and were not only 'not black and burly' but were sufficiently attractive for white girls of culture and refinement to fall in love with them as is well known to all.[64]

The article might have escaped state-wide attention had not the *News and Observer* publicized it. Democratic campaign speakers considered it the most vile and inflammatory material ever printed in the state, and carried copies of it with them to add gusto and crescendo to their racial harangues. Robert Glenn, Democrat and later governor, was reputedly famous for the way he interpreted the article: "To hear him read the Manly letter and to comment on it and to hear his tribute to the women in the rural districts, which he delivered in a voice that could be heard almost in the next county, was terrible and terrifying."[65] The Republican party was accused of endorsing the sentiments expressed in the article. The Democratic State Committee saw to it that reproductions reached the agricultural Populists, stating that it was an offense to white womanhood. An historian, and a keen political observer, wrote that "if it is an offense, it is one which is after all a mere statement of opinion."[66] Dr. Cyrus Thompson declared that the article was written four months before its publication by the Democratic press and was dragged out in the heat of the campaign because the Democrats feared defeat if they did not resurrect as much dirt as they could.[67] A white Republican paper added that the Manly article appeared in the spring of 1898 and not in August when Daniels publicized it.[68] Whether the article was the mere opinion of one man or whether it was published in the spring of 1898 did not matter to the Democratic party. The article, as Daniels intended it, intensified racial hatred in the closing days of the campaign.

In early October, there was projected into the campaign an editorial from the Atlanta *Constitution* written by Frank Weldon who had recently visited North Carolina:

It is no secret that colored leaders, ambitious for their race, have matured in their minds a plan by which they hope to obtain absolute control of [North Carolina's] legislative, executive, and judicial machinery, and then to rapidly carry out a scheme of colonization by which this will become a thoroughly negro sovereign State, with that population in the majority and furnishing all officials in the public service, from U. S. Senators and Governors down through judges, legislators, and solicitors, to the last constable and janitor. If their plans succeed, North Carolina is to be the refuge of their people in America. Their brethren from all the Southern States will be invited to come here, cast their lot among their fellows, and altogether to work out their destiny in whatsoever degree of prosperity and advancement they may be able to achieve for themselves.[69]

The Democrats did not investigate the truth, falsity, or possibility of the idea expressed in the editorial, but proceeded to make the most of it in the closing month of the campaign.

There appeared in the closing days of October a Democratic organization known as the Red Shirts. Men wore flaming red shirts, rode horses, carried rifles, paraded through Negro communities, and appeared at political rallies, especially at Republican rallies. There is division of opinion as to the origin and activities of the Red Shirt movement in North Carolina. There is, however, complete agreement on its purpose. The movement presumably had its origin in South Carolina where the Negro population exceeded the white, and at a time when Benjamin R. Tillman was ascending the crest of political popularity with his extreme anti-Negro attitude. Tillman was invited during the campaign to come to North Carolina to make his political tirades against the Negro in the interest of "white supremacy" and accepted the invitation. Marion Butler evidently condemned Tillman for this visit and his interference in another state's politics, because Tillman wrote Butler that as a private citizen he traveled where he pleased.[70] It was thought by the chairman of the State Democratic Committee that as a result of Tillman's visit and his story of how South Carolina had disfranchised the Negro, the Red Shirt organization took hold in North Carolina.[71] In opposition to the idea that Tillman's visit resulted in the introduction of the organization, it is remembered by a contemporary that there were no Red Shirts until after the Manly editorial of 1898; until after the declaration of the people of Wilmington; and until after the threat of the Negro senator from Edgecombe, W. L. Person, to lynch any Negro who voted the Democratic ticket.[72]

As to its purpose and membership, a recent historian writes as follows:

The whites were determined to put an end to Negro rule, and just as the Ku Klux Klan had come into existence in the State in 1868 to put the Negro "in his place," the Red Shirts now became prominent. . . . It was composed "in the main of respectable and well-to-do farmers, bankers, school teachers, and merchants—in many cases the best men in the community."[73]

It is held that the purpose of the organization was one of intimidation, being chiefly interested in routing Negro political rallies.[74] More recent investigation reveals that some Negroes were killed.[75] Contemporaries and historians hold that the organization functioned mainly in the southeastern part of the state.[76] This would include New Hanover, Brunswick, Columbus, and Robeson counties which are adjacent to South Carolina's borderline, and this geographical proximity lends some probability to the idea that the movement may have been transplanted from South Carolina.[77]

The activities of the Red Shirts became so pronounced that Governor Russell, hoping to prevent physical violence, issued an official proclamation two days before the last Democratic rally. He warned the people of North Carolina that the Constitution of the United States secured to every state protection from invasion; that the Constitution of North Carolina guaranteed to the people of the state the inherent right to regulate their own internal government; and that no turbulent mob using the weapons of intimidation and violence should usurp the authority of the courts. He affirmed that the campaign in progress had brought about lawlessness in certain counties; that certain counties lying along the southern border of this state had been actually invaded by armed and lawless men from another state; that political meetings had been broken up and dispersed by these armed men; that citizens had been fired on from ambush and taken from their homes at night and whipped; and that peaceful citizens were afraid to register preparatory to voting. He commanded all ill-disposed persons to desist from unlawful and turbulent conduct; all law-abiding citizens not to allow themselves to become excited by appeals made to their passions and prejudices; all officers of the law to apprehend and bring to speedy trial all offenders against the political and civil rights of any person; and all persons who may have entered this state from other states, in pursuance of any unlawful purpose, to disperse instantly and leave the state.[78]

The Democrats made elaborate plans for the final campaign rally which was held on October 28 in Goldsboro. The railroads of the state granted free transportation to all who wanted to attend. More than eight thousand persons were present. Amid tremendous enthusiasm and confusion, the political meeting began. Among the chief speakers of the day was W. A. Guthrie. His appearance on the Democratic bandwagon in 1898 is both interesting and humorous. He was a Republican before 1894, a Populist from 1894 to 1896, and a Democrat in 1898. There was no doubt that Guthrie was angry at the Populists because though they chose him as gubernatorial candidate in 1896, many of them had supported Republican Daniel L. Russell at election time. One cannot determine just when Guthrie turned Democrat. It is also difficult to reconcile his speaking for the Democrats in Goldsboro on October 28, 1898, with his letter of September 22 to Butler: "You would be amused, if not surprised, at the overtures coming from Democrats from many directions importuning me to take the stump in the campaign to help them out of the hole."[79] The Democrats welcomed him into the fold; however, in 1894 when they saw him turn Populist, they had stated jeeringly that his varied experience in all parties made him a valued adviser.[80] The story was different in 1898, for the Democrats were elated over Guthrie's pleasing "chameleon-like" versatility.

The Democrats drew up on that day a document contending that Negroes held one thousand offices in eastern North Carolina; that towns and cities were turned over to them to pillage; that the sanctity of white womanhood was endangered, business paralyzed, and property rendered less valuable; that Republicans had a second time proved their unfitness to govern; that Senator Pritchard was not justified in asking President McKinley to send troops to the state for the coming election; and that white men must and would rule North Carolina.[81] Thus the Democratic party had, at the close of the campaign, striven to convince the state that the vote of 1898 should be a racial vote.

The election of November 10 was a great victory for the Democrats,[82] and jubilee celebrations were held in many towns and cities. John Spencer Bassett wrote to a friend:

As to the election, I might write you a whole book. We are crowing down here like children because we have settled the Negro question. We don't see that we have not settled it by half. At best we have only postponed it. We have used a great deal of intimidation and a great deal of fraud; although it is hard to get information about the latter. I do not have the honor to agree with my fellow Anglo-Saxons on the Negro question. You must not be led astray by what you hear about Negro rule in N. C. When this campaign started, I had heard nothing of the evils of Negro rule. I took pains to ask about it from many sources. I learned that in some of the Negro counties there were magistrates, a few county commissioners, and some school committees. In no case did I hear that they were disposed to abuse the privilege.

The campaign has been one of passion. The Democratic press opened up on the Negro. Considering the violence of its attack, it seems to me that the Negro has acted admirably. Villified, abused, denounced as the unclean thing he has kept his peace; he has been patient. He has borne what no other people in history have borne. He has done it largely because he is a coward in the presence of the white man.[83]

The business element had rallied to the Democratic cause. Simmons' secret promise that their taxes would not be increased had done the trick. His secret promise to the denominational interests had secured their support. The magician, who pulled the promises from his hat right and left, admitted in later years that "in order to win the campaign I felt it necessary to make two promises which later became somewhat embarrassing."[84] Josephus Daniels frowned upon Simmons' secret promises. He commented, in part, that

The trade was akin to secret treaties, which have never wrought any good. I thought then, and think still, that the promise by Simmons and Jarvis was indefensible. They assumed the right of campaign managers to usurp secretly the powers of legislative bodies. The defense by Simmons does not justify the secret agreement. It convicted railroad executives and church leaders of taking advantage of politics to obtain ends the people would not grant after open discussion.[85]

One prominent Democratic paper, which proved to be a careful observer though it did not know of the secret promises, gave an interesting commentary titled "Post-Election Reflection," which reads in part:

In my opinion the business men of the State are largely responsible for the victory. Not before in years have the bank men, the millmen, and the business men in general—the backbone of the property interest of the State—taken such sincere interests. They worked from start to finish, and furthermore they spent large bits of money in behalf of the cause. For several years this class of men has been

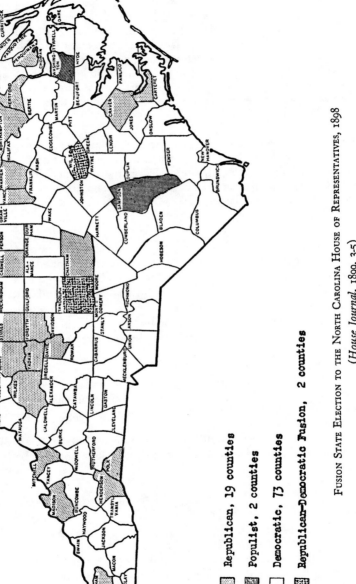

FUSION STATE ELECTION TO THE NORTH CAROLINA HOUSE OF REPRESENTATIVES, 1898

(*House Journal*, 1899, 3-5)

Republican, 19 counties

Populist, 2 counties

Democratic, 73 counties

Republican-Democratic Fusion, 2 counties

almost ignored. . . . When Democratic rallies were held, mills and shops were shut down so that the operatives could attend the speakings. . . . Indeed North Carolina is fast changing from an agricultural to a manufacturing State.[86]

Support of the business, railroad, and industrial groups precluded any attempt of the legislature of 1899 to curb their power. They were allowed to go their rugged individual way. The Democratic party in its desire to overthrow Negro participation in politics had given to these capitalistic elements the bridle by which to check progressive legislation. Democratic victory guaranteed to them a domination in politics which far exceeded their numerical strength. The opposition element within the Democratic party had lost in its fight for idealism at the turn of the century. Manufacturing, big business, and the railroad interests were safely in the saddle, thanks to Furnifold Simmons and the "corporation" Democrats.

One Republican, A. Eugene Holton, gave a fairly accurate interpretation of the Democratic victory of 1898 when he examined it from an economic point of view, although his interpretation was regarded at that time as the whimpering and rationalization of a defeated party. This chairman of the state Republican Executive Committee, held "that the defeat of the Republican party was charged to the negro, but the negro was only the torch light which the voters have observed, while the tar beneath, that produces the light has been obscured." He outlined three basic reasons why the capitalistic elements hated Fusion economic legislation and desired a Democratic victory:

In the first place the Legislature of 1895 reduced the rate of interest from 8 to 6 per cent. This in the banks of the State alone amounted to a loss of 2 per cent upon 12 or 15 millions and had the effect of depriving the banks of a large profit on rediscounts on papers that had heretofore been taken from private individuals and rediscounted in Northern banks, besides depriving the business interests of the State of a large volume of currency. This enlisted against us [Fusionists] the interest of both the bankers who loaned, and the business men who borrowed, besides the interests of a large number of individuals who were living off the interest of their money. To these individuals this legislation meant heavy loss.

In the second place the cities and towns of the State have for many years been accumulating heavy bonded indebtedness and the spirit of repudiation, as manifested in Oxford, Stanly, Wilkes and Buncombe county bond cases, was charged to Republicans and Populists. Therefore the people holding these bonds imagined that their interest lay in a change of administration, for they were confronted with the fact that North Carolina securities issued by cities, towns and counties could hardly be realized on. This line of securities also included mortgage bonds issued by railroads and parties holding them or seeking investments feared a policy of repudiation.

In the third place the revenue act of the last Legislature [1897] enlisted the business men against us by the taxation of capital stock upon face value, this having enormously increased their taxes. Nearly every business of the State, including cotton mills, tobacco manufacturers, merchants and other aggregations of capital have for several years been carrying on business almost entirely through these corporations and had their business capitalized in many instances above its actual value. Even the railroads did not feel secure from renewed attacks. In fact, every interest in the State representing capital was arrayed against us, or at least its moral support was withdrawn, all in great contrast to the campaign of 1896, when these same men, fearing Bryanism and Populism, either openly voted the Republican ticket or at heart wished Republican success and aided in bringing about the election of Senator Pritchard.

With the assurance of a legislative change of policies which the Democrats were ready to give to insure success, it was an easy matter for the Democrats to raise unlimited means with which to carry on an effective campaign. Even prominent and influential Republicans in the State made contributions.[87]

In view of the fact that many whites voted a racial ticket in 1898 based upon propaganda by the business, industrial, and railroad men—propaganda which was issued by the Democratic press aimed at Negroes and Negro office-holding—a confession made by the leading editor, Josephus Daniels, in 1944, is also necessary to a sound interpretation of the Democratic victory of 1898:

The News and Observer's partisanship was open, fierce, and sometimes vindictive, and was carried in news stories as well as in editorials. . . . The paper was cruel in its flagellations. In the perspective of time, I think it was too cruel. . . . Whenever there was any gross crime on the part of Negroes, *The News and Observer* printed it in a lurid way, sometimes too lurid, in keeping with the spirit of the times. . . . We were never very careful about winnowing out the stories or running them down . . . they were played up in big type.[88]

Notes to Chapter Ten

1. *News and Observer*, May 19, 1898.
2. *Ibid.*
3. *Charlotte Observer*, April 25, 1898.
4. *People's Party Handbook of Facts*, 1898, 36, 62-64.
5. The Populists described these men in the Democratic convention as a gathering of lawyers.—*Is The Democratic Party Honest? A Statement of Facts Issued By the People's Party State Central Committee* (University of North Carolina Pamphlet Collection), 21-24.
6. *Democratic Handbook*, 1898, 109; also *Is the Democratic Party Honest? A Statement of Facts Issued By the People's Party State Central Committee*, 17-18.

7. *Dr. Cyrus Thompson's Great Speech*, delivered in Clinton, North Carolina, August 19, 1898, 3.

8. Josephus Daniels, *Editor in Politics*, 122.

9. There is every reason to doubt that Mr. Daniels' attitude toward the Populists in 1944 is the same as it was in the 1890's. His editorial violence against them, as revealed in his *News and Observer* from 1895 through 1900, indicated his real attitude at the time. It can safely be concluded that his mild and sympathetic "return of the Prodigal Son" attitude toward the Populists in 1944 is a far cry from his editorials and newspaper reports in the 1890's.

10. *North Carolina Pamphlets, 1880-1899* (Duke University Library Pamphlet Collection), VI, No. 73.

11. *Democratic Handbook*, 1898, 194-96.

12. *Appleton's Annual Cyclopedia*, Third Series, III, 505; also *Democratic Handbook*, 1898, 195-96.

13. Dan Lacy, The Beginnings of Industrialism in North Carolina (Unpublished M.A. thesis, 1935), University of North Carolina Library, 128, 155, Figure 1.

14. *Ibid.*, 58, 64, 65, 156, Figure 2.

15. *Ibid.*, 117, 157, Figure 3.

16. *Ibid.*, 122-23, 158, Figure 4.

17. *Supra*, Chap. IV, 60-61.

18. Archibald Henderson, *North Carolina, The Old North State and The New*, II, 412.

19. Fred Rippy (ed.), *Furnifold Simmons, Statesman of The New South*, 23-24. The secret arrangement was not revealed until 1936, in *ibid.*, 29.

20. *Ibid.*, 29.

21. *Infra*, Chap. XIII, 200; Appendix, 228-29.

22. Rippy, *op. cit.*, 23-25.

23. *Citizens and Voters*, a circular issued by the People's Party, 1898 (Duke University Library Pamphlet Collection), 32.

24. *Wilmington Messenger*, September 18, 1898.

25. *Charlotte Observer*, September 25, 1898; and *News and Observer*, October 23, 25, 1898.

26. *Comments By The State Democratic Committee on The Handbook Issued By The People's Party State Executive Committee* (University of North Carolina Library Pamphlet Collection), 7, 18; also *Democratic Handbook*, 1898, 42.

27. Josephus Daniels, *Editor in Politics*, 284-85.

28. *News and Observer*, August 11, 18; September 20; October 5, 6, 12, 19, 20, 22, 28, 1898.

29. *Ibid.*, August 18, 19; September 30, 1898.

30. *Ibid.*, August 26; September 18, 22, 1898.

31. *Ibid.*, August 13, 30; September 4, 6, 8, 11, 27, 1898.

32. *Ibid.*, August 14, 16, 23, 24; September 21, 1898.

33. Mabry, "The Negro in North Carolina Politics Since Reconstruction," 45.

34. *Democratic Handbook*, 1898, 1-196.

35. *The Union Republican*, August 25, 1898.

36. *People's Party Handbook*, 1898, 7.

37. *Caucasian*, September 4, 1898.

38. *People's Party Handbook*, 1898, 90.

39. *Dr. Cyrus Thompson's Great Speech*, 22-23.

40. *The Union Republican*, September 15, 1898.

41. *People's Party Handbook*, 1898, 42-63.

42. *The Union Republican*, Issues of September and October, 1898.

43. *Ibid.*, September 25, 1898.

44. *Dr. Cyrus Thompson's Great Speech*, 18.

45. *Progressive Farmer*, September 7, 1898.

46. *Dr. Cyrus Thompson's Great Speech*, 11.

47. *Is The Democratic Party Honest? A Statement of Facts Issued by the People's Party State Central Committee*, 1898, University of North Carolina Library Pamphlet Collection.

48. James B. Lloyd to Marion Butler, September 24, 1898, Marion Butler Papers (Shorter Collection), University of North Carolina Library.

49. *Ibid.*, October 15, 1898.

50. E. J. Faison to Marion Butler, July 29, 1898, Marion Butler Papers (Shorter Collection), University of North Carolina Library.

51. Ransom Hinton to Marion Butler, July 30, 1898, Marion Butler Papers (Shorter Collection), University of North Carolina Library.

52. James B. Lloyd to Marion Butler, July 28, 1898, Marion Butler Papers (Shorter Collection), University of North Carolina Library.

53. B. F. Keith to Marion Butler, July 14, 1898, Marion Butler Papers (Shorter Collection), University of North Carolina Library.

54. J. Z. Green to Marion Butler, July 8, 1898, Marion Butler Papers (Shorter Collection), University of North Carolina Library.

55. R. L. Strowd to Marion Butler, August 4, 1898, Marion Butler Papers (Shorter Collection), University of North Carolina Library.

56. *Ibid.*, September 16, 1898.

57. *The Union Republican*, May 12, 1898.

58. *Ibid.*, August 18, 1898.

59. *Ibid.*

60. *Ibid.*, August 25, 1898.

61. *Ibid.*, September 1, 1898.

62. James Young to His Excellency, Daniel L. Russell, June 8, 1898, Governor's Papers, Department of Archives and History, North Carolina Historical Commission, Raleigh, N. C.

63. *The Union Republican*, September 1, 1898.

64. *News and Observer*, August 18, 1898; Josephus Daniels, *Editor in Politics*, 286. No copies of the *Record* are available.

65. Josephus Daniels, *Editor in Politics*, 297.

66. John Spencer Bassett to Herbert Baxter Adams, November 15, 1898 (photostatic copy of Herbert Baxter Adams correspondence preserved at Johns Hopkins University Library), Duke University Library Manuscript Collection.

67. *Dr. Cyrus Thompson's Great Speech*, 16.

68. *The Union Republican*, December 1, 1898.

69. *Appleton's Annual Cyclopedia*, Third Series, III (1898), 509; also *News and Observer*, October 5, 1898.

70. Senator Benjamin R. Tillman to Senator Marion Butler, November 3, 1898, Marion Butler Papers (Shorter Collection), University of North Carolina Library.

71. Rippy, *op. cit.*, 24.

72. Josephus Daniels, *Editor in Politics*, 293.

73. Hugh T. Lefler (ed.), *North Carolina History Told by Contemporaries*, 397.

74. Mabry, "The Negro in North Carolina Politics Since Reconstruction," 47; Hamil-

ton, *History of North Carolina Since 1860*, 287; and Ashe, *History of North Carolina*, II, 1205-6.

75. Lefler, *op. cit.*, 397.

76. Rippy, *op. cit.*, 24; Lefler, *op. cit.*, 397; and Hamilton, *History of North Carolina Since 1860*, 287.

77. While it is rumored that Tillman used Red Shirts in his political ascendancy in South Carolina and introduced, perhaps, the same into North Carolina, there is no mention made of Tillman and the South Carolina Red Shirts in Francis Butler Simkins' *The Tillman Movement in South Carolina*, 1926, or his more recent and elaborate *Pitchfork Ben Tillman, South Carolinian*, 1944, a scholarly treatment of everything good and bad that Tillman did.

78. Executive Papers, Governor Daniel L. Russell, Proclamation, October 26, 1898.

79. W. A. Guthrie to Marion Butler, September 22, 1898, Marion Butler Papers (Shorter Collection), University of North Carolina Library.

80. *News and Observer*, August 18, 1894.

81. *Ibid.*, October 29, 1898: "The Goldsboro Platform"; also *Appleton's Annual Cyclopedia*, Third Series, III (1898), 508.

82. See map, 152.

83. John Spencer Bassett to Herbert Baxter Adams, November 15, 1898 (photostatic copy from Herbert Baxter Adams' Correspondence preserved at Johns Hopkins University), Duke University Library Manuscript Collection; also published in W. S. Holt (ed.), "Historical Scholarship in the United States, 1876-1901: As Revealed in the Correspondence of Herbert Baxter Adams," *The Johns Hopkins University Studies in Historical and Political Science*, Series LVI, No. 4, 258.

84. Rippy, *op. cit.*, 29.

85. Josephus Daniels, *Editor in Politics*, 322.

86. *Charlotte Observer*, November 17, 1898.

87. *Charlotte Observer*, November 19, 1898.

88. Josephus Daniels, *Editor in Politics*, 145, 147, 253, 295-96.

CHAPTER ELEVEN

THE WILMINGTON RACE RIOT

ONE DIRECT REPERCUSSION of the Democratic victory of 1898 expressed itself in a race riot in the city of Wilmington. November 8 was election day and it passed quietly. However, on November 10, two days after the election, the city was in the throes of a race riot.

Without elaborate details or any attempt at this point in the analysis to separate allegations from things which admittedly happened, a composite story of the riot, as related by the Democratic press and the majority of state historians, is offered here. These sources told the story that Negroes were in the majority in Wilmington and voted slavishly the Republican ticket. They also related that the Fusionists permitted Negroes to hold many offices, insisting on substituting ignorant officeholders for intelligent ones; allowed Negro police flagrantly to arrest whites; willfully and maliciously turned the city over to Negro rule; and tried to force upon Wilmington social equality between the races. The story continued that the city was not able to pay off its bonded indebtedness and through extravagance, corrupt politics, and financial juggling, sank deeper into debt. White Democrats contended that they would not be kicked around by aggressive and insolent Negroes and their cohorts. Democratic opinion held that Alex Manly, Negro editor, had insulted white womanhood throughout the state by his incriminating remarks that some of these "big burly black brutes" (Democratic description of a Negro) were sufficiently good looking for white women to fall in love with and then cry rape when their love affairs were discovered. It seemed that tension reached fever pitch, and rumors circulated rapidly that Wilmington Negroes had purchased Winchester rifles with the avowed purpose of "shooting it out" on election day. It was reported that in the wake of the Democratic victory in Wilmington and New Hanover some of the prominent whites on the next day ordered Manly to leave the city within a few hours and that some worthless Negroes fired on the whites who were enroute forcibly to eject Manly and his press from the city. The incident developed into a riot. Some of the reports termed the Wilmington affair a rebellion rather than a riot in so far as it apparently demonstrated the determination of leading white citizens to liberate the city from black tyranny.[1]

This account of the riot has been given with such regularity and with such slight variation that it has become "standard" and, thus, generally accepted. A more careful investigation of the available information, however, renders it somewhat unreliable and requires some substantial revision of certain portions of the generally accepted story. Wilmington was a hotbed of racial tension because of its Negro majority in population in 1890 and its Negro parity at the close of the century. The city had two ebullient newspapers, *The Morning Star* and *The Messenger,* which constantly chanted the Democratic refrain that Wilmington had degenerated economically and socially under Negro rule. The *News and Observer* caught up the chants and amplified them for a larger audience. It sent reporters to the city to write up the Democratic side of city government. Some of the historians of this state have relied excessively upon the Democratic press in their treatment of the Wilmington riot.[2]

The Fusionists had no effective opposition newspaper in Wilmington or, for that matter, in the entire state. There were in that city two Negro editors, Alex Manly and Armond W. Scott (lawyer), who published *The Record* and *The Sentinel,* respectively.[3] The latter ceased publication before 1896, while the former continued as the champion of the Negro's cause in that locality. The daily *Record* fought unceasingly for better roads and better bicycle paths, and against the unsanitary conditions of the colored wards in the city hospital, and carried on frequent editorial tilts with the white editors of Wilmington's *Morning Star* and *The Messenger.*[4] Such editorial activities on Alex Manly's part did not enhance his popularity with Wilmington's white population who thought him radical, bold, and saucy. In 1898, a prominent Georgia white woman wrote an article demanding the lives of Negro rapists and enjoining Southern manhood to protect its women from lustful Negro brutes.[5] Alex Manly replied through his paper that white women were not any more particular in the matter of clandestine meetings with Negro men than white men with Negro women.[6] Into the tense Wilmington campaign of racial and political propaganda fell the Manly article circulated by the Raleigh *News and Observer.* While the article was not the cause of the upheaval, it served as an excellent pretext when election time came.

The tenseness of the situation resulted in Governor Daniel L. Russell's joining in a circular appeal to the Fusionists of New Hanover "to put no county ticket in the field; no negro nominees, but to have only State, Congressional and Senatorial tickets,"

Conditions are such in your county that we join in giving you this advice. Listen to us! Do not encourage any attempt to depart from the agreement made with the merchants and business men. They have taken down their Legislative Ticket for the House, and have put up their two Representatives. Let us make no objections to them or to their County Ticket. These merchants and business men have given their word that there shall be a free and fair and peaceful election. Now it is most important to you that you turn out and vote the Fusion Ticket for Judge and Solicitor, for Congressman and for State Senator. Do not listen to men who seek to divide you because they have personal grievances or disappointments. Let every Republican, every Populist, every Independent, every man who is opposed to the Democratic Machine and its methods, turn out and put in his vote. If you fail to do it, the consequence may be disastrous.

Vote for the Fusion Ticket, for Oliver H. Dockery for Congress, and R. B. Davis for Senate.

Do not hang around the polls on Election Day, vote and go to your homes.

J. C. PRITCHARD,
MARION BUTLER,
D. L. RUSSELL.

A. E. HOLTON,
Chairman Republican State Committee.

CYRUS THOMPSON,
Chairman Populist State Committee.

OLIVER H. DOCKERY,
Candidate for Congress.[7]

The statement that the Fusionists, as reported by the Reverend Mr. Kirk, Negro Republican, had no local ticket in the campaign in Wilmington or New Hanover is corroborated in effect by Locke Craig, "white supremacy" orator, who referred to the withdrawal of the Fusionist ticket in an address at Limestone Township, Buncombe County, on November 3, 1898.[8] Election day came and passed. It was declared that Negroes were absolutely obedient to the request to return quietly to their homes after casting their ballots; consequently all was peace on Tuesday of the election.[9]

It is always difficult, and sometimes impossible, to describe a riot in detail. Each participant or observer can tell only that part which he saw from his location. There are hundreds of angry men involved in a riot, and if each made a record of the startling things he saw, the records would differ in hundreds of ways. But the written records of participants are few, fragmentary, and partisan. To piece together what each observed and arrive at a plausible picture is the writer's task. Riots do not occur overnight. Tensions and conflicts precede these sociological abnormalities. They are but symptoms of a malignant growth.

One of the factors in the background of the riot, which historians have seemingly ignored, was the tension created in political circles by the Wilmington city charters of 1895 and 1897. The extra "police board" of 1895 (seven Fusionists) had precedence over the elected board of Democratic aldermen of 1894,[10] and this was a bitter pill for the Democrats. Through the charter of 1897, Wilmington was governed by a board of ten aldermen, five elected by the people and five appointed by the governor.[11] This arrangement displeased the Democrats equally because a Republican governor would appoint Republicans or Fusionists. In conformity with the provisions of the 1897 charter, the city held its election on March 25. The five wards elected respectively for aldermen Andrew J. Walker (Negro), W. E. Springer, Owen Fennell (Negro), W. E. Yopp, and Elijah M. Green (Negro). The five aldermen appointed by Governor Russell were Silas P. Wright, John G. Norwood (Negro), B. F. Keith, A. J. Hewlett, and D. J. Benson.[12] On March 26, the day after the election, the five aldermen appointed by Governor Russell, Andrew J. Walker of first ward, and Elijah M. Green of fifth, met, took the oath prescribed by law, and organized. They chose Silas P. Wright as mayor and H. C. Twining to fill the vacancy caused by Wright's resignation as alderman. Three of the elected aldermen, W. E. Springer, Owen Fennell, and W. E. Yopp, did not attend this meeting. However, on the same day these three met with the "runners-up" from five wards—Spencer, Munds, Catlett, Green, and Mann—organized themselves into a board of aldermen and chose H. L. McL. Green as mayor.[13] Wilmington then had two boards of aldermen and two mayors. The first board based its claim of legality upon the 1897 charter. The second board ignored the 1897 act and contended that, under the 1895 charter providing for ten elected aldermen, two from each ward, the winner and the "runner-up" were bona fide aldermen. The second board was clearly challenging the constitutionality of the 1897 charter and Governor Russell's power of appointment.

On the next day, March 27, the three elected aldermen (W. E. Springer, Owen Fennell, and W. E. Yopp), who on the day before had participated in the organization of the board which chose Green as mayor, gave notice to the other two elected aldermen (Andrew J. Walker and Elijah Green) of the first board, organized themselves into an alleged board of aldermen, and chose Walker Taylor, Democrat, as mayor.[14] Thus three mayors and three boards of aldermen were contesting the election of March 25. To add more confusion to the picture, the old Democratic board of aldermen held a meeting and formally resolved not to deliver possession of the city government to any of the various persons claiming to have been elected aldermen at the alleged election of March 25.[15]

Mayor Silas P. Wright and the first board of aldermen (two elected and five appointed) took possession of the city government. The old Democratic board of aldermen with W. N. Harriss as mayor instituted suit against Wright and his board, alleging the unconstitutionality of the act of 1897 governing Wilmington and demanding possession of their offices. The four contesting suits were consolidated at the April term of court, 1897, by an order of the court. The judge of the superior court who heard the case gave judgment to the plaintiffs, holding that the city charter of 1897 "was uncon-stitutional; the election for aldermen of the City of Wilmington held on March 25, 1897, was invalid; and the old board of aldermen, mayor, and their associates were entitled to hold office until their successors were duly qualified and elected."[16] This superior court verdict was a Democratic victory because the old board of aldermen was dominated by the Democrats and the Fusion legislature of 1897 had abolished the "police board" and restored the aldermen to supreme authority.

Silas Wright and his board appealed to the Supreme Court of the state, while refusing to turn the government back to the old board. At the Septem-ber term, four contentions were presented to the Supreme Court:

(1) Wright and his aldermen contended that the act of 1897 was con-stitutional and valid in its entirety, and the election was held under and pursuant to the said act and was a valid election:

(2) Taylor and his aldermen claimed the act of 1897 unconstitutional and void, in so far as it conferred upon the governor the power to appoint an alderman from each ward, but was constitutional and valid in so far as it provided for the election of five aldermen;

(3) Green and his aldermen contended that the provision of the 1897 act, which devolved upon the governor the appointment of one alderman from each ward was null and void, but the remaining portions of the act were good and valid; and the election as held under the provisions of the charter (1895) prior to 1897, entitled them (the "runners-up") to be duly elected aldermen; and

(4) Harriss and his board of aldermen, already adjudged by a lower court to be the rightful board, contended that the act of 1897 was uncon-stitutional and void in its entirety, that election held under the act was in-valid, and that they were entitled to hold office until their successors were *legally elected and qualified.*[17]

The lawyers for the Democratic board of aldermen were George Rountree and Iredell Meares and for the Fusion board were Addison Ricaud and E. R. Bryan. Chief Justice Faircloth, expressing the opinion of the court, held that Wright and his board of aldermen were the rightful occupants of the offices. Faircloth reasoned that sovereign power resides in the people, who in turn select their representatives to the legislature; the people have invested their representatives in the legislature with the power in question to be exercised at their discretion, with which the courts cannot interfere; and the constitution provides that the legislature may change or abrogate any city charter.[18] The Supreme Court thus reversed the decision of the lower court by a unanimous decision. The Democrats of the state looked in vain to Associate Justice Clark (Democrat) as their bulwark on the supreme bench. He concurred. Chief Justice Faircloth intimated that the criticism should be directed at the constitutional convention of 1875 which granted the legislature the power to govern cities and counties rather than at the legislature of 1897.[19] In 1875-76, the Democrats had sponsored the constitutional amendment vesting in the legislature the power to change, modify, or abrogate city and county governments, so that they could control Republican or Negro counties and cities. In the Fusion period, their impairment of local self-government proved to be a boomerang. The Supreme Court decision fanned the flames of confusion in Wilmington where a Republican mayor and his board of four Negro aldermen and six white aldermen held office.

Wilmington was governed by Fusionists who were supported by a large number of Negro voters. Many of these Democrats who resented Wilmington city government, were formerly very influential in the political and economic life of the city. The appointment of Negro police by Mayor Wright and his board added to the Democrats' disgust. Charles Norwood (Negro) was elected treasurer of New Hanover County for two years, 1896-98, and his office was in Wilmington. The fact that he paid all teachers (white and Negro) and all county employees (white and Negro) from his office intensified the Democrats' displeasure because they had to deal across the counter with him. Henry Hall (Negro) was elected assistant sheriff to Sheriff Manning (white) of New Hanover County, and his office was in Wilmington. Dan Howard, first Negro jailer of the city, was objectionable because he had the power to carry the keys to the jail. John Dancy, collector of the port of customs, and John Taylor, his bookkeeper (Negroes), had their offices in the city. David Jacobs (Negro) was a coroner of the county. The great majority of Wilmington whites resented Negro office-holding of any kind. Federal patronage, Fusion politics, and, of more consequence, the anti-Negro attitudes of the Democrats had created an explosive situation in Wilmington. These Negro officeholders and the factors involved in the long drawn out municipal election of 1897 hover in the background of the riot of 1898.

There is some evidence that economic tension existed in Wilmington. Many of the craftsmen of Wilmington were colored—bricklayers,[20] plasterers, carpenters, workers in the shipyard, and workers in the factory, who, perhaps, were willing to work for lower wages than their white competitors. It has been recorded that,

Negroes were given preference in the matter of employment for most of the town's artisans were Negroes, and numerous white families in the city faced bitter want because their providers could get but little work as brickmasons, carpenters, mechanics; and this economic condition was aggravated considerably by the influx of many Negroes, and Wilmington was really becoming a Mecca for Negroes and a city of Lost Opportunities for the working class whites.[21]

The city also had a considerable number of intelligent Negro business and professional men. There was spirited competition between Negro and white lawyers. Four prominent Negro lawyers, Armond W. Scott, L. A. Henderson, William A. Moore, and L. P. White, handled virtually all the Negro legal business, a situation which made the white lawyers envious.[22] A story survives that during the Fusion period, White, a Negro lawyer, told J. D. Bellamy, a white lawyer, after the judge had corrected the latter in a murder case, "Young man, you have got to go to school again. You are now talking to a lawyer."[23] Such a comment in the courts between white men may or may not have caused resentment, but here was a black man talking to a white man and that made the difference in North Carolina. It made a difference in the late 1890's when passion and race prejudice ran high; it made a difference in Wilmington where soon race prejudice produced a riot; and, last, it made a difference, no doubt, in the minds of other Wilmington white lawyers such as Rountree and Waddell.[24]

Alfred M. Waddell, staunch Democrat and defeated office-seeker, stated in defense of what he deemed intolerable conditions in Wilmington that "nigger lawyers are sassing white men in our courts; nigger root doctors are crowding white physicians out of business."[25] By word of mouth and dimmed with many years of memory, a Negro contemporary holds that the colored citizens of Wilmington were progressive and enterprising; that some negro property-holders were worth from five to forty thousand dollars; and that from negro ranks were furnished teachers, lawyers, physicians, clergymen, merchants, and business men.[26]

Many staunch Negro Republicans who were intelligent leaders lived there. Among them were John C. Dancy, collector of customs of the port of Wilmington; Armond W. Scott, graduate of Shaw University, admitted to the bar at the age of twenty-one, prominent lawyer,[27] now (1951) judge of the Twelfth Municipal District of Washington, D. C.; Alex Manly, editor of *The Record;* the Reverend Mr. I. J. Bell; Tom Miller; R. S. Pickens; Aaron Bryant; Carter Peamon; and Thomas Rivera. Aside from the fact that New Hanover sent one Negro to the legislature of 1897, the county had a treasurer, recorder of deeds, coroner, and some magistrates, while the city of Wilmington had four aldermen, a jailer, some policemen, and two paid fire companies (the Cape Fear and the Phoenix) who were Negroes. These Negro officeholders, functioning in a town with a majority Negro population, afforded an opportunity for the local Democrats to proclaim to the state that Wilmington was under "Negro domination." Edward A. Johnson, Negro alderman of Raleigh, reported that Negroes in Wilmington had pianos, servants, expensive carpets, lace curtains at windows, and that "white supremacy" orators of that city constantly asked from the platform, "How many of you white men can afford to have pianos and servants?"

After an elaborate comparison of the white man's property, wages, and physical comforts with the Negro's, with the greater emphasis upon those of the latter, the audiences were left under the assumption that Wilmington was the Negro's Utopia.[28]

Political confusion resulting from the Democrats' refusal to accept the city government act of 1897, economic competition between white and black labor, the violent opposition of whites to Negro office-holding, and the yellow journalism of the press made the city a veritable boiling pot. The orators of the "white supremacy" campaign fanned the flames of passion. A. M. Waddell is reported to have said in his address in Durham, near the end of the campaign of 1898: "We in Wilmington extend a Macedonian call to you to come over and help us. We will not live under these intolerable conditions. No society can stand it. We intend to change it, if we have to choke the current of Cape Fear River with negro carcasses."[29]

Rumors played as large a part in intensifying racial antagonism in Wilmington as any other single factor. In the closing days of the "'white supremacy" campaign, both Negroes and whites were reported arming themselves. The situation had become so acute that white hardware stores refused to sell ammunition to Negroes, while white customers preceding the Negro customers to the counters could buy it.[30] Some Negroes ordered guns from a Northern manufacturing concern which in turn sent the order to its North Carolina distributing agent, who in turn sent the letter to prominent Democrats of Wilmington.[31] It was reported that the Negroes had decided that, in case of Democratic victory, Negro servants would apply the torch to the white employers' homes; that Negro males would do the same to the cotton warehouse where bales of cotton were stored; and that Negroes had urged their fellow race members to use the bullet which has no regard for color.[32] It was reported by a contemporary that Democratic stump orators had secured the aid of poor whites in both city and rural districts by promising them that, by assisting to kill and chase the Negro from the city, the property owned by the colored citizens would be turned over to them.[33] Whether this last rumor was true or not, the economic consequences of the riot bear out the contrary; no property was seized.[34] It is not known whether the other rumors had any semblance of truth, but it may be generally stated that both races made some preparations. The Democrats maintained that they armed in defense against the Negroes, and the Negroes claimed that they armed in defense against the Democrats. On the other hand, one reporter stated the situation correctly, perhaps, when he wrote that "the fiat had gone forth 'The whites must rule.' . . . It was this fear of the Negro uprising in defense of his electorate that offered an ostensible ground for the general display of arms; but if the truth be told, the reason thus offered was little more than a fortunate excuse."[35] According to Armond W. Scott, of Wilmington, the chief concern of the Negro males in their meetings in October, 1898, was how should they plan protection for their wives and children.[36]

A Wilmington resident in 1898 wrote in 1942, "that for a period of six to twelve months prior to November 10, 1898, the white citizens of Wilmington prepared quietly but effectively for the day when action would be necessary."[37] A certain element of preparation stood out in the activities which preceded the riot indicating strongly that he was correct in his observation. There was organized in the city, prior to November 10, a self-styled committee of Democrats known as the "Secret Nine" which planned the agenda of activities for the day after election. The Secret Nine drew up a "Declaration of White Independence." The preamble proclaimed that the Constitution of the United States did not anticipate the enfranchisement of Negroes; that the North Carolina delegates to the constitutional convention did not contemplate their descendants being subjected to an inferior race; that the undersigned citizens of Wilmington would no longer be ruled by Negroes; that the 60,000,000 white people of the United States would not subject Wilmington whites to Negro rule; that the whites of Wilmington would refuse to pay taxes levied by Republicans and Negroes; that the Negro antagonized the white man's interest; and that the most progressive group in any community was the white population. Three resolves and an emphatic warning followed the preamble:

That we propose in the future to give to white men a large part of the employment heretofore given to Negroes because we realize that white families cannot thrive here unless there are many opportunities for the employment of the different members of their families.

We therefore owe it to the people of this community and city, as a protection against such license in the future, that *"The Record"* cease to be published and that its editor be banished from this community.

We demand that he leave the city forever within twenty-four hours after the issuance of this Proclamation. Second, that the printing press from which *The Record* has been issued be shipped from the city without delay; that we be notified within 12 hours of the acceptance or rejection of this demand.

If the demand is agreed to within twelve hours, we counsel forbearance on the part of white men. If the demand is refused or no answer is given within the time mentioned, then the Editor Manly, will be expelled by force.[38]

Immediately after the declaration was formulated, the Secret Nine appointed a committee of twenty-five to effect necessities which might arise therefrom. Alfred M. Waddell, "white supremacy" orator, was made chairman.[39]

The white committee of twenty-five invited thirty-two leading Negroes of the city to a meeting at 6 P. M., at the close of election, November 8, and presented to them the "Declaration of White Independence." The Negroes were told that they had until 7:30 A. M., November 10, to reply to the demands.[40] John Dancy, Negro, is supposed to have petitioned Chairman Waddell, white, for permission to ask a question relative to the declaration, and the latter is supposed to have replied that no Negro would be permitted to address the floor.[41]

The Negroes retired to Elijah Lane's barbership on the corner of Market and Water streets and served as a committee of colored citizens to reply to the demands. The Negroes recorded as present were Dr. J. H. Alston, physician; Richard Ashe, financier; John H. Brown; John Carroll, caterer; John Goings, associated with the Manly press; Elijah Green, alderman elected from the fifth ward, 1897-98; H. C. Green, merchant; Henry Green; James Green; Josh Green, coal and wood dealer; L. A. Henderson, lawyer; Dan Howard, first Negro jailer in New Hanover County; John Holloway, clerk in the post office; John H. Howe, contractor; John T. Howe, in the legislature of 1897 from New Hanover County; David Jacobs, coroner of New Hanover County; David J. Jones, wheelwright; J. W. Lee; the Reverend W. H. Leak, Methodist minister; Alex Mallett; Dr. T. R. Mask, physician; T. C. Miller, financier who made loans to white and colored; William A. Moore, lawyer; Carter Peamon, barber and politician; Brown Reardon; R. S. Pickens, magistrate; Isham Quick, coal and wood dealer; Robert Reardon; Thomas Rivera, mortician; Fred Sadgwar, financier and architect; Armond Scott, lawyer; and the Reverend J. W. Telfair, manager of the James Sprunt Cotton Press.[42]

The committee of Negroes drafted a reply to A. M. Waddell and mailed it instead of carrying it to him. This is the reputed copy of the letter:

Hon. A. M. Waddell,
Chairman Citizens Committee
Wilmington, N. C.
Dear Sir,
We the colored citizens to whom was referred the matter of expulsion from this community, of the persons and press of A. M. Manly, beg most respectfully to say that we are in no wise responsible for nor in any way endorse the obnoxious article that called forth your activities. Neither are we authorized to act for him in this matter, but in the interest of peace we will most willingly use our influence to have your wishes carried out.
                    Very respectfully,
                    The Committee of Colored Citizens.[43]

The mailed letter did not reach Waddell on November 10, 7:30 A. M., the deadline. It has been held by contemporaries that this letter was delayed through the intentional neglect of Armond W. Scott, Negro lawyer.[44] Scott, who served as secretary to the Negro committee, formulated the reply to the white committee. He contends that the letter herein cited is not the original reply.[45] The author of the reputed letter states that it was unthinkable for any Negro to enter the white settlement to deliver the letter that night for fear of loss of life; consequently, he mailed it.[46] On November 10, thirty minutes after the expired time, at 8 A. M., Waddell led bands of men to the Wilmington Light Infantry Armory, armed them, and proceeded to Manly's office. The building was burned. The riot began. Fighting raged in the streets, and word was sent to Governor Russell asking for the state militia.

From eye witnesses come accounts of some segments of the riot. H. Ditzler, special correspondent of *Collier's Magazine*, was on the spot at the time of the riot. The pictures apparently taken on the day of the riot, show the Manly office with the top floor burned away and standing in front of it were white boys and men, apparently ranging from the early teen age to middle age, dressed in collars, hats, ties, and fashionable garments of the period, armed with shot guns and sticks.[47] These pictures best demonstrate that the mob was not composed of white hoodlums.

The Reverend Mr. Kirk, Negro minister and eye witness, declared that on the day of the riot men, women, and children rushed to the woods and swamps, and there slept on the ground in November weather; streets were dotted with dead bodies, some of which were lying in the street until the day following the riot, others of which were discovered later under houses by their stench; colored men who passed through the streets had either to be guarded by one of the crowd or have a written permit giving them the right to pass; little white boys searched Negroes and took from them every means of defense, and, if the Negroes resisted, they were shot down by armed white males who looked on with shot guns; rioters went from house to house looking for Negroes whom they considered offensive and killed them, and poured volleys into fleeing Negroes like sportsmen firing at rabbits in an open field; Negro churches were entered at the point of a cannon and searched for ammunition; and white ministers carried guns.[48]

Thomas Rivera was in his mortuary when he heard the excitement in the streets. Upon rushing to his door, he found his front blocked by two armed whites who told him "to get the hell back inside if he wanted to live." He then went out by the back entrance to a white Republican's drugstore. This Republican friend urged him to leave the city for a while. Rivera returned home about noon, gathered his important papers, fled in the afternoon to the white cemetery, and spent the night there. When he was asked what happened to his wife and children during the riot, he replied that the whites were not interested in harming women and children, but seemingly vented their spleen upon males. Rivera returned to his establishment the next day.

Daniel Wright was killed when he refused to come out of his house. "Dan was a politician," said Rivera, "and when he refused to come out, the mob fired several shots toward the attic where they thought he was. Dan, in turn, using a smokeless and noiseless rifle, fired into the group killing two members of the Red Shirts, Hill Terry and George Bland.[49] The house was set fire to, and when Dan finally fled he was shot." His body was turned over to Rivera for burial. Dan's wife, who came out of the house and stood in the street, related the incident to Rivera. The latter said that he had a personal conference with A. M. Waddell, on the day after the riot, and asked for protection which Waddell promptly granted and guaranteed until the confusion abated in the city.

Rivera heard the story that, on the day of the riot, whites approached the Sprunt Cotton Press with guns to kill the 800 Negroes employed there; that James Sprunt, owner of the factory, ordered the foreman to barricade the doors; that he then ordered the four guns of his pleasure cruising yacht to be turned on the armed Democrats who then moved on; and that at night, November 10, the Negroes came out and fled.[50]

Armond W. Scott was sitting on his porch on the morning of the riot when a white Democrat hastened to warn him that his name was on the proscribed Democratic list and that he had better flee the city for his life. Money, which he refused, was offered him to facilitate his escape. When he reached the station, he found mobs of Red Shirts who threatened him. Frank Steadman, a leader of the Democratic mob, ordered the Red Shirts to desist from their threats. After Scott boarded the train for Rocky Mount, Conductor Capehart dared a Democratic interloper, searching the train, to touch him.[51]

Lieutenant Colonel Walker Taylor, commander of the Second Regiment of the State Guard located at Wilmington, was asked to restore order to the city. His report to the adjutant general is offered here:

Nov. 11, 1898, I wired you about 9 o'clock as follows:
"Situation here serious. I hold military subject to your prompt orders." The relations between the races at this time was very strained and, shortly after the sending of the foregoing message, a negro shot a white man on Harnett between 3rd and 4th streets. Following this I received your telegram ordering me to take command of Captain Jones's company (Company C, Second Regiment, N. C. S. G.) and preserve peace and order, which I at once proceeded to do as best I could. At this time the feeling was intense, and believing the presence of military in the district where the tragedy occurred would deter the rioters from further violent acts, I assumed personal command and marched the company to the point

referred to and beyond, following the gathering crowd. I was joined by the Wilmington Division of the Naval Reserves in charge of Commander Geo. L. Morton, which continued a separate and distinct command until about 4 o'clock P. M., when he reported to me in pursuance of your telegraphic orders directing him to do so. In the meantime Commander Morton marched the Naval Reserves through a part of the territory in which renewed trouble threatened and, with the Infantry company, I made search for rioters in contiguous blocks. A building from which someone or more were firing at citizens on the street was surrounded and four negroes therein discovered were arrested and safely jailed. One negro, the fifth therein, refused to surrender after repeated commands to do so, and fleeing from the building was shot. This was the only firing done by the military, and afforded the very best results, in proof of which I mentioned the fact that no further shooting from buildings or death followed. At this point I took a detail of ten men, proceeded to the suburbs of the city, and closed all stores and shops and learned all I could of the situation. Threatening crowds were encountered, but none offered determined resistance. They sullenly dispersed when ordered to do so, but gathered at other points. Considering the situation very serious, I wired you for reinforcements, and your advices that the Clinton and Maxton Companies and Kinston Naval Reserves were ordered here very much simplified the work demanded for the night near at hand. Until the arrival of these troops and during Thursday night I used the troops in hand for patrol duty in the riot section of the city.

Upon arrival of the Maxton Company about 11 P. M. I assigned it to duty at the City Hospital for the protection of the wounded—this was done in consequence of threats made by the negroes to kill the two wounded white men and recover the negroes wounded, four in number, placed there for treatment. About 11:30 P. M. the Clinton Company arrived and, at the request of the Mayor, it was ordered to do duty at the jail, where the prisoners arrested in the afternoon were incarcerated. The Kinston Naval Reserves reached Wilmington about 2:30 A. M. Friday, and were assigned to patrol duty for a few hours following which they relieved Company A, (Clinton Company) on duty at the jail. . . .

The services rendered by the troops were entirely satisfactory, and promptly assured the citizens of the city that they were present for a purpose agreeable to all who desired peace and order; and hence there was honest cooperation during the entire time the troops were on duty, as evidence by the attentions shown by the citizens in furnishing food, bedding and other comforts.[52]

Walker Taylor, Democrat, was elected mayor by the third board of aldermen as a result of the contested municipal election of 1897. He never served because the Supreme Court threw out the contesting mayors and their boards of aldermen in the *Harriss et alia* v. *Wright* case. This is the same Walker Taylor whose duty it was to quell the riot. No doubt many whites ministered to the comfort of his troops with the full realization that the State

Guard was on their side. The crowning proof that this Democrat, Taylor, was in sympathy with the rioters is the fact that not one white man was arrested during the riot. Estimates of the number of Negroes dead varied from eleven to thirty,[53] while some held that hundreds of Negro bodies were dumped into Cape Fear River.[54] The enigma remains as to why Governor Russell did not put Wilmington under martial law. The military went in but only in aid of the civil authorities.

The political result of the violence was that A. M. Waddell and other prominent Democrats marched to the city hall and county courthouse in the afternoon of the riot and forced the Fusionists to resign and elected themselves to office. In reality, the Democrats effected a *coup d'état*. Waddell, leader of the riot, became mayor; H. P. West, B. F. King, A. B. Skelding, Charles W. Worth, William H. Sprunt, Preston L. Bridgers, and the Reverend J. W. Kramer became aldermen; Edgar G. Parmele was named chief of police by the new board with M. F. Heiskel Gouvenier as assistant and John F. Furlong as captain of the police.[55] Waddell gave this specious explanation of how the Democrats took over the positions when the Fusionists' terms of office had not expired:

In order to accomplish this legally, a meeting was held, and the old Board of Alderman resigned by wards. One alderman would resign; that would make a vacancy; and then the Mayor [Fusionist] would ask if there were any nominations for the vacancy; and one of his own men would nominate a man he knew we wanted for the ward, and so on, in succession, through each ward in town. We [Democrats] really didn't have anything to do with it. They asked us whom we wanted. Successively they resigned, and our men were elected. The room was as quiet as a room in a private home.[56]

In spite of the four hundred armed men, hundreds of armed Red Shirts, death, violence, and a *coup d'état*, Waddell had the audacity to state that "there was no intimidation used in the establishment of the present city government."[57]

The Democratic press of the state interpreted the riot as being necessary, yet differed in the analysis of the consequences. The *News and Observer* hailed it as absolutely necessary to save Wilmington from degradation.[58] The *Charlotte Observer*, a more rational Democratic paper, stated that the situation in Wilmington was intolerable but regretted the riot.[59] The *Wilmington Messenger* hailed the heroic efforts of the white people in liberating themselves from black tyranny.[60] A Republican newspaper questioned the motives of the Democratic activities in Wilmington. If the purpose of the riot was to eject Manly and his press from the city as the white committee's Declaration stated, *The Union Republican* concluded that this step might have been taken earlier. It stated that

The Manly article was written several months before the election and before the campaign propaganda began. Why was it not right and proper to expel Manly when the article appeared? If the Democrats had been sincere, Manly and his press would have been ejected long before November 11. If the riot aimed only at Manly, what were the reasons in driving White officials out of the city and leaders of the Republican party? [61]

The Northern press, on the whole, condemned the riot as an act of barbarism, unjustifiable and needless.[62] One newspaper termed the outbreak between the races a disgrace to the country and a refutation to North Carolina's claim to a capacity for self-government.[63] Another charged that the Southern white man had fallen in the intellectual and material plane, and belonged to a race totally inferior to that of his Anglo-Saxon predecessors and in general degenerate.[64] A Brooklyn paper commended the Wilmingtonians on the use of force and advocated immediate disfranchisement of the Negro.[65]

The opinions of contemporaries at the time of the riot ranged from undue praise to severe condemnation. The opinions of A. M. Waddell, self-appointed Democratic mayor and leader of the riot, immediately after the event should be compared with those published in 1902. He stated in 1902 that it was the most orderly and quiet riot he had ever seen or heard of; that perfectly sober men participated in it; that defiant and armed Negroes occupied the streets; that a Negro deliberately and without provocation shot a white man; and that the riot was the unanimous act of all the white people prompted solely by the overwhelming sense of its necessity in behalf of civilization and decency.[66] Immediately after the riot, he averred "I have sent messengers of both races out in the surrounding woods, where it is said fugitives are hiding, begging the people to come back. Self appointed vigilantes are responsible for much of this misery, because of the indiscriminate way they have gone about banishing objectionable persons; and in some instances, unscrupulous whites have gratified their personal spite in dealing with negroes."[67]

Daniels, whose paper contributed to the inflammatory background of the riot, hailed it as the salvation of the city of Wilmington from degradation.[68] Henry G. Connor, prominent Democrat in the campaign of 1898 and later chosen as speaker of the House of Representatives in 1899, wrote to his friend that "the politicians stirred the minds and feelings of the people more deeply than they intended."[69] John Spencer Bassett, brilliant North Carolina historian and independent in politics, wrote as follows: "The campaign has been one of passion. It has ended in a riot at Wilmington—justifiable at no point, a riot directly due to the 'white man's' campaign," and further added, with historical and constitutional justification, "The whole thing was not necessary because in two months the Democratic Legislature will meet and can and will change affairs in Wilmington."[70]

In reference to the beginning of the violence, the military reported that Negroes fired first.[71] Professor Bassett wrote, "It was claimed that Negroes fired first. I don't think many white people who understand things in the State believe the charge."[72] Daniels, appraising the occurrence forty years later, concluded that if the Democratic allegation is true that Negroes precipitated the riot, "they did not fire until four hundred armed white men led by Colonel Waddell marched to the *Record* office to destroy it."[73] A local paper absolved the mob from the blame for the burning of Manly's building by declaring that it was accidental.[74] Some present day historians avoid placing the blame on any source by such general conclusions as "during the disturbance the building was found to be on fire and it was completely destroyed, the origin of the fire never being discovered."[75] One Democratic paper, known for fair play, stated that "It was claimed at that time and has been claimed ever since that the fire was accidental. We have our doubts about that; it seems much more probable that the fire was deliberately applied by some irresponsible member of the mob."[76] Daniels stated in 1944 that probably many applied the torch.[77]

Recent evidence indicates that Manly did not write the article so widely used by the Democrats in the campaign of 1898. William L. Jeffres, associate editor of *The Record,* claims that he wrote it.[78] This confession came too late to spare Manly. Recent memoirs assert that Thomas Clawson, white, Democrat and editor of the *Wilmington Messenger,* owned the printing press which Manly used and the Democrats destroyed. The author of this revelation ascribes to himself the credit for saving the two Manly brothers from being lynched. He emphasizes the fact that they conducted a creditable paper supported largely by the liberal advertisement from the white businesses of Wilmington.[79] The paradoxes of life become more confusing when an attempt is made to explain why a white Democratic editor furnished a Negro Republican editor with a printing press when the political propaganda generated from each press was diametrically opposed. Furthermore, the same Democratic white editor reprinted the Manly article and sent it to the *News and Observer* for wider circulation designed solely to engender hatred for Manly and his race; yet, in the beginning of the riot, he gave the victim a timely warning on how to escape from the city to avoid death.

The white Democrats of Wilmington maintained that the city was dominated by ignorant Negroes. New Hanover County's Negro male literates numbered 1,906 against 1,202 illiterates,[80] a higher literacy ratio than in any of the "black counties" in the state. Contrary to the Democratic accusation that ignorant Negroes dominated politics, hence the Democratic command that they must flee the city, stands out the undeniable fact that in the tumult of the riot, the shiftless and illiterate Negroes were allowed to remain. The men who have been identified before as prominent—Tom Miller, Aaron

Bryant, the Reverend I. J. Bell, Armond W. Scott, R. S. Pickens, John Dancy, John Taylor, the Manly brothers, McLain Laughton, Carter Peamon, and Isaac Loften—were forced to leave the city. Such activities indicate strongly that the Democrats were chiefly interested in eliminating men of college training, some wealth, and local renown. These men not only excelled in Wilmington, but also continued to excell in other areas.[81] The only charge made against them was that they antagonized the best interests of the whites.

The Wilmington race riot had dire repercussions on the city, the state, and the South. Most of the influential Negroes of Wilmington sold or gave away their personal holdings, packed bag and baggage, and moved to other parts of the state or out of the state. This migration left an apathetic Negro citizenry, fearful of and resentful toward the whites. So many of these Negro employees refused to return to their former white employers that the Democratic legislature of 1899 enacted a vagrancy statute for Wilmington, a coercive measure to force Negroes into white employment.[82] Hayden aptly summarized its effects on the state and the Southland when he concluded that there were few Negroes who dared exercise their rights of suffrage after the racial whirlwind of 1898 had blown the ballots from their hands.[83] While the campaign of intimidation, misrepresentation, vilification, and violence restored the state to the Democrats in 1898, so was Wilmington, in like manner but to a greater degree, restored to the local Democrats.

NOTES TO CHAPTER ELEVEN

1. Personal condensation of the Democratic point of view as gathered from:
Samuel A. Ashe, *History of North Carolina*, II.
Clawson's Memoirs, North Carolina Historical Commission, Raleigh, North Caroline, deposited May 29, 1944.
Josephus Daniels, *Editor in Politics*.
Democratic Handbook, 1900.
J. G. deR. Hamilton, *History of North Carolina Since 1860*.
News and Observer, July, August, September, and October, 1898.
Fred Rippy (ed.), *Furnifold Simmons, Statesman of the New South*.
Florence E. Smith, Populism and Its Influence in North Carolina (Unpublished Ph.D. dissertation).
James Sprunt, *Chronicles of the Cape Fear River, 1660-1916*.
Alfred M. Waddell, *Some Memories of My Life*.

2. Ashe, *History of North Carolina*, II, 1206-7; Hamilton, *History of North Carolina Since 1860*, 295-97; Henderson, *The Old North State and The New*, II, 421-22, who relies upon Hamilton, *History of North Carolina Since 1860*.

3. Interview with Judge Armond W. Scott, Judge of the Municipal Court, Washington, D. C., October 27, 1945.

4. Jack Thorne (pseudonym of David Bryant Fulton), *Hanover; The Persecution of The Lowly: A Story of The Wilmington Massacre*, 13.

5. *Ibid.*, 13-14.

6. *Supra*, Chap. X, 147-48; Chap. XI, 158.

7. J. Allen Kirk, *A Statement of Facts Concerning the Bloody Riot in Wilmington, North Carolina, Thursday, November 10, 1898*, 4-5.

8. Locke Craig Letters, Papers, and Scrapbook, 1880-1923, Duke University Library Manuscript Collection.

9. Kirk, *op. cit.*, 5.

10. *Private Laws*, 1895, Chap. 121, 158-60; also *Supra*, Chap. IX, 127-28.

11. *Private Laws*, 1897, Chap. 150, 282.

12. *W. N. Harriss et al.* v. *S. P. Wright et al.*, North Carolina Reports, CXXI (1897), 157.

Andrew J. Walker cited as Negro in the Clawson Memoirs; Elijah Green and Owen Fennell by Thomas Rivera, and John G. Norwood by *Wilmington Messenger*, October 2, 1897.

13. *Ibid.*, 157-58.

14. *Ibid.*, 158.

15. *Ibid.*, 158.

16. *Ibid.*

17. *Ibid.*, 158-59.

18. *Ibid.*, 160.

19. *Ibid.*, 160-61.

20. John T. Howe, Negro, Representative from New Hanover County in the legislature of 1897, secured for the Negro bricklayers' brotherhood an act of incorporation. *Public Laws, 1897*, Ch. 428, 617.

21. Henry Hayden, *The Story of the Wilmington Rebellion*, 2.

22. Interview with Judge Armond W. Scott, Washington, D. C., October 27, 1945.

23. Interview with Thomas Rivera (mortician in Wilmington, North Carolina, 1890-1899), Durham, N. C., May 20, 1944; further attested, Thorne, *op. cit.*, 78.

24. Rountree and Winston in the General Assembly of 1899 fought hard to frame the suffrage bill to disfranchise the Negro and offered their legal knowledge in constructing an election law laden with intricacies and technicalities aimed at the Negro.

25. Thorne, *op. cit.*, 21.

26. Interview with Mrs. Hattie Shepard, Durham, N. C., July 24, 1944.

27. As testimony to his popularity, Scott tried thirty-six cases in the last session of court before the riot.—Interview with Judge Armond W. Scott, Washington, D. C., October 27, 1945.

28. Edward A. Johnson, *History of the Negro Soldiers in the Spanish American War and Other Items of Interest*, 140.

29. Interview with Mr. J. E. Dickson (white, Democrat), Superintendent of Buildings and Grounds, North Carolina College, Durham, North Carolina, July 25, 1944. Further attested as one of Waddell's chief campaign statements, Hayden, *op. cit.*, 9; and Josephus Daniels, *Editor in Politics*, 301.

30. Interview with Judge Armond W. Scott, Washington, D. C., October 27, 1945.

31. *News and Observer*, October 22, 1898.

32. Henry L. West, "The Race War in North Carolina," *Forum*, XXVI (January, 1899), 580.

33. Thorne, *op. cit.*, 17.

34. Interview with Judge Armond W. Scott, Washington, D. C., October 27, 1945.

35. West, *op. cit.*, 582.

36. Interview with Judge Armond W. Scott, Washington, D. C., October 27, 1945.

37. Clawson Memoirs, North Carolin Historical Commission, Raleigh, North Carolina, deposited May 29, 1944.

38. Hayden, *op. cit.*, 11.

39. *Ibid.*, 12.

40. *Ibid.*, 15.

41. Interview with Thomas Rivera, Durham, North Carolina, July 20, 1944; substantiated by Judge Armond Scott, Washington, D. C., October 27, 1945.

42. Names obtained from Hayden, *op. cit.*, 13; positions obtained from readings and interviews with Thomas Rivera, Durham, North Carolina, July 20, 1944, and Armond W. Scott, Washington, D. C., October 27, 1945.

43. Alfred M. Waddell, Private Papers, University of North Carolina Library Manuscript Collection, n.d., n.p. There is no proof that this is the original.

44. Hayden, *op. cit.*, 14.

45. Judge Scott declared that L. A. Henderson, Negro lawyer, attempted to tell the white committee that *The Record* had ceased publication two weeks earlier but was denied the privilege of finishing his remarks. The Negro committee retired to Elijah Lane's barber shop and selected Scott as secretary to formulate a reply to the white committee. The secretary stated that it was agreed to reiterate the explanation which Henderson had attempted to give. He, therefore, wrote the white committee that *The Record* had ceased publication two weeks earlier, Manly had agreed not to publish it again, there was no necessity to eject the editor and his press, and the committee was happy to say that the alleged basis of conflict between the races had been eliminated.— Interview with Armond W. Scott, Washington, D. C., October 27, 1945. He further stated that his letter was written in long hand, Armond W. Scott to Helen G. Edmonds, February 26, 1946.

46. Interview with Judge Armond W. Scott, Washington, D. C., October 27, 1945.

47. *Collier's Magazine*, Library of Congress, Washington, D. C., XXII, No. 8 (November 26, 1898), 3.

48. Kirk, *op. cit.*, 9-11.

49. This is the only specific mention of loss of white lives. The Adjutant General's Report cites two whites wounded. *Supra*, 169-70.

50. James Sprunt, Democrat, who owned this cotton press, related the story of the riot in his *Chronicles of the Cape Fear River, 1660-1916*, 554-55, and omitted any reference to the story told by Rivera. Sprunt's treatment of the riot is taken *verbatim* from A. M. Waddell, *Some Memories of My Life*, 242-43. That Rivera was not in error is attested by Thorne, *op. cit.*, 82-83.

51. Interview with Judge Armond W. Scott.

52. *Public Documents*, 1899, Document 9, 29-30; report dated November 22, 1898.

53. Josephus Daniels, *Editor in Politics*, 307, estimates eleven; Hamilton, *op. cit.*, 296, twelve; J. S. Bassett to H. B. Adams, November 15, 1898, twelve; Waddell, *Some Memories of My Life*, 242, (a participant), "between twenty and thirty."

54. Kirk, *op. cit.*, 17.

55. Hayden, *op. cit.*, 18.

56. Alfred M. Waddell, "The North Carolina Race War," *Collier's Magazine*, XXII, No. 8, 5 (November 26, 1898).

57. *Ibid.*

58. *News and Observer*, November 12, 13, 1898.

59. *Charlotte Observer*, November 16, 1898.

60. *Wilmington Messenger*, November 13, 1898.

61. *The Union Republican*, December 1, 1898.

62. "The North Carolina Race Conflict," *The Outlook*, LXIII (November 19, 1898), 709.

63. *The New York Mail and Express;* cited from Hayden, *op. cit.,* 24.

64. *The New York Press;* cited from Hayden, *op. cit.,* 25.

65. *The Brooklyn Citizen;* cited from Hayden, *op. cit.,* 24.

66. Waddell, *Some Memories of My Life,* 242-43.

67. Waddell, "The North Carolina Race War," 4.

68. *News and Observer,* November 13, 1898. The editor appraised it forty years later with a more moderate use of words as "an armed revolution of white men of Wilmington to teach what they believed was a needed lesson."—Josephus Daniels, *Editor in Politics,* 307-8.

69. Mabry, "The Negro in North Carolina Politics Since Reconstruction," 48 (citing from Henry G. Connor to George Howard, November 25, 1898, Henry G. Connor Papers in possession of R. D. W. Connor, University of North Carolina, Chapel Hill, North Carolina).

70. John Spencer Bassett to Herbert Baxter Adams, November 15, 1898 (photostatic copy from Herbert Baxter Adams Correspondence preserved at Johns Hopkins University), Duke University Library Manuscript Collection; also published in W. S. Holt (ed.), "Historical Scholarship in the United States, 1876-1901: As revealed in the Correspondence of Herbert Baxter Adams," 259.

71. *Public Documents,* 1899, Document No. 9, 29.

72. John Spencer Bassett to Herbert Baxter Adams, November 15, 1898, *loc. cit.*

73. Josephus Daniels, *Editor in Politics,* 307.

74. *Wilmington Messenger,* November 13, 1898.

75. Hamilton, *History of North Carolina Since 1860,* 295; also Mabry, "The Negro in North Carolina Politics Since Reconstruction," 54; citing from Rountree's "Recollections," in possession of J. G. deR. Hamilton, University of North Carolina, Chapel Hill, North Carolina.

76. *The Charlotte Observer,* March 14, 1899.

77. Josephus Daniels, *Editor in Politics,* 307-8.

78. *Ibid.,* 297.

79. Clawson Memoirs, North Carolina Historical Commission, Raleigh, North Caroline, deposited May 26, 1944.

80. United States Department of Commerce, *Bureau of Census,* I, Part I (1900), 992-93.

81. Armond W. Scott became Judge of the Municipal Court of Washington, D. C., in 1937, under Franklin D. Roosevelt.

John C. Dancy became Recorder of Deeds in Washington, D. C., 1901-11; John C. Dancy, Jr., Director of the Urban League in Detroit, Michigan, was gubernatorial appointee on several Michigan committees for interracial betterment, 1945.

Alex Manly and his descendants are reputed to be among Philadelphia's most industrious and civic-minded citizens.—Interview with Dr. Leon F. Sarjeant, of Philadelphia, Pennsylvania, June 2, 1944.

82. *Supra,* 174.

83. Hayden, *op. cit.,* 26.

CHAPTER TWELVE

THE LEGISLATURE OF 1899

THE NOVEMBER ELECTION OF 1898 restored North Carolina to Democratic control. The General Assembly of 1899, which met on January 4, was composed of ninety-four Democrats, twenty-three Republicans, and three Populists in the House of Representatives; and forty Democrats, seven Republicans, and three Populists in the Senate.[1] Four Negroes were elected to the House and one to the Senate in spite of the violent anti-Negro campaign of 1898. This was the largest number of Negroes elected in the 1890's.[2] The triumphant party gained five seats in the United States House of Representatives, while the Republicans retained three and the Populists one.[3] The Second Congressional District re-elected George H. White, Negro.[4]

Henry G. Connor was chosen as speaker of the House and Charles A. Reynolds as president of the Senate. Not one Republican, Populist, or Negro was placed on an important House or Senate committee. So great was the spirit of revenge that one Democrat, on the second day of the session, proposed a resolution to repeal all laws enacted by the Fusionists.[5] The Democrats refused to consider the resolution.[6] Senator Glenn's resolution, that a joint committee be appointed to examine Fusion laws and make the necessary recommendation, was passed.[7]

Governor Russell sensed fully the spirit of the legislature of 1899 and the effectiveness of the cry of Negro office-holding. In his biennial message on January 5, he dedicated himself to the task of explaining his activities in regard to Negro appointments:

By the constitution and laws of the State, the power of appointment to office is vested in the Governor as to many constitutional and statutory offices. It has been charged in the public press in other States, and the impression seems to prevail among many people in various sections of the United States and perhaps, in foreign countries, that North Carolina has been under negro government, and that the Governor of the State has appointed large numbers of colored persons to office. It appears from an account made of the commissions issued from the executive office to persons appointed by the Governor, that I have appointed in the two years [1896-1898] to civil office eight hundred and eighteen (818) persons, of whom not more than eight (8) were colored.[8]

His explanation had no effect upon an Assembly pledged to abolish Fusion handiwork.

The Democratic objectives as stated in the campaign of 1898 were the repeal of the Fusion election law, the abolition of Fusion county and municipal government, and the elimination of Negro domination. There was a fourth objective high on the agenda of legislative activities of 1899, although denied by the Democrats in the campaign, namely, to disfranchise the Negro by a constitutional amendment. The economic needs of the state were subordinate to the Negro question. The speaker of the House chose well the committee to handle the four big questions in true Democratic fashion. On the county and municipal government committee were George Rountree, H. W. Stubbs, Francis D. Winston, "white supremacy" orators; on the election law committee were H. W. Stubbs, Francis D. Winston, Frank Ray, and Locke Craig, "white supremacy" campaigners; and on the constitutional amendment committee were George Rountree, Francis D. Winston, and Lee Overman, "white supremacy" advocates.[9]

The process of disfranchisement had already taken root in the South by 1899. Mississippi and South Carolina provided for disfranchisement in the new state constitutions of 1890 and 1895, respectively; and Louisiana in an Amendment in 1898. These disfranchising provisions were operating unrestricted by court interference.[10] Mississippi and South Carolina had incorporated the educational qualification for voting which required that an elector be able to read and write the constitution, to have paid his poll tax, and to own property; yet, an exception was made for those who could not read, write, or own property if they were able to understand and give a reasonable interpretation of the constitution when it was explained to them. Louisiana had incorporated the educational qualification of reading and writing but also added the "grandfather clause," viz, that electors could vote who voted or whose ancestors voted prior to January 1, 1867. North Carolina faced the task of choosing between the Mississippi-South Carolina plan and the Louisiana plan, or venturing into untried realms of constitutional experiments.

Francis D. Winston, originator of the "white supremacy" clubs of 1898 and solicitor of George H. White's (Negro) aid in securing a judicial appointment in 1890, presented on January 6 in the North Carolina legislature the first suffrage bill designed to disfranchise the Negro.[11] Both Democratic and Republican newspapers reported that the Winston suffrage bill was patterned substantially after the Louisiana disfranchisement amendment with a changed verbiage to suit North Carolina's county and township government in that it required educational and property qualifications, poll tax receipt by March 1 in election years, and an exemption of these qualifications to persons, their sons, and their grandsons who voted prior to 1867 and who served in the army of the United States prior to 1867; the entire amendment bill to be voted on at the general election in 1900.[12]

The original Winston bill was debated, modified, and amended from January 6 to February 17. The Republican press attacked the bill immediately. It contended that "the Democrats are determined that rights and privileges shall be dependent upon property, that money must be respected. The minister of the Gospel who is not blessed with a certain amount of the world's goods, the young man who is starting out in life and those against whom the tide of mis-fortune has set shall no longer be protected by the constitution. It is a bold step toward the supremacy of money over manhood and character."[13] The Populists, gleeful in seeing come to pass what they had prophesied in the campaign of 1898, pointed the old "I-told-you-so" finger at North Carolinians.[14] The Republicans, deriding the Democrats for going back on their campaign pledge of no disfranchisement, stated that "our present legislature is wholly destitute of moral obligations and has deceived the people."[15]

In the meantime, Isaac Smith, Negro legislator from Craven County, seeking an effective means of reducing the severity of the bill, asked that a Negro committee be permitted to appear before the committee on constitutional amendments.[16] Permission was granted and Smith, the Reverend Mr. Leak, and Professor Crosby of Shaw University appeared. Crosby said, "You want to disfranchise enough Negroes to make it certain that good government will prevail. Do that and stop. Do not go to the extent of persecution." The Reverend Mr. Leak stated that "Negroes are allowed to work and earn their money together with whites in the South, but not spend it together, while in the North Negroes are not allowed to make their money together, but can spend it together. I like the condition here better."[17]

The Negroes were not unaware of the motives of the Democratic legislature. Five days after the appearance of the Negro committee, Republican Negroes held a meeting in Raleigh for the purpose of discussing their plight and framing a memorial to be sent to the legislature. The group termed itself the Negro State Council. George H. White, Negro congressman, presided over the meeting and John Dancy, collector of customs of the port of Wilmington, served as secretary. There were eighty-nine delegates present, principally from the eastern counties. Every effort was made by White and some others to secure a resolution advising Negroes to emigrate in case the Democrats "made their stay in North Carolina intolerable," and agreeing that each would aid the other in so emigrating. The Reverend Mr. W. H. R. Leak and Dr. L. A. Scruggs thought the resolution too strong and, upon failure of the group to modify it, left the convention. John Dancy and more conservative elements mustered enough sentiment to delete the threat of emigration. The vote on the resolution resulted in forty-two against it and thirty-sven for it. The Negro State Council sent a memorial to the legislature.[18] A reporter covering the Negro gathering wrote,

Tonight White and Dancy signed an address to the Negroes of North Carolina. Included in this is a memorial to the Legislature asking it not to pass any laws the effect of which would be to 'blunt our aspirations, ruin our manhood and lesson our usefulness as citizens, but guarantee us an equal chance with other men to work out our destiny.' . . . The address urged the negroes not to be too hasty in seeking any changes in their present surroundings and plans but to quietly and industriously fill all contracts with landlords and otherwise, and where necessary, enter into new ones for the current year.[19]

The appearance of a Negro group,[20] for the second time, before the amendment committee and the memorial from the Negro State Council had no effect on the Democratic legislature. On February 16, the final bill was ready for a vote. Smith, Negro, made an open appeal in the House to public opinion by relying heavily upon a mixture of religious warning, constitutional justification, and patriotic fervor: "The King that judgeth the poor his throne shall be established forever. The poor illiterate colored man of North Carolina is to be disfranchised. On the other hand this same poor man is not to be relieved from paying a poll tax, which goes to support a government, which to him has proven false. If this be not taxation without representation, what is it?" He hinted that the federal government might enforce the Fourteenth Amendment and "you would cause this State to become only entitled to five congressmen instead of nine as it now has." Smith implored, "If you, the white people hold all the offices in the State, created by State statute, except such colored men as might be elected to the General Assembly and to Congress, would this give satisfaction? I understand this would. You do not want nor do you need any constitutional amendment to accomplish this end. Remember your word and your promise during the last campaign, that if the Democratic party won, the colored men would not be disfranchised. Of all sad thoughts, the saddest is the very people I have held up to my race as their best friends are now about to disfranchise them."[21]

The Winston *Union Republican* felt that Smith was in error when he termed the Democrats the Negroes' best friends. This paper reasoned that "if it is friendship to the Negro to keep him illiterate and compel him to serve only in the capacity of menial slaves, then their's is friendship. But if it is friendship to the colored race to allow him to cultivate and aid him in developing the natural capacities which the Creator has given him, then their's is not friendship."[22]

On February 17, J. Y. Eaton, Negro from Vance County, urged that his race was steadily becoming more intelligent and should not be penalized for its ignorance: "Wasn't it a law put upon the statute books in North Carolina in 1831 making it a crime for a Negro to learn to read and write? This law was in force until 1865. Now thirty-three years afterward, you are making the result of your own wrong, the pretext for disfranchising the Negro."

J. H. Wright, Negro from Warren County, entered his protest and termed the suffrage bill "a great sledge hammer of political death." W. W. Hampton, white Republican from Surry County, contended that North Carolina was taking a step backward, as universal suffrage prevailed in all the United States except perhaps Rhode Island and Massachusetts. H. S. Williams, white Republican of Yadkin County, said that he knew that nothing he could say or do would have any effect on the result, but he felt that he would be untrue to the trust reposed in him by his people if he did not rise to oppose the suffrage bill. Rountree, Democrat and part-framer of the final bill, read from the constitution of Massachusetts the educational qualification for suffrage and the provision that the descendants of all persons who could vote on May 1, 1867, could vote, adding, "there's not the slightest difference of principle between that law and the one we now have under consideration. Our's is to protect us against ignorant negroes, their's to protect them against ignorant foreigners." Winston, Democrat, closed the debate in the House: "I care not to discuss the constitutional side of this question. Every man who talks of white supremacy must show his faith by his works. Have we so soon forgotten New Bern, Greenville, Tarboro, Wilmington?"[23] By a vote of eighty-one for and twenty-seven against, the suffrage bill went to the Senate.[24]

Opposition in the Senate was mild compared to that in the House. The Democratic senators in their caucus meeting before February 17 had settled their differences on the original Winston suffrage bill. Robert Glenn, of Forsyth, and M. H. Justice, of Rutherford, had opposed the bill on the grounds that the "grandfather clause" would work a tremendous hardship on the western part of the state in that white illiteracy was high in that section, these illiterates would not be literate by 1906, and therefore the "grandfather clause" should be a permanent exemption.[25] The compromise reached by H. G. Connor, Locke Craig, and George Rountree of the House, who felt that permanent exemption was without precedent, was that the "grandfather clause" would become inoperative after December 1, 1908.[26] Senator J. A. Goodwin, a Populist of Chatham County, attempted on February 18 to secure for all disfranchised persons exemption from all civil and military duties and the poll tax.[27] This was lost by a vote of forty-two to six. Senator J. A. Franks, Republican from Swain, sought on the same day to delete the poll tax requirement and was ignored.[28] Some Republicans presented a substitute providing that the Negro be allowed to vote but not hold office.[29] This would not destroy the Negro as a political asset of the white Republicans. An offer to disfranchise, coming from the Democrats, and efforts to disqualify him as an officeholder, coming from his supposed friends the white Republicans, placed the Negro "between the devil and the deep blue sea." Senator T. O. Fuller, Negro, made the last speech in the Senate against the amendment. He opposed it because it was unnecessary, unconstitutional, impractical, impolitic, unwise, unjust, and contrary to the genius and spirit of American institutions. He cited experiences from national and state history to support his opposition.[30] Opposition sentiment to the amendment availed nothing. The final suffrage bill required that every registrant must be able to read and write any section of the constitution in the English language, and must have paid his poll tax by March 1 in the election year, that no male registrant who voted or whose ancestor voted before January 1, 1867, could be disfranchised provided he registered before December 1, 1908, and that the amendment must be submitted to popular referendum in the election of 1900.[31]

T. O. Fuller stated that North Carolina studied the Mississippi, South Carolina, and Louisiana plans but preferred the last. In so far as the Mississippi and South Carolina plans relied strongly upon the literacy test for voting, the Negro senator felt that North Carolina dared not use any scheme which would require property qualification or literacy because "the standard of intelligence among the Negroes of North Carolina was considerably higher than in Mississippi and South Carolina, with referenece to the great agricultural masses; and, too, the thrift of North Carolina Negroes in addition to their education might enable them to qualify under the 'understanding clause,' consequently the Carolinians decided to insert into their Constitution what was known as the Grandfather Clause."[32]

Obviously the bulk of Negroes would be disfranchised as a result of three factors: first, the free Negro who began voting in North Carolina in 1776 was disfranchised in 1835,[33] hence had no official access to the ballot before 1867;[34] second, many Negroes who had white fathers and grandfathers, who voted before 1867, and who would be legally entitled to vote under the "grandfather clause" would find it both difficult and embarrassing to prove their white ancestry, although the color of their skin would be ample evidence; and, third, 47.6 per cent of the adult Negro males, a total of 67,481, were classified as illiterates.[35]

On the very day of the passage of the suffrage bill, the historian, John Spencer Bassett, wrote to his friend:

The "white man's" government is in full blast in this State. They are arranging a suffrage amendment which will disfranchise the Negro and not disfranchise the ignorant whites. At best it is an enameled lie. If it honestly provided for an intellectual standard for suffrage it would be a good thing. It is one more step in the educating of our people that it is right to lie, to steal, and to defy all honesty in order to keep a certain party in power. . . . They introduced a jim crow car law and it will pass. They introduced a jim crow bed law—i. e., a law to prevent white men and negro women occupying the same bed—but that is hung up in the committee. It will not pass for fear it would overthrow the "white man's" government.[36]

Since the suffrage amendment would be submitted to popular vote in the election of 1900, the Democrats set about to frame a Democratic election law. Some wanted a strong election law. Some wanted to resort to the old methods of fraud and intimidation which had proved satisfactory in maintaining "white supremacy." But D. C. Allen, Rountree, and Craig stated emphatically that the old methods would not suffice, and that strong measures were necessary.[37] The result was an election law which resorted to centralized control of election machinery.[38] It prescribed that seven discreet men chosen by the legislature constitute the State Board of Elections which in turn would appoint three men in each county as the County Board of Elections. The county boards would appoint registrars and judges of elections in their counties and alter and creat new precincts unhampered by the Fusion requirement of a precinct voting place for every 350 electors. The judges, not registrars, were to be men of different political parties.

Besides centralized control of election machinery, the Democratic law also facilitated party control of elections by intricate registration procedure. It required that a new registration be made before the election of 1900 and

That in all cases the applicant for registration shall be sworn by the registrar before being registered and shall state and answer his age, place of residence, stating ward if he resides in an incorporated town or city, number of his house if numbered, and if not numbered then a designation of its localities by streets; and if not the owner, then the name of the owner or renter. If not a resident of an incorporated town or city he shall then state his place of residence in the election precinct; and if he is not the owner of the house in which he lives then he shall state the name of the person who does own the same or upon whose land he lives; the time of his residence in the said county, ward or election precinct; his avocation, place of business, where and by whom employed if employed; if new comer from whence he comes, and his post office address before removal; whether he has been disqualified as a voter by judgment or decree of any court, if so by what court reinstated; whether he has listed for taxation his poll for the current year in which he proposes to register, and for the next year preceding . . . and any other questions which may be regarded by the registrar as material upon the question of identity and qualifications of the said applicant . . . if the applicant is duly qualified and entitled to register, the name shall be entered giving his race opposite his name on the registration book.[39]

Such registration requirements in the Southern states led Stephen Weeks to write in the 1890's, "It will be noticed that the complexities of these laws are enough to confuse a mind better trained than that of the average Negro. To him they are beyond comprehension."[40] There were interesting possibilities in the power of the 1899 registrar to ask "any other questions which may be regarded as material upon the question of identity and qualification" of the applicant. The registration books were opened for inspection and challenges on the first Saturday preceding election; however, challenges could be made on election day. This brought about the old system of confusion wherein the "challenged" voter had Monday and Tuesday, election day, to clear himself. Ballots found in the wrong box were void, although the judges of registration deposited the ballots and not the voters. In case of a tie vote, the county board of elections determined the winner, and this was an instrument for Democratic advantages. County canvassers, who counted the total precinct vote and formed abstracts two days after the election, were restored. The Democrats were too well pleased with the intimidation and results of the Red Shirts in the campaign of 1898 to incorporate in their new law the Fusionist prohibition of armed men assembling at the polling places on election day. The election time was changed from November to the first Thursday in August. The Democrats wanted to forestall the possibility of having to defeat national Republican influence in 1900 at the same time it was battling for survival in state politics. The intricate Democratic election law[41] was designed to curb the Fusionist vote and insure victory for the suffrage bill. A Raleigh reporter for the *Charlotte Observer* wrote

A prominent citizen informs me that he had heard that there is a movement on foot to require every grown male in the State to contribute one dollar towards defeating the constitutional amendment. "But," he added, "this will hardly counter balance the loss of 50,000 illiterate votes under the new election law."[42]

The legislature was puzzled as to how to change the Fusion system of county government. Avowedly they were for a change because of Negro office-holding. But the Fusion ideal of popular election of county officers had much appeal for many white Democrats. Predicated upon the assumption that the Fusionists had made a debacle of things, the legislature of 1899 titled their act as one "to restore good government to the counties of North Carolina."[43] The law was simple and terse in form but potent in meaning. Justices of the peace were elevated to the chief positions, county commissioners were subordinates; the legislature appointed the justices of the peace, and this arrangement applied only to Washington, Granville, Caswell, Bertie, Vance, Warren, Craven, Edgecombe, Perquimans, Franklin, Montgomery, Pasquotank, and New Hanover counties. In ten of these thirteen counties, the Negro population was over 50 per cent.[44] The remaining six "black counties" received individual treatment. Halifax, Northampton, Pitt, and Pender were assigned numerous Democratic justices of the peace.[45] Anson was restored to specific legislative control.[46] Hertford with three Republican commissioners, duly elected in 1898, had five additional ones of Democratic persuasion imposed upon the county; and a vote of the majority of the board controlled all action.[47] Scotland, a new "black county" created in 1899 from

THE DEMOCRATIC ELECTION LAW OF 1899:
CENTRALIZATION

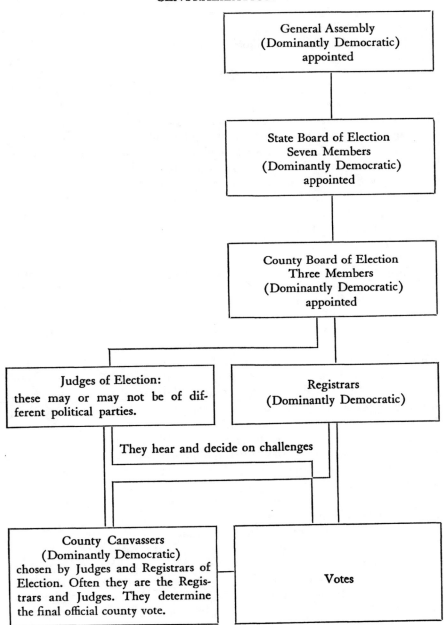

Richmond and Robeson, was granted two Democratic commissioners who had to hold meetings with the commissioners of Richmond and Robeson.[48]

The Democrats made specious and ingenious changes in sixty-five counties including strong centralization in those wherein the Negro was a political factor. The legislature found no uniform way of handling county government. Variations provided by laws included the appointment of county commissioners by the legislature,[49] the popular election of county commissioners,[50] an increase in the number of commissioners,[51] legislative appointments of the justices of the peace,[52] popular election of the justices of the peace,[53] appointment of additional commissioners by the judge of the superior court,[54] election of commissioners by the justices of the peace,[55] and appointment of commissioners by the clerk of the superior court.[56] Thirty-two counties were left undisturbed in the enjoyment of local self-government through popular election of county officials, a tribute to the popularity and idealism of Fusion county government.

The Democratic county government system did not go unchallenged, but the Fusionist minority was ineffective. Republican Snipes, of Hertford, made a spirited protest and called upon Fusionists to support him. Isaac Smith, Negro Republican, shrieked to Snipes that he was well pleased with the Democratic process.[57] The Republicans ordered their protest spread upon the Journal stating that the undemocratic system of Democratic county government was a violation of the rights of free people.[58] A Republican newspaper, seeing Hertford with three legally elected Republican commissioners and a Fusion majority vote over three hundred, stated that the Democratic legislature by appointing five Democratic commissioners was so hungry for the crumbs of public office that "they are practicing legal thievery for offices to which the people have refused to elect them."[59]

There is one factor which raises the question as to the Democrats' intention. Had they intended to muzzle only the sixteen "black counties," they could have provided for popular election of county officials in all save the "black counties," and their actions would have been sanctioned by the constitution of the state and the courts.[60] The very fact that the legislature interfered with the government of "white counties" showed rather conclusively that an important objective was party centralization and Democratic perpetuation. The Negro scare served as an effective smoke screen behind which the Democrats seized governmental control of white Republican as well as Negro counties.

Municipal government suffered from the same irregularities as Democratic county government. Raleigh, Wilmington, New Bern, Edenton, and Greenville had been characterized as under Negro domination during the campaign of 1898. In reality, Raleigh had a bare Negro majority in 1890 and a white majority in excess of 2,000 in 1900. The Democrats allowed Raleigh to retain four wards, which were drastically redistricted; four aldermen from each ward; and a mayor, city clerk, and tax collector elected by the popular vote of the city.[61] The redistricted wards rendered the Republican vote impotent. Thus Raleigh retained popular elections with Democratic domination guaranteed through the use of the gerrymander.

Wilmington was restored to the Democratic system in use there in 1894— five redistricted wards, each electing two aldermen, and the aldermen choosing the mayor.[62] In order to render the incumbent Negro magistrates impuissant, the 1899 provision stated that no person arrested by the city police could be tried before any other person than the mayor. Since Negroes were hesitant to work for whites after the riot, the mayor was empowered to order all tramps and vagrants to find employment within twenty-four hours or leave the city.

So anxious were the Democrats to rid New Bern of its lone Negro councilman and Negro magistrates that they provided a temporary measure whereby five white Democrats—W. Dunn, S. H. Cutter, T. A. Green, K. R. Jones, and G. H. Roberts—were designated as trustees invested with authority to take over and preserve the real, personal, and mixed property of New Bern until further directed by law.[63] Fusionists, whose terms did not expire until 1901, were warned that failure to turn over city property carried a penalty of $500 and six months' imprisonment. Later in the legislative session, New Bern was redistricted and allowed six wards electing two aldermen each who in turn chose the mayor. Fusionist officeholders were warned again that their attempts to maintain offices carried a penalty of $1,000 and one year's imprisonment.[64]

Edenton was allowed to keep four wards which were redistricted, and four councilmen from the four wards chose the mayor from the city at large.[65] Greenville, which had a white majority of 2,400 but also four Negro councilmen during Fusion, was redistricted into five wards, the first and fifth electing one alderman each and the second, third, and fourth two each. The eight aldermen chose a mayor and tax collector.[66] In five towns accused of Negro domination one was allowed to elect the mayor by popular election, and four were compelled to choose theirs by their aldermen. Redistricting insured Democratic supremacy.

In towns and cities where whites outnumbered Negroes, and no Negroes held office, the Democratic changes were made to insure Democratic domination and not specifically "white supremacy." Goldsboro, Durham, Burlington, Kinston, Mt. Airy, Salisbury, and Wilson were redistricted and the powers of the aldermen enlarged.[67] The city of Asheville represented a startling exception in the activities of the Democratic legislature. The city was allowed three aldermen and a mayor, and all major city officials were popularly elected. Fusion officeholders whose terms had not expired were specifically allowed to remain in office until expiration of terms.[68] The Democrats' refusal to alter the provisions of popular election in this white city indicated strongly that they wanted and needed the western part of the state to help them carry the disfranchisement amendment and the election of 1900.

A logical result of the 1898 campaign was the Jim Crow car law, the first of its kind in the state's history since the Civil War. The first segregation bill was styled an act "to promote the comfort of passengers on railroad trains by requiring separate accommodations for the white and colored races."[69] Isaac Smith, Negro, asked that there should be a special prohibition in the bill against officers of the law taking white prisoners into the cars set apart for Negroes.[70] The request was lost. Winston, white Democrat, wanted the bill amended to make it mandatory that all railroads and steamboats should provide separate but equal accommodations for white and colored under such regulations and requirements as the Railroad Commission of the state should establish, and to require that violation be interpreted as misdemeanors.[71] The Winston amendments were lost because railroad influence was too strong in the legislature of 1899 to subject the operation of railroads to a commission which might be hostile. The big question was not whether there was to be such a bill, but how should it be titled. Other titles offered were acts "to provide separate cars for white and black passengers on the railroads of the State," "to promote the comfort of passengers on railroad trains," and "requiring separate accommodations for white and colored races on railroads."[72] The railroads opposed the bill on the grounds that it meant the construction of separate cars, and unnecessary additional expense, and that it would be difficult to make exceptions in cases where the Negroes were travelling as servants of the more favored race.[73] Economic gains, to the railroad interests, were more important than establishing racial barriers in travel. Efforts were made to reduce the objections to segregation by inserting pleasing "catch" phrases into the final measure: "An act to promote the comfort of travellers on railroad trains, and for other purposes." The Jim Crow car law required that there be separate but equal accommodations for the white and colored races either by separate passenger cars or by compartments in passenger cars; that it should not apply to Negro servants in attendance on their employers or to officers or guards transporting prisoners; and that when any coach for one race was completely filled and there was no extra coach for additional passengers, the conductor would set apart a portion of the car of one race for the passengers of the other race.[74]

It has never been fully determined in what respects these separate accommodations shall be equal. It has often been a subject of debate whether it meant an equal number of seats or the same type and quality of accommoda-

tions. Senator T. O. Fuller, Negro Republican, fought the Jim Crow proposal. The execution of the Jim Crow car law justified his later contentions:

It has been noted that the coaches set apart for colored people were not so well
equipped as others; and that the lavatories were neglected and often conveniences
for men and women were very close together. The coaches for colored people are
too often encroached upon by the news Butcher, or conductor, who uses the choice
seats for his own work. The location of the coaches for colored people is usually
near the engine which subjects them to smoke and the dangers that follow wrecks
and collisions.[75]

That Fuller's comments were true was attested by a contemporary who wrote:

After the law went into effect, there was a feeling that the Southern Railway was
trying to enforce it in such a way as to make it so unpopular that its repeal could
be secured. . . . After the law was seen to be permanent, most of the railroads
were indifferent to giving clean cars and equal facilities to their Negro patrons.[76]

The Democratic legislature of 1899 exhibited a different attitude toward
Negro emigration than previous Democratic legislatures. In 1891, it had prevented their leaving through circuitous prohibition. When the industrial
areas of the North and Middle West were anxious to use cheap labor in the
1880's, corporations sent agents south to recruit Negro labor. Tenant farmers,
sharecroppers, and underpaid workers, spurred on by the agricultural depression of the 1880's, began to seek their fortunes elsewhere. North Carolina,
faced with a drain on its labor supply, prohibited Negro emigration by requiring of labor recruiters a license in each county to ply their trade. The
license for operation in each county cost $1,000. The punitive consequences
for violation were a fine not less than $500 and not more than $5,000 or imprisonment in the county jail or in the state prison from four months to two
years for each offense.[77] A state historian describes the situation in these
words:

From the close of the war it had been the habit of white people to express the wish
that all negroes would leave the state, but when a very small movement of the
sort began, there was widespread alarm and angry opposition. The state could not
dispense with negro labor, particularly when it was not being replaced by white
labor. So the negro was at first advised not to leave, and later, when the movement seemed somewhat more serious, almost commanded to stay.[78]

The years between 1891 and 1899 were fitful years in the history of North
Carolina. Senator Fuller, Negro, offered a bill in 1899 to repeal the stringent
provision of 1891.[79] The Senate, weary of the race problem, was ready to

accept the repeal but not from a Negro. Two white Democrats proposed the same bill in the House. The discussion of the bill evoked a variety of comments in the House. Thompson of Onslow County favored the repeal. Democrat Ray of Macon said he thought the present law a good one and that it stopped speculation in labor. Curtis of Buncombe favored the repeal, saying that he didn't care if all the Negroes left the state. Ray, apparently dodging the confession that the white man of North Carolina wanted and needed Negro labor in 1891, rationalized that "the intention of the law in 1891 was good, being so enacted as to prevent all able-bodied laborers from leaving the State, thereby leaving the decrepit as a charge on the community."[80] Council of Watauga stated that the 1891 measure had served its purpose and that he favored repeal. Carraway of Lenoir favored free trade and thought the largest liberty ought to be allowed. Gilliam of Edgecombe stated that the law never represented the opinion of the state, but was enacted peculiarly for the benefit of Edgecombe County. Smith, Negro of Craven, said he favored letting all men go and come as they pleased.[81] The 1891 law was repealed[82] and Fuller was robbed of having the initiative in the repeal. Negroes were considering the question of emigrating.[83]

The legislature elected Democrats to offices held by Fusionists whose terms did not expire until 1901. These cases went to the Supreme Court. In some instances, the legal rights of the incumbents to the offices were upheld by the court over strong Democratic protest. Judge Clark, the lone Democrat in the Fusion court, was the only member who dissented from the majority opinion at times. In thirty-nine office-holding cases, he alone gave twelve dissenting opinions.[84] Fuller, the Negro senator, declared that Fusionist officeholders were made to resign by extraordinary pressure and when places were not vacated by this method, the legislature either abolished the offices or changed the names of them modifying the duties so as to give the appearance of legal procedure.[85]

Professor John Spencer Bassett was not in error when he wrote his friend that the Democrats had introduced a Jim Crow bed law, to prevent white men and Negro women from occupying the same bed, and that it was hung up in the committee.[86] Francis Winston of Bertie County meant to go all the way in the separation of the races when he proposed, on January 21, "to punish fornication and adultery between the negroes and whites by jail imprisonment of not less than four months or penitentiary imprisonment of not more than five years, and make the violation a felony."[87] The bill was referred to the Committee on the Judiciary. One week later, Winston presented the bill again, and this time it was placed on the Calendar.[88] Although the bill passed its first, second, and third readings, and was ordered engrossed and to be sent to the Senate, a "clincher" was put on it by a motion to reconsider and lay it on the table.[89] The motion carried. What had happened was that the bill had evoked considerable comment. The vote of sixty-two for and twenty-four against the bill evidenced the lack of unanimity in the actual desire to separate the races. A vocal minority had protested. A Raleigh reporter for *The Union Republican* summarized the protest as follows: "A fight occurred in the House on Saturday over the bill to prevent co-habitation of the Caucasian and negro races. The bill was savagely fought by almost every leading Democrat, especially the eastern ones, such as Judge Allen of Wayne, Rountree of New Hanover, Gilliam of Edgecombe, Gattis of Orange, Ray of Macon, and Justice and Council from the west. Representatives Petree and Williams, Republicans, twitted the Democrats with fighting a bill that looked to the real separation of the races. Justice of McDowell made the astounding charge that there was hardly any one in the House who had not in his life been guilty of this sin; and of all the Democratic members, only three plead exemption of the charge."[90]

On February 3, Winston's co-habitation bill which had passed the House with a majority vote was referred to the original committee. It decided that "the prevalence of this crime in North Carolina does not warrant the passage of the bill."[91] Although the Democratic legislature felt that the prevalence of the crime of miscegenation did not warrant a statute, George H. White, Negro congressman from the Second District, simultaneously announced in the United States House of Representatives that the increasing number of mulattoes was ample evidence that the crime of co-habitation between the races was great in the entire Southland, and White invited his fellow congressmen to follow him to his home, North Carolina, to witness the results for themselves.[92]

The Republican press did not fail to chide the Democratic legislature for its failure to pass the Winston bill. It stated that, "You wanted a complete separation of the races, and loudly did you boast in the campaign of how you would separate them. And yet you refuse to suppress that crime which is responsible for the existence of a mixed race."[93]

The last discussion of racial implication undertaken by the legislature of 1899 was the attempt to clarify an earlier Fusion statute. A law of 1897 granted unclaimed cadavers to the medical colleges in the state. In so far as the Leonard School of Medicine (Negro), a division of Shaw University, Raleigh, enjoyed this privilege, Democratic condemnation held that such a loosely worded law allowed white bodies to go to the Negro school and evidenced the Fusion theory of racial equality.[94] A spirited discussion arose in 1899 when the Democrats presented their version of the "dissection bill." The *News and Observer* titled the discussion "Boiling Bones."[95] The complete racial separation of cadavers, however, was not effected until 1903.[96]

The Democrats wanted to make an attempt at railroad regulation and thereby assure themselves that never again would the Populists have the cry of discrimination in railroad rates as a reason for leaving the Democratic fold. They abolished the railroad commission[97] and established a corporation commission with wider powers for administration but no punitive powers to curb railroad influence.[98] Special rates, rebates, and receiving greater or lesser compensation than what the law allowed were deemed unjust discriminations. The appearance of the law was more stringent than the application.[99]

The legislature of 1899, in dismantling the Fusion edifice, amended or repealed thirty-three sections of the North Carolina Code[100] and one hundred fifty-three public laws of 1895 and 1897.[101] A summary of what happened to Fusion legislation is found in these words of Locke Craig: "We effected the great transformation and went home. Within six months there were scarcely an act of that great body left; a few stock laws, some bills to protect fish in Hanging Dog Creek, a few dispensary bills and acts of incorporation."[102] Henry G. Connor, speaker of the House, who supported ratification of the suffrage amendment although he was not enthusiastic about all the provisions, stated aptly the concerted opinion of the Democratic legislators with reference to the proposed amendment:

That it is not perfect none know better or appreciate more fully than ourselves; that it is the best possible outcome of the situation, we believe to be true. We also believe that it is the basis upon which we may be able to build a safe, stable and intelligent system of suffrage in this State. We submit it to the people for their ratification.[103]

The legislature did not adjourn *sine die* but closed to meet in an adjourned session on June 12, 1900.[104]

NOTES TO CHAPTER TWELVE

1. *Appletons' Annual Cyclopedia*, Third Series, III (1898), 512. Names listed in *House Journal*, 1899, 7-11; *Senate Journal*, 1899, 506.

2. *Supra*, Chap. VII.

3. *Biographical Directory of the American Congress 1774-1927*, 463. Party affiliations obtained from biographical sketches in the Directory.

4. *Supra*, Chap. VI, 84-89.

5. *House Journal*, 1899, 25.

6. Locke Craig, Democratic member of the House in 1899, later Governor, 1913-17, stated that it was Dan Hugh McLane, of Harnett County, who desired to repeal all Fusion laws at one stroke; and Craig further added in true Democratic satire "but the Legislature thought those laws should be treated as well as Sodom was treated. You remember that God promised to spare Sodom if there were five righteous men in the city, and we thought that peradventure there might be five righteous laws in the whole lot, so we spared them as a whole."—*Memoirs and Speeches of Locke Craig*, 32-33.

7. *Senate Journal*, 1899, 13.

8. *Public Documents,* 1899, Document No. 1, Governor's Biennial Message to The General Assembly Session of 1899, 23.

9. *House Journal,* 1899, 1279, 1278, 1278.

10. Frank Johnson, "Suffrage and Reconstruction in Mississippi," Mississippi Historical Society *Publications,* VI (1902), 220-23; David D. Wallace, *The South Carolina Constitution of 1895,* 22; and *Constitution of Louisiana* (1898), 79.

11. *House Journal,* 1899, 49.

12. *The Union Republican,* January 12, 1899; *News and Observer,* January 7, 1899. It was characteristic of some Southern state constitutions to include an "old soldier" clause in the disfranchisement provisions. The preservation of suffrage rights to illiterate Confederate veterans was the motive which inspired the clause. The original Winston bill, section 7, used the phrase "United States Army" and the writer has found no explanation for it. Such a phrase was deleted from the final disfranchisement amendment as submitted to the North Carolina electorate in 1900.

13. *The Union Republican,* January 12, 1899.

14. *Caucasian,* January 29, 1899.

15. *The Union Republican,* January 19, 1899.

16. *House Journal,* 1899, 83.

17. *Charlotte Observer,* January 14, 1899.

18. *Charlotte Observer,* January 19, 1899.

19. *Ibid.*

20. Some participants of the group: W. A. Byrd, C. S. Brown, John Crosby, J. H. Hannor, E. A. Johnson, C. E. Lane, R. B. McRay, A. M. Moore.—*News and Observer,* January 19, 1899.

21. *Charlotte Observer,* February 16, 1899.

22. *The Union Republican,* January 19; February 23, 1899.

23. *Ibid.,* February 18, 1898: Debate in the House of Representatives. The original address of J. Y. Eaton against the proposed Amendment is in the possession of Mrs. J. Y. Eaton, Henderson, North Carolina.

24. *House Journal,* 1899, 655.

25. *Charlotte Observer,* February 10, 1899.

26. *Ibid.,* February 12, 1899.

27. *Senate Journal,* 1899, 493, 494-95.

28. *Ibid.*

29. *Ibid.*

30. Fuller, *Twenty Years in Public Life 1890-1910,* 80-91.

31. *Public Laws,* 1899, Chap. 218, 341-43.

32. Fuller, *A Pictorial History of the American Negro,* 281-82.

33. John Hope Franklin, *The Free Negro in North Carolina,* 101-19.

34. "Even though the free Negro was disfranchised in 1835, when issues were slim and the aspirants of small stature, the electioneers pulled the free Negro vote out of the proverbial closet and not infrequently assisted in sounding the death knell of this or that candidate."—*Ibid.,* 120.

35. United States Department of Commerce, *Bureau of Census,* I, Part I (1900), Table 92, 992-93.

36. John Spencer Bassett to Herbert Baxter Adams, February 18, 1899 (photostatic copy from Herbert Baxter Adams' Correspondence preserved at Johns Hopkins University), Duke University Library Manuscript Collection; also published in Holt, "Historical Scholarship in the United States, 1876-1901: As Revealed in the Correspondence of Herbert Baxter Adams," 265-67.

37. *Charlotte Observer*, January 11, 1899.

38. *Public Laws*, 1899, Chap. 507, 658-687.

39. *Ibid.*, 660.

40. Stephen Weeks, "The History of Negro Suffrage in the South," *Political Science Quarterly*, IX (1894), 695.

41. See chart, 186.

42. *Charlotte Observer*, March 14, 1899.

43. *Public Laws*, 1899, Chap. 488, 641.

44. Negro population:

	1890	*1900*
Bertie	58.9	57.6
Caswell	58.6	54.6
Craven	65.1	60.2
Edgecombe	64.7	62.4
Franklin	49.0	49.5
Granville	50.5	51.1
Montgomery	20.1	25.9
New Hanover	58.0	50.8
Pasquotank	51.6	51.4
Perquimans	49.2	49.6
Vance	63.4	58.5
Warren	69.6	68.5
Washington	51.4	50.6

45. *Public Laws*, 1899, Chap. 515, 701-4; Chap. 700, 887; Chap. 731, 902; Chap. 346, 477.

46. *Ibid.*, Chap. 292, 434; Chap. 428, 567.

47. *Ibid.*, Chap. 145, 271-73.

48. *Ibid.*, Chap. 127, 256-62.

49. *Ibid.*, Chap. 301, 440; Chap. 241, 362; Chap. 167, 308.

50. *Ibid.*, Chap. 467, 593.

51. *Ibid.*, Chap. 187, 320; Chap. 297, 437; Chap. 346, 477.

52. *Ibid.*, Chap. 179, 316; Chap. 181, 316; Chap. 202, 330-31; Chap. 204, 331.

53. *Ibid.*, Chap. 519, 712.

54. *Ibid.*, Chap. 333, 470.

55. *Ibid.*, Chap. 166, 308.

56. *Ibid.*, Chap. 297, 437-38.

57. *News and Observer*, January 18, 1899.

58. *House Journal*, 1899, 755-57.

59. *The Union Republican*, January 18, 1899.

60. *Harriss et al. v. Wright et al., North Carolina Reports*, CXXI, 156-63.

61. *Private Laws*, 1899, Chap. 153, 325-60.

62. *Ibid.*, Chap. 213, 591-96.

63. *Ibid.*, Chap. 30, 30-31.

64. *Ibid.*, Chap. 82, 151-66.

65. *Ibid.*, Chap. 48, 64-66.

66. *Ibid.*, Chap. 115, 222-32.

67. *Ibid.*, Chap. 171, 422-39; Chap. 235, 647-67; Chap. 200, 552-58; Chap. 180, 455-76; Chap. 324, 905; Chap. 186, 483-523; Chap. 297, 832.

68. *Ibid.*, Chap. 239, 672-82.

69. *House Journal,* 1899, 736.

70. *Ibid.,* 736.

71. *Ibid.,* 737.

72. *Ibid.,* 512-13.

73. Col. Warren G. Elliott, President of the Wilmington and Weldon Railroad, made a spirited defense on behalf of the Railroad interests.—*News and Observer,* January 25, 1899.

74. *Public Laws,* 1899, Chap. 384, 539-40.

75. Thomas O. Fuller, *Bridging the Racial Chasm,* 10.

76. Josephus Daniels, *Editor in Politics,* 331-32.

77. *Public Laws,* 1891, Chap. 75, 77.

78. Hamilton, *History of North Carolina Since 1860,* 205.

79. *Senate Journal,* 1899, 58.

80. *The Union Republican,* January 12, 1899.

81. *Ibid.*

82. *Public Laws,* 1899, Chap. 381, 536.

83. The *Charlotte Observer* carried in its issues of March, April, May, and June, 1899, reports of Negro meetings and Negro speakers on the question of emigration. That the Negro threat of emigration concerned prominent white Democrats is attested by the excerpt from the address: *The Problem of The Hour: Will The Colored Race Save Itself From Ruin* by Julian S. Carr, an address delivered at the Commencement Exercises before the Trustees, Faculty, and students of the North Carolina College of Agriculture and Mechanic Arts for Negroes, Greensboro, North Carolina, May 1899, Duke University Library Pamphlet Collection.

"I violate no confidence when I tell you that I am regarded as a friend of the black man in this State, and these are times of unrest in your race. But you may confide in my words, when I declare to you that the home best suited for the black man, everything considered, and beyond all comparison, is the Southland."—33.

84. See Appendix, 237-38.

85. Fuller, *A Pictorial History of the American Negro,* 278.

86. *Supra,* 191-92.

87. *The Union Republican,* January 26, 1899.

Listed in the *House Journal* 1899, 177, as H.B. 461 to amend Section 1041 of The Code.

88. *House Journal,* 1899, 267.

89. *Ibid.,* 274-75.

90. *The Union Republican,* February 2, 1899.

91. *Ibid.,* February 9, 1899.

92. *Congressional Record,* Fifty-sixth Congress, First Session, XXXIII, Part 2, 1507, 2151-54.

93. *The Union Republican,* March 23, 1899.

94. *Supra,* Chap. IV, 63.

95. *News and Observer,* January 11, 1899.

96. *Public Laws,* 1903.

97. The Railroad Commission was under indictment because Governor Russell dismissed James W. Wilson and S. Otho Wilson, railroad commissioners, inasmuch as they were charged with tainted influence in the railroad interest. The legislature of 1899 reinstated these Democrats, then gave them the opportunity to resign.—*House Journal,* 1899, Joint Session, 1093-97. The majority of the Democrats present knew the men were guilty, but Republican Russell was their target.

98. *Public Laws,* 1899, Chap. 164, 291-307.

99. Simmons admitted that a harsher measure was under consideration, and he personally had to remind the committee of the campaign pledge. Rippy (ed.), *Furnifold Simmons, Statesmen of the New South,* 29.

100. *Public Laws,* 1899, 997-98.

101. *Ibid.,* xi-xxiv; the number would be larger if the writer were to enumerate all Private Laws amended or repealed.

102. May F. Jones (ed.), *Memoirs and Speeches of Locke Craig,* 61.

103. *House Journal,* 1899, 1260.

104. *Ibid.,* 1263.

CHAPTER THIRTEEN

THE ELECTION OF 1900 AND DISFRANCHISEMENT

THE DAWN OF THE TWENTIETH CENTURY found the political parties in North Carolina contending for supremacy. The press of the state had intermittently built up sentiment for and against the suffrage amendment during the summer and fall of 1899. North Carolina politics reverberated in the halls of the United States Congress. Jeter C. Pritchard, Republican of North Carolina, introduced into the United States Senate on January 8 the resolution "that enactment by any State which confers the right to vote upon any of its citizens because of their descent from certain persons or classes of persons, and exclude other citizens because they are not descended from certain persons or classes of persons, having all the qualifications prescribed by law, in the opinion of the Senate is violation of the fourteenth and fifteenth amendments to the constitution of the United States."[1] Populist Senator Marion Butler, of North Carolina, who was constantly at odds with Pritchard because the former was a silver and anti-trust man and the latter was a gold and high tariff man, joined hands with Pritchard on the manhood suffrage question as it related to North Carolina. The resolution was defeated. Pritchard offered it again on January 22, and Butler again supported him. The resolution evoked a spirited debate and Southern senators whose states had already incorporated a disfranchisement amendment delivered philippics against the resolution. Senators H. DeSoto Money of Mississippi, Benjamin R. Tillman of South Carolina, Samuel D. McNery of Louisiana, and John T. Morgan of Alabama[2] fought the resolution with might and main. Again it was defeated. On February 6, Butler discussed manhood suffrage in North Carolina and declared that the suffrage bill was unconstitutional and a broken pledge of the Democratic party, adding further, "if there had been any negro domination then the popular thing to have done to secure votes would have been to promise the people to devise some scheme to limit suffrage as soon as they got to power. Did they do that? No!"[3] The Populists in North Carolina submitted the suffrage bill to numerous senators in the United States Senate and asked for written replies. The replies were published, at least those which the Populists desired to publish, stating that the amendment was unconstitutional in its entirety, but, if technicalities availed, the educational test might remain valid but the "grandfather clause" would fall.[4] This very analysis had been arrived at by the Populists in the state and had been their chief point of attack against the suffrage bill during the first six months of 1900.[5] The Democrats in the state were not unaware of the reverberations from the nation's capital nor could they be complacent about the rumor that Pritchard had urged President McKinley to supply federal troops to supervise the election of 1900.

The Democratic state convention met on April 11 in Raleigh. Furnifold Simmons, titular leader of the party and aspirant for the United States Senate, sounded the keynote of the coming campaign when he reminded the group that one thousand Negroes held office two years before, that a few Negro magistrates whose terms had not expired remained yet, and that Negro rule in North Carolina must cease.[6] The theme of the campaign of 1900 was unmistakably set forth—"white supremacy." Charles Brantley Aycock, who had demonstrated his oratorical ability in the campaign of 1898, was chosen as gubernatorial nominee; W. D. Turner, lieutenant governor; J. Bryan Grimes, secretary of state; B. R. Lacy, auditor; B. F. Dixon, auditor; and R. D. Gilmer, attorney general.[7] The platform urged adoption of the suffrage amendment, condemned Negro rule, and praised the Democratic administrations since 1876.[8]

The remnants of the Populist party met on April 18 in Raleigh and chose Cyrus Thompson and A. C. Shuford to head the ticket. Butler had admonished the party as early as January 8 to fuse with the Republicans,[9] but no official action was taken at the convention. The platform denounced the suffrage amendment on the grounds that the only part of it which would remain valid would be the literacy test and that this would not only disfranchise native whites, but would dignify the right of suffrage with the most vicious, troublesome, and obnoxious class of Negroes. It also denounced the legislature of 1899 for denying local self-government; affirmed the basic fact that the Populist party in North Carolina was a white man's party; proposed the elimination of Negro office-holding by amending the state constitution to read "that all negroes and all persons of negro descent to the third generation inclusive are disqualified for office"; and pointed out that since the Supreme Court of the state had declared in the *Harriss* v. *Wright* case that the General Assembly could provide local self-government for white counties, towns, and cities and maintain a legislative system of control for "black counties," the white people through this arrangement would always have complete control.[10]

The Republicans met in convention on May 1 in Raleigh. Spencer B. Adams was chosen as candidate for governor and Claudius Dockery for secretary of state. The Republicans again as in 1896 had a skeletal ticket. The platform denounced the Democratic allegation of Negro rule and maintained that it had never existed in North Carolina; it denounced the suffrage amendment as unconstitutional and an abrogation of the state's pledge when readmitted into the Union after the Civil War; it denounced the Democrats for violation of local self-government; it denounced the election of 1898 as one of fraud, intimidation, and violence; and it endorsed fusion administration.[11]

The campaign which followed the political convention highlighted the suffrage amendment and "Negro domination." The Democrats had sent Josephus Daniels to Louisiana in early May to report on how the disfranchisement worked there. The party leadership thought the visit advisable since North Carolina had patterned its "grandfather clause" after Louisiana's. Daniels reported that the Louisiana plan of suffrage had put politics on a higher plane, left no necessity for fraud, caused the Populists to return to the Democratic party, liberated white women from black tyranny, eliminated the ignorant Negro from politics, and provided all white men with the ballot.[12] These reports were used by "white supremacy" orators to show that North Carolina needed a disfranchisement amendment. Louisiana's suffrage law had not been tested before the courts; hence, the North Carolina Democrats found themselves searching for arguments which would substantiate the constitutionality of their proposed amendment. Some Republican lawyers in the state questioned the constitutionality of both parts of the amendment, while some Democratic lawyers held that it was constitutional in its entirety.[13] Marion Butler wrote Furnifold Simmons on April 10 asking him for a joint debate at any place in the state so the public could hear both sides at the same time. Simmons declined the invitation; thereupon, Butler heralded the invitation and the refusal to the public and accused Simmons of fear of a public discussion.[14]

The Democrats tried to make it appear that if the public endorsed disfranchisement, then it was opposed to Negro domination, and vice versa. The Democrats stood four square in support of their measure. The Republicans stood four square against it. The Populists chose the middle ground of attack, that courts would leave only the literacy test standing and illiterate whites would thereby be disfranchised. The issue of a literacy test fell upon fertile soil in areas where white illiteracy ran high. The census reports of 1890 classified 60.1 per cent of the Negro and 23.1 per cent of the white population as illiterate; and those of 1900, 47.6 per cent Negro and 19.5 per cent white.[15] A further analysis reveals that North Carolina's male adult literate Negro population was 59,597 and illiterate 67,481. The male adult literate white population was 232,478, and illiterate 54,334.[16] Hence, one-fifth of the white adult and more than one-half of the Negro adult population were illiterate.[17] It would not be fair to say that every white and colored male adult voted in the 1890's, since the aggregate number of male adults of both races totalled 417,578[18] while the total gubernatorial votes in 1892, 1896, and 1900 were 280,500, 330,196, and 312,916, respectively.[19] If the Supreme Court should overthrow the "grandfather clause" and leave the literacy test standing, the true application of that test would have disfranchised 54,334 whites, and this would have been a terrible political blunder. The Democrats further realized that 59,597 literate Negroes alone, supporting the Republicans and Populists, would be an effective aid to further Fusion political victory.

George Rountree, upon hearing intimations that the Supreme Court might invalidate the "grandfather clause" dismissed them nonchalantly in 1899 with these words: "Your committee did not think this worthy of consideration."[20] By summer, 1900, the ghost of judicial invalidation had become more real, and the Democrats were far from being nonchalant. To offset the danger of white disfranchisement and to weaken the attack of the opposition on the amendment, the legislature met in adjourned session on June 12 to 14, July 24, and July 30 and sought, by amending the suffrage law, to block judicial overthrow of their suffrage plans:

That this amendment to the constitution is presented and adopted as one indivisible plan for the regulation of the suffrage, with the intent and purpose to so connect the different parts, and to make them so dependent upon each other, that the whole shall stand or fall together.[21]

The *Democratic Handbook* admitted that the legislature deemed it expedient to set at rest all such groundless apprehensions by proposing an entire and indivisible plan of suffrage and that, by such legislative action, the prop was knocked from beneath the Fusionists who sought to defeat the amendment by saying the courts would hold inoperative the "grandfather clause" and leave the literacy clause.[22] The poll tax requirement for registration and the proviso for all whites to register under the "grandfather clause" prior to December 1, 1908, remained.

The adjourned session augmented the cumbersome and latitudinous election law of 1899. To the long list of registration requirements were added the registrant's place of birth and proof of his identity to the satisfaction of the registrar,[23] where formerly the oath of two witnesses sufficed to substantiate both. The Democrats hailed this change as very necessary.[24] The legislature feared an interpretation of their election law by the Supreme Court of the state which had a Republican-Populist majority. Hence, they specified that no judge could restrain an election official by mandamus or injunction from performing his duties until the fact had been submitted to a jury at a regular term of the superior court and that, when a jury had found the facts and the judge issued a restraining order, the election official had the right to appeal to the state Supreme Court and continue to perform his election duties until the Supreme Court had pronounced a decision.[25]

The intent was to restrain the courts in checking on the activities of election officials, or at least to make the court's participation so long and drawn out that the election would be over before it could compel a registrar to do his duty. While Democratic sources stated that the changes were designed to restrain the courts, Senator Pritchard claimed that the Democratic legislature's attention was directed to the courts because of a Republican conference held in Greensboro in June before the meeting of the Adjourned Session. Jeter C. Pritchard, A. E. Holton, R. S. Linney, and W. P. Bynum agreed in the Greensboro conference that, since the Democratic election law gave unlimited power to the registrar, the Republican voters could by mandamus compel him to place their names on the registration books.[26] The repercussions from this conference supposedly spurred the Democrats to render court interference in elections ineffectual.

Johnson, Populist from Sampson County, made futile efforts on June 13 to obtain amendments providing for county election boards nominated by three political parties, a precinct for every four hundred voters, poll-holders upon request to put ballots in the proper boxes, and appeals from the decisions of the registrars. Johnson was not trying to protect the Negro voter, for he declared "the white people should and would rule. The election law would disfranchise not only the negroes in the east, but a great many white people in the State. I am not here to defend the negroes, they ought never to have been given the right of suffrage when they were." Isaac Smith, Negro Republican from Craven County, and an aggressive controversialist, asked Johnson specifically, "Do you represent the idea of the Populist party when you say the Negro has no right to vote?" Johnson evaded the issue. Smith, exaggerating some of the facts in the case but justified because of the fusion agreement of 1900, added,

The gentleman from Sampson holds a certificate and warms his seat now by the votes from my race. His party—if he has a party—has in the United States Senate today a representative that is there by negro vote. I refer to Senator Butler, whom we put there in connection with your little part. . . . For you we've done much, and you might at least keep quiet, or at most, not say more against us than Amen when somebody else abuses us.[27]

The Democrats used this polemic argument between Populist Johnson and Republican Smith in the campaign to their own advantage. It was set forth as proof that "even the Populists did not favor negro rule."[28] Senator Fuller, Negro, protested without avail that the election law "made it possible for the will of the majority of the people of North Carolina to be thwarted by an organized minority."[29]

During the meeting of the adjourned session, Governor Russell was asked to express himself on the suffrage amendment. He replied:

No, I shall not vote for it. I am against it for many reasons. One good reason is enough. That one is that it violates the fifteenth amendment. . . . It will be adopted and unless restrained by the Federal courts it will be put into operation . . . with a free and fair vote it would be defeated. There is no way to prevent it, the Democratic managers have got passion and prejudice aroused and have established a reign of terror in many localities.

Then came the question to him: "Will the negroes try to register?"

No, I do not believe they will to any great extent. My advice to the colored people is to let the amendment thing alone. They are helpless. Let them leave it to the whites. It is going to be adopted and remain so until set aside by the courts and their opposition only makes bitterness against them and puts them in peril. I advised against the policy of permitting this amendment to be made a party issue.[30]

The Democrats, in urging the adoption of the amendment, used an effective document in the form of a catechism designed to answer all objections to the measure. A sample will illustrate the nature of the campaign document:

Question: Will the Amendment, if adopted, disfranchise the negro?
Answer: The chief object of the Amendment is to eliminate the ignorant and irresponsible negro vote. . . . There are . . . between eighty and ninety thousand negroes who will be disfranchised by the educational clause.
Question: Will the Amendment disfranchise the uneducated white man?
Answer: Why, certainly not . . . it gives every white man who registers before December, 1908, the right to vote for all time thereafter, though he may never know a letter in the book or become able to write a word.[31]

The insertion of the indivisibility clause into the suffrage amendment caused the Fusionists to shift the emphasis of their attack upon the amendment. While continuing to hold that the entire plan of suffrage was unconstitutional, they projected the fear that, if it should be held operative, illiterate whites and their illiterate descendants would be disfranchised after 1908.[32]

A Negro periodical of the state added its bit of condemnation to the amendment. It reasoned that, if North Carolina had put a limited education within the reach of all and then disfranchised Negroes because they had failed to take advantage thereof, no rational colored citizen would have had the slightest objection. But to foster illiteracy for years and then punish that illiteracy by constitutional enactment, denying the right of franchise to one race because it could not read and write, yet granting it to another race similarly circumstanced because its ancestors voted, was a travesty on justice.[33]

Irrespective of the legislature's indivisible plan of suffrage, the catechism's defense, and the cry of Negro domination, the Democrats were not assured of maximum white support at the polls. "White supremacy" orators took to the field in June and did not cease until election. Charles Brantley Aycock of Wayne County, the Democratic gubernatorial candidate, opened the campaign at Laurinburg, a campaign which forced him to travel 4,000 miles by railroad and 1,000 miles by buggy to deliver more than a hundred speeches heard by 75,000 people.[34] The campaign speeches of Aycock deserve special analysis. When he delivered his acceptance of the gubernatorial nomination on April 11, in Raleigh, the burden of that address was centered on Negro domination, the unfitness of the Negro to govern, and the need of good government.[35] Aycock began his tour of the western part of the state on April 16, at which time he stated in Burlington, "The issues we are discussing this year amount to but one thing, the negro question."[36] His subsequent addresses at Winston, Greensboro, Hickory, Asheville, Murphy, Bryson City, Waynesville, Shelby, and Charlotte on April 17, 18, 19, 21, 23, 24, 26, and 28, respectively, rehearsed the necessity of the disfranchisement amendment as the only suitable instrument to eliminate the ignorant Negro from politics.[37] Aycock returned to the eastern part of the state and on May 2, 4, 5, and 8, emphasized at Wilmington, New Bern, Elizabeth City, and Washington the evils of Negro rule.[38] His addresses in the eastern part of the state were devoted to Negro officeholders and the need of good government and in the western part of the state to the necessity of the disfranchisement amendment.

Counties in the western part of the state, with high percentages of illiteracy, became apprehensive of an amendment which would deny the ballot to white illiterates who had not registered by 1908 and to their children who might be illiterate after 1908. Aycock was cognizant of these western repercussions and was forced, from June 26 through July 15, to retell the Democratic story in the western part of the state. While the tenor of his speeches partook of the evils of Negro domination, Aycock found himself spending less time in abusing Negro officeholders and more time making the disfranchisement amendment palliative by promising that no white child would be disfranchised by 1908 because of the lack of an education. He said in Waynesville, a western town, "If you vote for me I want you to do so with the distinct understanding that I shall devote the four years of my official term to upbuilding the public schools of North Carolina. I shall endeavor for every white child in the State to get an education."[39] He said in Asheville, another western city, "You are to ignore the Republican talk that white children, now under thirteen, will be disfranchised after 1908 if they cannot read and write. If I am elected, my administration pledges itself to abolish illiteracy."[40]

The sudden emphasis which Aycock gave to education in the western part of the state was the direct result of the rising fear on the part of white illiterate voters that the restrictive provision of the amendment limiting their registration to 1908 would work a hardship on future illiterate white children. It is to be remembered that western Democrats had urged at the time of the passage of the suffrage bill that there should be no time limit assigned to registration.[41] The Fusionists lost no opportunity in playing up the fact that, after 1908, the illiterate white man stood on the same footing with the illiterate Negro.[42] Western repercussions forced the Democratic party to scrutinize more carefully the "1908 provision for registration limitation." A large number of Democrats feared that they might lose the election, and there arose an agitation to delete the provision from the amendment. Aycock's biographers stated that the gubernatorial candidate "was in the midst of his campaign in the western part of the State where he was devoting much of his time advocating it. When he learned of the movement to have it struck out he promptly declared his opposition to such a course in terms that could not be misunderstood. He accepted the nomination, he asserted, with the understanding that the Democratic platform was a solemn pledge to the people that the Amendment would be submitted to them as adopted by the legislature" and "if his party should repudiate its pledge by making the proposed change in the Amendment, he would withdraw from the campaign."[43] The result was that the "1908 registration limitation" remained, but the succeeding campaign speeches of Charles B. Aycock were more than ever dedicated to the promise that the schools of the state would be opened for four months out of every year, and the white boy who could not vote by 1908 would have no excuse.[44]

If the Democratic party had wanted to show its high and noble impulse for a better educational system, then it would have done so from March, 1899, when the suffrage bill was first ratified, to June, 1900. The very omission of any reference in the campaign speeches of such "white supremacy" orators as Locke Craig,[45] Furnifold Simmons,[46] and Alfred M. Waddell[47] to a promised educational renaissance, and a comparison of Aycock's speeches in the eastern part of the state before June 10 with those in the western part of the state after June 10[48] evidence the fact that the Democratic party had been forced by political expediency to make public education a cornerstone of the Democratic campaign of 1900.[49]

As election time neared, the Red Shirts appeared again in the heavily populated "black counties." They prevented Republican speakers from appearing and, at times, used strong measures.[50] "White supremacy" clubs organized again, as in 1898, but this time the issue of Negro office-holding was linked with an appeal to vote for the amendment. The lines between the pro-amendment and the anti-amendment forces were drawn sharply.

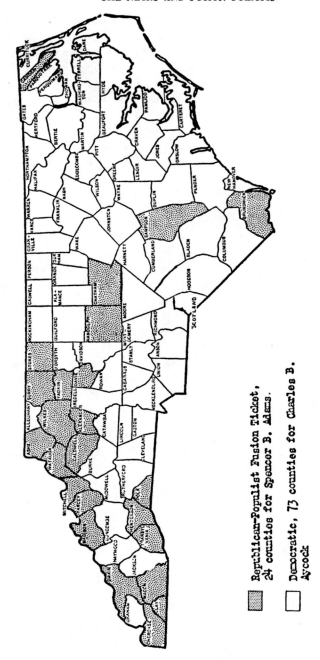

GUBERNATORIAL ELECTION, 1900
(*North Carolina Manual*, 1913, 1005-6)

Republican-Populist Fusion Ticket, 24 counties for Spencer B. Adams.

Democratic, 73 counties for Charles B. Aycock

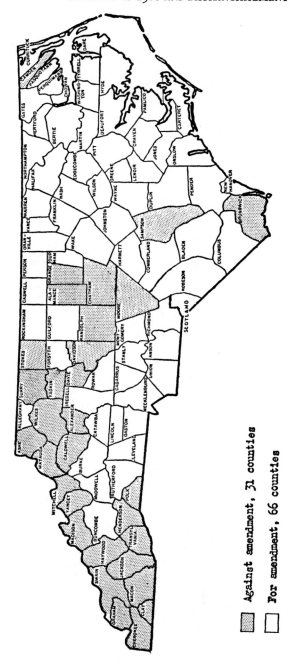

Against amendment, 31 counties

For amendment, 66 counties

VOTE ON DISFRANCHISEMENT AMENDMENT, 1900

(*North Carolina Manual*, 1913, 1016-18)

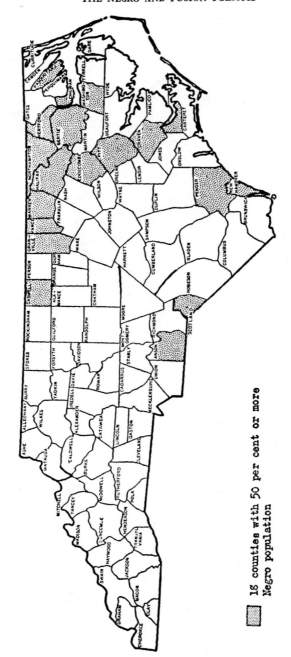

BLACK COUNTIES, 1900

(United States Bureau of Census, *Negro Population, 1790-1915*, 784, 785)

18 counties with 50 per cent or more
Negro population

The Democratic agencies propagated the idea that a vote against the amendment was tantamount to a vote favoring Negro rule. Such an hypothesis placed some Democrats and many Republicans in a dilemma.

The August election returned a Democratic victory, 186,650 votes for Aycock and 126,296 for Adams.[51] The popular electorate returned 182,217 votes for the suffrage amendment and 128,285 against it.[52] Aycock carried seventy-three counties, yet only sixty-six of these voted for the amendment. Adams carried twenty-four counties, yet thirty-one voted against the amendment. The seven counties evidenced a dislike for the Republican nominee, yet favored the nominee's platform; and likewise favored Aycock, yet disliked his platform, clearly indicating that the suffrage question had cut across party lines.[53] The thirty-one counties which voted against the amendment were "white counties," located in the central and western parts of the state. When it is reflected that the campaign of 1898 and the repercussions of the Wilmington race riot had intimidated Negro voters; that the intricate Democratic election law of 1899 augmented complexity for the voter and latitude for the registrar in 1900; that the poll tax requirement and the Red Shirt movement reduced the Negro vote in 1900; and that Governor Russell advised the Negroes not to try to vote against the amendment but leave it

COMPARISON TABLE OF NEGRO VOTE IN 1896 AND 1900*

	FOR AMENDMENT	AGAINST AMENDMENT	1896		1900	
			REPUBLICAN RUSSELL	DEMOCRATIC WATSON	REPUBLICAN ADAMS	DEMOCRATIC AYCOCK
Anson	2,124	496	1,158	1,681	522	2,015
Bertie	2,649	944	2,009	1,372	996	2,675
Caswell	1,437	1,277	1,699	1,310	1,313	1,421
Chowan	1,138	917	1,134	722	948	1,055
Craven	2,662	955	2,867	1,656	932	2,611
Edgecombe	3,781	374	2,736	1,807	385	3,758
Granville	2,459	1,610	2,196	1,896	1,527	2,540
Halifax	6,280	899	3,979	1,997	877	6,618
Hertford	1,407	397	1,436	879	429	1,368
New Hanover	2,967	2	3,145	2,218	3	2,963
Northampton	2,469	1,059	2,312	1,660	1,096	2,438
Pasquotank	1,542	892	1,510	938	926	1,502
Pender	1,255	294	1,159	1,089	276	1,260
Pitt	3,414	2,042	2,462	2,538	2,096	3,433
Scotland	1,803	7	—	—	25	1,065
Vance	1,343	913	1,815	1,093	944	1,304
Warren	1,807	1,356	2,171	922	1,069	2,133
Washington	1,037	547	1,270	591	571	976

*North Carolina Manual, 1913.

to the courts, it is reasonable to assume that the vote of 128,285 against the amendment was substantially and in large majority the vote of white men.

There were eighteen "black counties" in 1900[54] and not one defeated the amendment. New Hanover, with a Negro majority of 50.8 per cent, registered two votes against the amendment and three votes for Republican Adams; and Scotland, with a majority of 53.5 per cent, registered seven votes against the amendment and twenty-five for Adams. The Negroes in the "black counties" which had aided in the Republican victory of 1896 were not dead in 1900; yet, these Republican "black counties" "supported" the amendment and voted against "their" Republican nominee as the comparison table shows.[55] Where had the Republican gains of 1896 in the "black counties" disappeared in 1900? The Negroes had not emigrated because the Negro percentage in population for 1900 was 34.7 per cent, 1.7 per cent over 1890. It is not enough to say the Populists returned to the Democrats in 1900, hence a small vote for Republican Adams and against the amendment, because the "black counties" were not predominantly Populist. The answer lies in the realm of intimidation, racial intolerance, the Red Shirt movement, the partisan election law, and the repercussions of the Wilmington race riot of 1898.

The Negro was disfranchised. Prominent North Carolinians had different interpretations relative to the election of 1900 and the amendment. A Democratic editor felt that disfranchisement was a great blessing to the state.[56] John Spencer Bassett condemned the Democrats for their physical terror used against Negroes and their social terror used against whites in the election of 1900; considered the methods used in securing the amendment as far worse than the amendment itself; maintained his contention that the small number of Negro officeholders was miscalled "Negro rule"; and added, "there can be no defense, no apology and no excuse for the methods employed to secure its adoption."[57] He had commented in early April that the disfranchisement amendment would pass "because it will be voted on under the new election law which is the worst since Reconstruction."[58] As evidence of fraud in the election of 1900, forty-five registrars were arrested on various charges and bound over to the federal court.[59] Henry G. Connor, speaker of the House of Representatives which framed the suffrage bill, was rather despondent upon realizing that the amendment, supposedly designed to eliminate illiterate Negroes, had proscribed the entire Negro race. He wrote,

I fear that the shrinkage in the number will make the Negro absolutely indifferent to his political interests and welfare and the whites will be emboldened to oppress him in his material and educational interests. It is a serious question whether 100,000 freemen can maintain any satisfactory status in North Carolina without any political power or influence.[60]

The necessity of the disfranchisement is a matter of opinion. If it were designed to prevent Negro office-holding, other methods could have been used. The Populists had offered the specious proposal of insertion into the state constitution of a prohibitive clause against Negro officeholders. On the other hand, the legislature could have set up legislative control over the "black counties" and popular elections for the "white counties." The constitution of North Carolina permitted legislative control,[61] the Supreme Court of North Carolina confirmed it,[62] and the Democrats had used it in overcoming Negro majorities from 1876 to 1894. If it was designed to eliminate the Negro as a voter, and at the same time crush his self-respect, then it was necessary. The formulation of the amendment was predicated upon the elimination of the Negro officeholder, but the application of the amendment reduced the Negro to a political nonentity.

The victory of the Democratic forces in 1900 spurred the legislature of 1901 to eradicate the last possible barrier to the application of the disfranchisement amendment. The Supreme Court—three Republicans, one Populist, and one Democrat—was attacked. Since the Court had rendered many decisions unfavorable to the Democrats from 1895 through 1898 and had specifically reversed some Democratic legislation of 1899 which pertained to office-holding,[63] many Democratic legislators felt that the Court was bent on destroying their legislative effectiveness through judicial means. Locke Craig stated in an extremely partisan manner that "every single political decision that court made, was made in antagonism to destroy the Legislature of 1899,"[64] and Josephus Daniels wrote, "From Fusion Judges, Good Lord Deliver Us."[65]

The closing blow of the legislature of 1901 was the impeachment and trial of Chief Justice D. M. Furchess and Associate Justice R. M. Douglass, Republicans. The basis for impeachment was the fact that the Supreme Court had retained Theophilus White as shell-fish inspector on October 17, 1900,[66] when the office had been abolished in 1899 and a Democratic officeholder had been given the same duties under a new title.[67] Judge Clark, lone Democrat in the Court, offered the only dissenting opinions in many office-holding cases and furthered the Democrats' suspicions of the Court.

The fact that Theophilus White received his salary over the Democratic protest involved the two Republican judges, the treasurer, and the auditor. The impeachment resolution condemned all four.[68] It cut across party lines in the Democratic House where some desired censure; others, impeachment; and others, acquittal. However, impeachment won out. Five charges were made against the judges.[69] Of the fifty senators comprising the court, a vote of thirty-eight was necessary to pronounce judgment of removal from office. The necessary vote was not obtained on either article.[70] Since there were eleven Republicans in the Senate, and the "not guilty" vote on each article was more than eleven, it is evident that the trial cut across party lines.

F. H. Busbee, attorney for the respondents, perhaps summarized best the atmosphere of the trial when he argued that "the impeachment was political prosecution and instituted to prevent apprehended dangers, rather than to punish past offenses."[71] After a trial of seventeen days, the judges were acquitted.

Governor Russell had advised the Negroes to refrain from voting against the amendment and to leave it to the courts. Whether Russell had information on the individual judges' views about the constitutionality of the amendment, no one knew. The Democrats believed that the salvation of the Democratic program demanded "unpacking" the Court and Democratizing it.

The year 1900 closed the issue of the Negro as a political factor in North Carolina. Strong men of the Negro race counseled their followers to forbearance, thrift, economy, and education. Dr. James E. Shepard, a federal Negro officeholder, with his characteristic approach to realism in solving the race question, admonished both races to vote against the suffrage amendment without rancor or bitterness and to pursue the higher paths of education. He appealed to the white people especially to temper their intolerance with the understanding that Negroes had paid over $245,000,000 annually in taxes, had 2,750,000 children in school, 37,000 teachers, 400 newspapers, several banks, and some factories. The most violent anti-Negro newspaper editor of the period agreed that Dr. Shepard's speech was a "temperate and well-worded appeal," a speech of "appeal and reasoning."[72]

John Dancy, former collector of the port of customs at Wilmington, realizing that the morale of the Negro group needed a factual boost in 1901, stated that "we constitute a third of the population of this State and contribute to its productive wealth. Our own hands till the soil and produce five-sixths of the cotton crops, the major portion of the cereals which constitute our food supplies, as well as sustenance for our increasing stock. It proves, if it proves anything, that as a race we are not lazy, we are not drones in the hives of industry, we are not nonetities in the industrial world." To increase the self-respect of the group, Dancy warned, "certain duties are to be performed which will aid greatly in the solution of our problem. We need to learn first of all, that there is a vast difference between liberty and license. We have the liberty to exercise all the rights guaranteed by the law, but we have no license to violate the law. . . . In reference to education, I urge eternal vigilance along that line. We need to keep every school house open to us, filled with our children. We need to make sacrifices, and supplement the efforts of the State by running the school longer terms than the present meagre support furnished them will permit. . . . The inauguration of mechanical and trade schools, and schools giving training in technology—and the recognized disposition to go into the trades as a means of providing and insuring a livelihood, suggests a departure along right lines which means much for use in the future. If we succeed along these lines, we will have taken another step in the solution of our great problem."[73]

The Republican party proved its disloyalty to the Negro group after the election of 1900. The Negro who could qualify to vote under the disfranchisement amendment was forgotten, and the party marched thereafter under the banner of a "lily white" party. Jeter C. Pritchard, who relied indirectly upon the aid of Negro voters in 1894 and 1896 to secure his senatorial election, declared in 1902 that the existence of the Republican party demanded that the Negro question remain buried.[74] It cannot be overlooked that some of the intelligent Negroes perceived the double-crossing activities of their Republican leaders. From the private correspondence of John C. Dancy comes this illuminating letter demonstrative of the fact that Pritchard knew how to play shuttlecock:

Tuskegee Institute
Tuskegee, Alabama
October 7, 1902

Personal
My dear Mr. Dancy,

I have received your letter. Among other things that I wanted to see you about was to ask you what you consider and understand to be the attitude of Senator Pritchard toward our people. He has done a great deal of harm in this State, in fact he congratulated the State convention over the fact that the Republican party had gotten rid of the Negro. As I have not seen any account of any protest or any adverse action made by the colored Republicans of North Carolina I take for granted that in some way they must have faith in Senator Pritchard, but judging by his words and actions in this State I do not believe that we have any more dangerous enemy in the whole country than Senator Pritchard, and the time has come, it seems to me, when we want to speak out. Of course you may know things regarding him that I do not. One thing, however, I do know, and that is that he is not representing the views of the President in regard to our race although he has been posing as a representative of those views. I think your relationship with Senator Pritchard rather puts you in an awkward position, and I am very anxious for your sake as well as for that of the race, to have the situation cleared up as much as you feel that you can clear it up.

Yours truly,
Booker T. Washington[75]

A concluding evidence that the Republican party had no thought of seeking the enfranchisement of the Negro was that part of its platform in 1906 which declared the party "in favor of extending the operation of what is known as the 'grandfather clause,' in the recently adopted amendment, to the year 1920" and the party pledged itself to do all in its power to carry out this resolution, and have it enacted into law.[76] While the Republican party was anxious to protect illiterate whites, there was no mention of the literacy clause which affected Negroes, or any disposition to retreat from its "lily white" position which affected educated Negroes.

The national Republican administration's indifference to the disfranchisement of Negro Republicans in North Carolina did not pass unnoticed. The opinion of some of the educated Negroes was that "our friends are still in possession of the National Government but they have not done as much for our race as they have led us to hope."[77]

NOTES TO CHAPTER THIRTEEN

1. *Congressional Record*, Fifty-sixth Congress, First Session, XXXIII, Part 1, 670; Part 2, 1027-38.

2. Alabama did not have a suffrage amendment in 1900, but looked forward to effecting one.

3. *Ibid.*, 4052-59.

4. *The Proposed Franchise Amendment, Some Constitutional Discussions with Declarations* (Duke University Library Pamphlet Collection), 1900, 1-75.

5. *Caucasian*, issues of January, February, March, April, May, and June, 1900.

6. Rippy (ed.), "An Address to the Democratic Convention of 1900," *Furnifold Simmons, Statesman of the New South*, 88-96.

7. *Public Documents*, 1901, II, Document No. 28, Abstract of Votes for State Officers.

8. *Democratic Handbook*, 1900, 22-24.

9. *Caucasian*, January 8, 1900.

10. *The Proposed Suffrage Amendment: Platform and Resolutions of the Peoples' Party* (University of North Carolina Library Pamphlet Collection), 1-16.

11. *Appleton's Annual Cyclopedia*, Third Series, V (1900), 444-45.

12. *News and Observer*, May 12-28, 1900; also Josephus Daniels, *Editor in Politics*, 374-80.

13. W. A. Guthrie, *Opinions of A Lawyer on the Constitutionality of the Proposed Amendment* (Duke University Library Pamphlet Collection), 1-16.

14. *Some Correspondence Between State Chairmen of Two Political Organizations* (Duke University Library Pamphlet Collection).

15. United States Bureau of Census, *Negro Population 1790-1915*, Table 27, 428.

16. United States Department of Commerce, *Bureau of Census*, I, Part 1 (1900), Table 92, 992-93.

17. The question of determining what constitutes literacy is a tedious one to analyze in any census returns. Many Negroes were termd illiterate when they could not read, though some of them could write. While it cannot be proved that this was the case in North Carolina, there is this reminder as stated in the census reports, in reference to literacy: "It is not improbable that in certain sections of the South white enumerators have been inclined to assume where specific answers were not obtained to the inquiry, and especially when the person enumerated was not directly interrogated, that whites were able and that Negroes were unable to write, and thus to class the former as literate

and the latter as illiterate."—United States Bureau of Census, *Negro Population 1790-1915*, 403.

18. United States Department of Commerce, *Bureau of Census*, I, Part 1 (1900), Table 92, 992-93.

19. *North Carolina Manual*, 1913, 1006.

20. *Great Speech of George Rountree, Esq., Delivered Before the House of Representatives on the Subject of the Constitutional Amendment* (Duke University Library Pamphlet Collection), 16.

21. *Public and Private Laws and Resolutions, Adjourned Session*, 1900, Chap. 2, 55.

22. *Democratic Handbook*, 1900, 86.

23. *Public and Private Laws and Resolutions, Adjourned Session*, 1900, Chap. 1, 27.

24. *Democratic Handbook*, 1900, 87.

25. *Public and Private Laws and Resolutions, Adjourned Session*, 1900, Chap. 1, 53-54.

26. *Congressional Record*, Fifty-sixth Congress, Second Session, XXXIV, Part 4, 3275.

27. *Ibid.*, June 14, 1900.

28. *The Negro Smith Scores Populist Johnson* (Campaign Pamphlet, University of North Carolina Library, Southern Historical Collection, evidently published and used by the Democrats for campaign material in 1900).

Smith had a similar disagreement with Republican Snipes, white, of Hertford County, in the legislature of 1899 when Snipes held that, although Hertford was a Black county, Negro office-holding had never obtained there and never would.—*News and Observer*, January 18, 1899.

The Democrats used this argument between a white and a Negro Republican to the disadvantage of the Fusion party in the campaign of 1900 under a cartoon titled: "Isaac Smith Goes A-Snipe Hunting."—University of North Carolina Library Pamphlet Collection.

29. Fuller, *A Pictorial History of the American Negro*, 938-39.

30. *Charlotte Observer*, July 20, 1900.

31. *Catechism*, 1900 (University of North Carolina Library Pamphlet Collection).

32. *Caucasion*, issue of August, September, and October, 1900.

33. *African Methodist Episcopal Zion Quarterly* (June, 1900), 38-40.

34. Charles Brantley Aycock Papers, 1899-1912, memorandum, North Carolina Historical Commission, Raleigh, North Carolina.

35. *Ibid.*; R. D. W. Connor and Clarence Poe, *The Life and Speeches of Charles Brantley Aycock*, 212-17; *News and Observer*, April 12, 1900.

36. *News and Observer*, April 17, 1900.

37. Charles Brantley Aycock Papers, 1899-1912, addresses in the original form and excerpts from addresses, North Carolina Historical Commission, Raleigh, North Carolina; also *News and Observer*, April 17, 18, 19, 20, 25, 27, 29, 1900.

38. *News and Observer*, May 3, 5, 6, 10, 1900.

39. Charles Brantley Aycock Papers, 1899-1912, addresses in the original form and excerpts from addresses as printed by the Raleigh *News and Observer*, North Carolina Historical Commission, Raleigh, North Carolina.

40. *Ibid.*

41. *Supra*, Chap. XII, 178-83.

42. *Caucasian*, June, July, 1900.

43. Connor and Poe, *The Life and Speeches of Charles Brantley Aycock*, 86.

44. *News and Observer*, June 26; July 1, 4, 7, 1900.

45. Locke Craig Letters, Papers, and Scrapbook, Duke University Library Manuscript Collection.

46. Furnifold Simmons Papers, Duke University Library Manuscript Collection; also Rippy (ed.), *Furnifold Simmons, Statesman of the New South*.

47. Alfred M. Waddell Private Papers, University of North Carolina Library Manuscript Collection; also Waddell, *Some Memories of My Life*.

48. Charles Brantley Aycock Papers 1898-1912, North Carolina Historical Commission, Raleigh, North Carolina; also *News and Observer*, May, June, July, 1900.

49. While Aycock proved to be North Carolina's great "Educational Governor," it is doubtful if his interest in educational improvements was evolutionary. His record at the University of North Carolina after his first year is hardly average (Charles Brantley Aycock Papers 1898-1912, Academic Record). He was a member of the School Board of Goldsboro, 1887-1901, serving as chairman from 1891-1901; yet, an answer to his biographers' inquiry: "What influence did Aycock have on the schools of Goldsboro?" brought forth the reply: "The schools continuously grew in importance, no particular feature."—J. E. Avent to R. D. W. Connor, April 12, 1912, Charles Brantley Aycock Papers 1898-1912, North Carolina Historical Commission, Raleigh, North Carolina.

50. Hamilton, *History of North Carolina Since 1860*, 312.

51. *North Carolina Manual*, 1913, 1006; map, 206; also Table 3, Appendix: Vote for Governor.

52. *Ibid.*, 1018, map, 207; also Table 4, Appendix: Disfranchisement vote.

53. Alamance, Davidson, Graham, Haywood, Jackson, Moore, and Orange.

54. Negro Population in North Carolina in 1890 and 1900: map, 208, also Table I, Appendix.

55. See Appendix, Table 4, 233.

56. *News and Observer*, August 6, 1900.

57. *The Outlook*, LXV, No. 15 (August 11, 1900), 843.

58. John Spencer Bassett to Herbert Baxter Adams, April 3, 1900, *loc. cit.*

59. Hamilton, *History of North Carolina Since 1860*, 313.

60. Henry G. Connor to George H. Howard, November 3, 1902 (citing from William A. Mabry, "White Supremacy and the North Carolina Suffrage Amendment," *North Carolina Historical Review*, XIII, No. 1 [January, 1936], 23), Henry G. Connor Correspondence in possession of R. D. W. Connor, University of North Carolina, Chapel Hill, North Carolina.

61. *Constitution of North Carolina*, Article VII, Section 14.

62. *W. N. Harriss et al.* v. *Silas P. Wright et al.*, North Carolina Reports, CXXI, 156-63; *Tate* v. *Commissioners*, CXXII, 814; *Gattis* v. *Griffin*, CXXV, 334; and *State* v. *Shank*, CXXV, 632.

63. *Supra*, Chap. XII, 178.

64. Jones (ed.), *Memoirs and Speeches of Locke Craig*, 61.

65. Josephus Daniels, *Editor in Politics*, 396-98.

66. *White* v. *Hill*, North Carolina Reports, CXXV, 194-202.

67. *Public Laws*, 1899, Chaps. 18 and 19, 110-16; and *Public and Private Laws and Resolutions, Adjourned Session*, 1900, 82.

68. *House Journal*, 1901, 319.

69. *Trial of David M. Furchess, Now Chief Justice, and Formerly Associate Justice, and Robert M. Douglass, Associate Justice of the Supreme Court of North Carolina, On Impeachment by the House of Representatives for High Crimes and Misdemeanors 1901*, li.
Article I Two judges were guilty of unlawfully and wilfully violating those parts of

the State Constitution which declare the legislative, executive and judicial powers ought to be forever separate; the Supreme Court can hear claims against the State but its decision is purely recommendatory; and no money could be withdrawn from the State treasury except through legislative enactment.

Article II They intended to bring the General Assembly of North Carolina into ill-repute by disregarding Chapter 21, *Public Laws, 1899.*

Article III They wilfully ordered Theophilus White to be paid.

Article IV They directed writs to issue unlawfully and contrary to practice of courts because first, the claim was one against the State and should have been carried originally to the Supreme Court; second, statutory requirements for writs of mandamus were ignored; third, the writs were issued in disregard of Supreme Court procedure; fourth, Chapter 21, *Public Laws, 1899,* was ignored; and, fifth, an associate justice was denied the right to file a protest and dissent.

Article V They intended to defeat legislative will in respect to many office-holding cases by repealing acts of the General Assembly.

70. *Ibid.,* 681-721.

71. *Ibid.,* 793.

72. Josephus Daniels, *Editor in Politics,* 336.

73. *Address of John C. Dancy To the Colored Industrial Fair,* November 2, 1901, Raleigh, North Carolina, John Dancy Papers.

74. *The Brightest Day of Republicanism in North Carolina,* Address of Honorable Jeter C. Pritchard Delivered Before the Republican State Convention at Greensboro, North Carolina, August 28, 1902 (University of North Carolina Library Pamphlet Collection).

75. Booker T. Washington to John C. Dancy, October 7, 1902, John C. Dancy Papers, in possession of John C. Dancy, Jr., 606 E. Vernor, Detroit, Michigan.

76. *Speech Delivered By Spencer B. Adams, Chairman State Republican Executive Committee at Asheville, North Carolina, August 25, 1906, Together with the Platform of the Republican Party Adopted at Greensboro, July 10, 1906,* 24 (University of North Carolina Library Pamphlet Collection).

77. *African Methodist Episcopal Zion Quarterly* (December, 1900), 52.

CHAPTER FOURTEEN

CONCLUSIONS

A RESURGENCE OF THE NEGRO in politics occurred in North Carolina 1895-1901, a situation which obtained in no other Southern state. The resurgence was a result of the movement of agrarian discontent which projected the Farmers' Alliance into politics. The Populist party in North Carolina was a protest against social and political grievances which the Bourbon Democratic party did little to alleviate. Conservative men were in control of the Democratic party and were in alliance with railroad and manufacturing interests. The majority of these men had used the state, between 1876 and 1894, to further their own business interests and were content to rest on their chief accomplishment—redemption of the state from Yankees and Negroes.

The results of the election of 1892 indicated that the combined forces of the Populists and the Republicans could defeat the Democratic party. The Republican party, however, had a large Negro element in the eastern counties of the state and substantial white support (native North Carolinians) in the western counties. The question of fusion brought the Populist party face to face with the Negro as a voter, and the possibility of the Negro as an officeholder. After 1892, Populists could have returned to the Democratic fold, existed as an independent party, or clasped hands across the racial chasm and cooperated with the Republicans. The energetic element of the party was made up of political realists who favored fusion with the Republican party. Fusion politics was, therefore, based upon the arithmetics of political bargaining.

The Populist movement in North Carolina was not a revolt against "white supremacy," and to think for one moment that the party fused with the Republican party to inaugurate an era of political or social equality for the Negroes who formed an element of that party is failure to understand the confusion and complexity of the 1890's. Fusion was sound on the surface, but beneath were personalities and prejudices, which constituted a problem. Even these might have been overcome for political expediency had not the Democrats sabotaged the effectiveness of the Fusionists' program by attacking them in their chief vulnerable spot, the Negro question. The architects of Fusion never found an effective means of counteracting Democratic propaganda. Democratic historians have dwelled too much upon the "unlikes" of the Fusion parties and have ignored the fact that these "unlikes" pertained chiefly to national party issues. Their "likes" on state issues, with the exception of the Negro question, extended to well-recognized grievances: the need of a uniform rate of interest, a fair election law, and the restoration of local self-government.

Fusion victory in politics in 1894 and 1896 resulted in many fundamental changes among which were the election law, the system of county and municipal government, more active Negro participation in politics, Negro office-holding, and the first and last Republican governor since 1876. The Fusion election law was framed upon the assumption that every man could cast one vote and have that vote count as cast. It was designed primarily for the interest of both parties, and the fact that the Negro enjoyed wider political participation was incidental and resulted from the fact that he was a member of one of the parties seeking to promote its self-interest. The Fusion change in county government from Democratic centralized legislative control to popular local control was ideal, although effected to guarantee Republican and Populist representation in local affairs on a fair and equitable basis and not to put the Negro in control of county government. Fusion municipal government lacked that uniformity which was characteristic of Fusion county government. The glaring differences in administrative arrangements for localities with preponderant Negro populations discredit the charge that towns were turned over to Negro rule.

It is well to understand that the participation of Negroes in North Carolina politics was nothing new. Constantly from 1876 to 1894, there was a North Carolina Negro either in the state legislature or in the Congress of the United States. Some few Negroes had supported their Democratic overlords, although the Democratic party has been insistent in its denial that such was ever the case. Negro officeholding was not new in the state, but what was new was the increased voting power of the Negro, and his ability in the 1890's to support more effectively his white Populist and Republican leaders.

There is no term more calculated to strike terror to the hearts of Southern whites than the expression "Negro domination." Southern necromancers sometimes resort to the black magic of reducing any political issue into one of "Negro domination" and social equality. This political trick never fails to send all but the very brave and the very foolish into a panic and to check political advancement and racial adjustment. The remedy is not some countermagic, but an examination of facts. An examination of "Negro domination" in North Carolina revealed that one Negro was elected to Congress; ten to the state legislature; four aldermen were elected in Wilmington, two in New Bern, two in Greenville, one or two in Raleigh; one county treasurer and one county coroner in New Hanover; one register of deeds in Craven; one Negro jailer in Wilmington; and one county commissioner in Warren and one in Craven. There were a few Negroes in minor positions as assistant deputies to the sheriff, register of deeds, and coroner. The largest number of Negro officeholders was included under magistrates, who were largely powerless under the Fusion county government law. Through federal patronage one Negro was collector of the port of customs in Wilmington, one was deputy collector of internal revenue in Raleigh, and some were post-masters. But the public offices held by Negroes were neither sufficiently important nor numerous to warrant the Democratic cry of Negro domination.

Statistics and mathematics throw light upon the question of Negro domination in county government in North Carolina. The census reports show that in 1890 the Negro numbered 33 per cent of the total population and 34.7 per cent in 1900. Sheer mathematics shows that 67 per cent could not be out-voted by 33 per cent in 1890, nor could 65.3 per cent be out-voted by 34.7 per cent in 1900. The Negro was not a numerical threat. The large white percentages were divided, and a considerable portion united with the smaller Negro percentages as did the white Republicans and Populists in the elections of 1894 and 1896. There was Fusion domination but not Negro domination. In leaders, officeholders, and party conventions the Republican party itself was largely controlled by whites.

The sixteen "black counties" in which Negroes numbered more than half the population sent to the United States Congress one Negro as compared with ten whites sent by the remainder of the counties. They sent to the North Carolina House of Representatives a total of six Negroes (one served two terms) as compared with twenty, nineteen, and seventeen whites, respectively. They sent to the North Carolina Senate a total of three Negroes while contributing to the election of eighteen, sixteen, and seventeen whites during the Fusion elections of 1894, 1896, and 1898. Negro domination did not exist in the state, and the cry was a technique of Democratic propaganda. One of the chief grievances was not Negro domination but the fact that whites had to transact legal business with Negro officeholders in any county or city.

There is no doubt that Democratic propaganda of the most vitriolic and damaging kind sabotaged the effectiveness of the Republican and Populists parties which had concrete programs when they entered office in 1895. The Fusionists failed not because some of their reforms were worse than the previous Democratic record, but because among other shortcomings they had the tedious Negro question to deal with and no party press effective enough to counteract Democratic propaganda.

The Wilmington race riot was justifiable at no point, the disfranchise-ment amendment was unnecessary, and the impeachment of two justices of the state Supreme Court was a fiasco. The impact of the race question upon the politics of the period had produced these unpleasant situations. In so far as the legislature had the power to control county government in individual cases, and the Supreme Court had sanctioned that authority, the legislature had the power to render the Negro vote in the "black counties" ineffective and disfranchisement unnecessary. But the fact that the Democratic legislature of 1899 chose to nullify local self-government in some "white" as well as "black" counties strongly indicates that their cry of Negro domination was false, and their hidden fear of Fusion domination was real. The disfranchisement amendment came after a broken Democratic campaign pledge and was predicated upon the specious assumption that "white supremacy" is dependent upon a one-party state and a one-party state dependent upon "white supremacy."

There was definitely an economic aspect to the restoration of the state to the Democrats. The financial contributions of the industrialists and the capitalists to the decisive campaign of 1898 were urgently solicited and given on the assurances of no legislative attacks on the business, manufacturing, and railroad interests. Their economic ascendancy behind the glare of race hatred contributed to the transformation of North Carolina from an agricultural to an industrial state.

In the redemption of the state to Democratic control, the denominational interests saw an opportunity to cripple the University of North Carolina, the capitalistic interests saw an opportunity to evade taxation, and the Democrats saw an opportunity to deal a death blow to opposition parties.

The Democratic accusation that the Populists were Negro-lovers is false. The Populists were, in the main, dissatisfied Democrats; and their racial attitudes were as distinct as the party from whence they came—avowedly anti-Negro. To achieve their political goals, they sacrificed their racial and social theories and joined hands with the Republican party to which Negroes belonged. The chief Populist newspaper carried too many anti-Negro tirades, and Populist legislators in the state legislature and in the United States Senate uttered too many negative statements to classify the party as a supporter of Negro office-holding. The Populists' concern, in the great fight to defeat the disfranchisement amendment, was never how many Negroes would be denied the ballot; but how many illiterate whites would be affected.

The Democrats knew that the Populists had no desire to see Negroes hold office, but they accused the Populists of supporting Negro domination because it was the vulnerable spot in the Fusion armor. While it is fundamentally true that the association of the Populist party with the Negro question hastened its demise, it cannot be overlooked that the party stood for reforms and compelled the Democratic party to champion reform.

The Republican party and the Negro shared a closer relationship. That party had a difficult role in that it had to contend with the dissatisfaction not only of the Populists, but also of the Negroes themselves. Historians who uphold the idea that Negroes voted the Republican ticket with a slavish fanaticism must not overlook the fact that there was never complete harmony between party leaders and Negro party followers during the Fusion period.

The various Negro meetings setting forth the well-recognized grievance that they did not share in the rewards of political patronage in proportion to their voting strength, and the opinions of living contemporaries, evince the fact that the Negroes were not satisfied. They voted largely as a bloc in the face of the threat of restoration of Bourbon control. That white Republican leaders had no desire to see Negroes hold office and double-crossed them is attested by the few and minor positions Negroes held in city, county, and state government; by the contrasting tenor of their speeches in states farther to the South and in North Carolina; and by the party's change into a "lily white" Republican party after 1901. The Negro during the Fusion period had to steer his frail political vessel between the Scylla of Democratic opposition, both personal and political, and the Charybdis of double-crossing white Republican political leaders. Necessity compelled the Republican party to seek Negro support and, in turn, accord him some *minor* considerations.

The Democrats used the Negro scare to return to the helm of state, to seize control of the white Republican as well as "black counties" and cities, and to disfranchise the Negro and weaken the Republican party, thereby reducing political opposition. Democratic propaganda was a double-edged sword—when slashing at the Republicans, it condemned them for Negro officeholding; when slashing at the Populists, it ridiculed them as minority Populists, tail of a Republican kite, and Negro lovers; and when condemning the Negroes, it reminded them of their well-recognized grievance that white Republicans secured the best positions while depending upon them for support. The overthrow of the Fusionists, the Wilmington race riot, the disfranchisement amendment, and the intimidation of the judiciary occurred between 1898 and 1902 and made North Carolina virtually a one-party state. All were the results of the Negro's attempt at political equality in a white man's country. All were illustrations of Democratic strategy and marked the road to Democratic supremacy and white domination in North Carolina. While the disfranchisement amendment aimed to eliminate the Negro from politics, it was the fear of the defeat of that amendment which forced the Democratic party to pledge itself to universal education for white children.

Had the Negroes used the ballot wisely? According to the Democrats, they had voted into office unscrupulous, office-hunting exploiters. Had the mass of ignorant rural white Democrats used the ballot wisely when they from 1876 to 1894 kept in power a party which made no reforms at a time when significant reforms were needed? It appears that the Negroes committed political suicide by supporting one party. They, at that time, felt that they were right in the light of their historical past and their psychological fears. It may be questionable whether a minority group should vote a straight party ticket if it is outnumbered by its opponents who are bent on destroying its effectiveness.

APPENDIX
BIBLIOGRAPHY
INDEX

APPENDIX

TABLE 1

NEGRO POPULATION IN NORTH CAROLINA, 1890–1900*

COUNTY	NEGRO POPULATION		INCREASE		PERCENTAGE NEGRO IN TOTAL POPULATION	
			NUMBER	PER CENT		
	1890	1900	1890–1900	1890–1900	1890	1900
Alamance	5,583	6,723	1,140	20.4	30.6	26.2
Alexander	842	856	14	1.7	8.9	7.8
Alleghany	460	466	6	1.3	7.1	6.0
Anson	9,789	11,674	1,885	19.3	48.9	53.4
Ashe	595	684	89	15.0	3.8	3.5
Beaufort	9,203	11,336	2,133	23.2	43.7	42.9
Bertie	11,291	11,821	530	4.7	58.9	57.6
Bladen	8,117	8,223	106	1.3	48.4	46.5
Brunswick	4,761	5,044	283	5.9	43.7	39.9
Buncombe	6,626	8,120	1,494	22.5	18.8	18.3
Burke	2,561	2,676	115	4.5	17.1	15.1
Cabarrus	5,459	6,101	642	11.8	30.1	27.2
Caldwell	1,554	1,931	337	24.3	12.6	12.3
Camden	2,320	2,191	−129	−5.6	40.9	40.0
Carteret	2,297	2,127	−170	−7.4	21.2	18.0
Caswell	9,389	8,199	−1,190	−12.7	58.6	54.6
Catawba	2,616	2,985	369	14.1	14.0	13.5
Chatham	8,199	8,339	140	1.7	32.3	34.9
Cherokee	274	432	158	57.7	2.7	3.6
Chowan	5,156	5,850	694	13.5	56.2	57.0
Clay	142	134	−8	−5.6	3.4	3.0
Cleveland	3,093	4,820	1,727	55.8	15.2	19.2
Columbus	6,052	6,476	424	7.0	33.9	30.4
Craven	13,358	14,543	1,185	8.9	65.1	60.2
Cumberland	12,341	12,571	230	1.9	45.2	43.0
Currituck	2,016	1,777	−239	−11.9	29.9	27.2
Dare	406	574	168	41.4	10.8	12.1
Davidson	3,528	3,174	−354	−10.0	16.3	13.6
Davie	2,852	2,635	−217	−7.6	24.5	21.7
Duplin	7,087	8,528	1,441	20.3	37.9	38.1
Durham	7,329	9,749	420	33.0	40.6	37.2
Edgecombe	15,599	16,584	985	6.3	64.7	62.4
Forsyth	8,999	10,541	1,542	17.1	31.6	29.9
Franklin	10,335	12,438	2,103	20.3	49.0	49.5
Gaston	4,836	7,242	2,406	49.8	27.2	26.0
Gates	4,713	4,804	91	1.9	46.0	46.1
Graham	25	26	1	—	0.8	0.6

APPENDIX

NEGRO POPULATION IN NORTH CAROLINA, 1890–1900*—Continued

COUNTY	NEGRO POPULATION		INCREASE		PERCENTAGE NEGRO IN TOTAL POPULATION	
			NUMBER	PER CENT		
	1890	1900	1890–1900	1890–1900	1890	1900
Granville	12,360	11,887	−473	−3.8	50.5	51.1
Greene	4,758	5,778	1,020	21.4	47.4	48.0
Guilford	8,223	11,103	2,880	35.0	29.3	24.4
Halifax	19,293	19,733	440	2.3	66.7	64.1
Harnett	4,220	5,058	838	19.9	30.8	31.6
Haywood	517	613	96	18.6	3.9	3.8
Henderson	1,378	1,759	381	27.6	10.9	12.5
Hertford	7,944	8,391	447	5.6	57.4	58.7
Hyde	3,941	4,014	73	1.9	44.3	43.3
Iredell	5,939	7,332	1,393	23.5	23.3	25.2
Jackson	518	591	73	14.1	5.4	5.0
Johnston	7,322	8,171	849	11.6	26.9	25.3
Jones	3,518	3,760	242	6.9	47.5	45.7
Lenoir	6,362	8,046	1,684	26.5	42.8	43.2
Lincoln	2,558	2,961	403	15.8	20.3	19.1
McDowell	1,825	1,893	68	3.7	16.7	15.1
Macon	665	673	8	1.2	6.6	5.6
Madison	710	551	−159	−22.4	4.0	2.7
Martin	7,383	7,327	−56	−0.8	48.5	47.6
Mecklenburg	19,526	23,873	4,347	22.3	45.8	43.2
Mitchell	553	536	−17	−3.1	4.3	3.5
Montgomery	2,257	3,682	1,425	63.1	20.1	25.9
Moore	6,479	7,849	1,370	21.1	31.6	33.2
Nash	8,521	10,619	2,098	24.6	41.2	41.7
New Hanover	13,935	13,109	−826	−5.9	58.0	50.8
North Hampton	12,018	12,118	100	0.8	56.6	57.3
Onslow	2,911	3,610	699	24.0	28.3	30.2
Orange	5,242	5,261	19	0.4	35.1	35.8
Pamlico	2,379	2,637	258	10.8	33.3	32.8
Pasquotank	5,546	7,027	1,481	26.7	51.6	51.4
Pender	6,546	6,909	363	5.5	52.3	51.6
Perquimans	4,574	5,003	429	9.4	49.2	49.6
Person	6,899	7,023	124	1.8	45.5	42.1
Pitt	12,327	15,492	3,165	25.7	48.3	50.2
Polk	1,093	1,207	114	10.4	18.5	17.2
Randolph	3,347	3,672	325	9.7	13.3	13.0
Richmond	12,959	7,763	−5,196	−40.1	54.1	49.0
Robeson	14,672	16,917	2,245	15.3	46.6	41.9
Rockingham	10,164	11,617	1,453	14.3	40.1	35.0
Rowan	6,980	8,115	1,135	16.3	28.9	26.1
Rutherford	3,692	4,441	749	20.3	19.7	17.7
Sampson	9,136	9,130	−6	−0.1	36.4	34.6
Scotland	—	6,710	6,710	—	—	53.5
Stanly	1,507	1,799	292	19.4	12.4	11.8
Stokes	2,813	2,991	178	6.3	16.4	15.1
Surry	2,348	2,904	556	23.7	12.2	11.4

NEGRO POPULATION IN NORTH CAROLINA, 1890-1900*—*Continued*

COUNTY	NEGRO POPULATION		INCREASE		PERCENTAGE NEGRO IN TOTAL POPULATION	
			NUMBER	PER CENT		
	1890	1900	1890–1900	1890–1900	1890	1900
Swain	225	174	−51	−22.7	3.4	2.1
Transylvania	513	615	102	19.9	8.7	9.3
Tyrrell	1,225	1,462	237	19.3	29.0	29.4
Union	5,547	7,999	2,452	44.2	26.1	29.5
Vance	11,143	9,755	−1,388	−12.5	63.4	58.5
Wake	23,109	24,358	1,249	5.4	47.0	44.6
Warren	13,480	13,069	−411	−3.0	69.6	68.2
Washington	5,238	5,366	128	2.4	51.4	50.6
Watauga	431	391	−40	−9.3	4.1	2.9
Wayne	10,984	13,419	2,435	22.2	42.1	42.8
Wilkes	2,042	2,437	395	19.3	9.0	9.1
Wilson	7,760	9,905	2,145	27.6	41.6	42.0
Yadkin	1,368	1,187	−181	−13.2	9.9	8.4
Yancey	292	283	−9	−3.1	3.1	2.5
TOTAL	561,018	624,469	63,451	11.3	34.7	33.0

*United States Department of Commerce, *Bureau of Census, Negro Population, 1790–1915*, 784–85. For comparative purposes, the white population 1890, 1,055,382; the white population 1900, 1,263,603.

TABLE 2

LITERACY FOR NORTH CAROLINA, 1900, TOTAL MALES TWENTY-ONE YEARS AND OVER, BY COUNTIES*

COUNTY	AGGREGATE	NATIVE WHITE		NATIVE NEGRO	
		LITERATE	ILLITERATE	LITERATE	ILLITERATE
Alamance	5,730	3,815	558	599	739
Alexander	2,285	1,742	373	76	94
Alleghany	1,613	1,219	302	42	50
Anson	4,370	1,935	352	905	1,168
Ashe	3,969	3,015	822	54	68
Beaufort	6,337	3,174	568	1,231	1,336
Bertie	4,352	1,759	378	957	1,247
Bladen	3,576	1,834	334	708	697
Brunswick	2,868	1,427	332	537	537
Buncombe	10,239	7,002	1,135	1,134	735
Burke	3,805	2,535	752	200	264
Cabarrus	4,835	3,148	453	553	666
Caldwell	3,345	2,311	646	182	198
Camden	1,284	626	175	237	239
Carteret	2,931	2,082	377	272	185
Caswell	3,320	1,351	306	532	1,125
Catawba	4,525	3,325	606	288	286
Chatham	5,176	2,975	630	683	868
Cherokee	2,531	1,841	578	40	51
Chowan	2,338	875	207	530	715
Clay	958	704	220	18	13
Cleveland	5,345	3,366	955	452	560
Columbus	4,459	2,527	629	764	458
Craven	5,805	2,060	351	1,705	1,627
Cumberland	6,225	3,260	563	1,316	1,046
Currituck	1,649	1,029	199	208	210
Dare	1,218	838	227	75	71
Davidson	5,189	3,524	975	286	388
Davie	2,754	1,711	467	261	308
Duplin	4,745	2,514	757	603	854
Durham	6,065	3,280	590	984	1,136
Edgecombe	6,019	2,022	474	1,316	2,177
Forsyth	8,475	4,962	965	1,409	1,073
Franklin	5,484	2,319	746	1,114	1,302
Gaston	5,994	3,777	621	834	704
Gates	2,121	968	319	328	503
Graham	869	647	191	1	2
Granville	4,855	2,098	494	868	1,390
Greene	2,692	1,119	383	500	685
Guilford	9,516	6,165	758	1,411	1,088
Halifax	7,287	2,478	377	1,644	2,750
Harnett	3,335	1,915	516	410	486
Haywood	3,417	2,465	799	84	50
Henderson	3,104	2,292	393	199	185
Hertford	3,014	1,144	290	683	889
Hyde	2,101	1,094	196	412	394
Iredell	6,387	4,191	648	702	827
Jackson	2,596	1,744	609	66	61
Johnston	7,025	4,088	1,294	697	921

LITERACY FOR NORTH CAROLINA, 1900—*Continued*

COUNTY	AGGREGATE	NATIVE WHITE		NATIVE NEGRO	
		LITERATE	ILLITERATE	LITERATE	ILLITERATE
Jones	1,850	906	192	411	331
Lenoir	4,306	2,049	545	800	897
Lincoln	3,186	2,128	485	328	239
McDowell	2,689	1,835	462	161	205
Macon	2,444	1,840	479	47	69
Madison	4,212	2,992	1,076	85	53
Martin	3,405	1,496	408	590	908
Mecklenburg	12,586	6,687	653	2,475	2,585
Mitchell	3,106	2,154	816	64	62
Montgomery	3,179	1,896	506	350	417
Moore	5,286	3,138	489	855	737
Nash	5,839	2,728	814	970	1,313
New Hanover	6,564	2,997	162	1,906	1,202
North Hampton	4,661	1,756	425	1,020	1,450
Onslow	2,749	1,618	426	404	300
Orange	3,414	1,894	412	493	611
Pamlico	1,861	1,036	239	327	254
Pasquotank	3,206	1,430	221	806	719
Pender	2,864	1,287	255	605	704
Perquimans	2,278	1,001	206	641	422
Person	3,429	1,524	601	334	963
Pitt	6,872	2,973	815	1,276	1,804
Polk	1,511	976	303	109	118
Randolph	6,277	4,465	1,037	394	361
Richmond	3,477	1,611	279	662	910
Robeson	8,511	3,696	855	1,599	1,601
Rockingham	7,159	3,877	985	873	1,383
Rowan	7,343	4,769	633	919	961
Rutherford	5,304	3,688	762	472	377
Sampson	5,502	3,031	933	649	877
Scotland	2,716	1,102	263	542	772
Stanly	3,096	2,116	593	206	174
Stokes	4,201	2,429	1,174	188	406
Surry	5,613	3,578	1,411	261	333
Swain	1,778	1,151	394	19	16
Transylvania	1,479	1,163	175	65	63
Tyrrell	1,171	657	187	165	156
Union	5,561	3,361	681	665	844
Vance	3,551	1,390	281	771	1,071
Wake	12,800	6,226	1,358	2,555	2,528
Warren	3,889	1,208	185	1,076	1,365
Washington	2,404	1,033	234	563	573
Watauga	2,773	2,108	578	35	49
Wayne	6,992	3,401	758	1,523	1,262
Wilkes	5,528	3,506	1,567	208	239
Wilson	5,372	2,526	764	873	1,193
Yadkin	3,092	2,166	660	124	137
Yancey	2,360	1,587	707	24	41
TOTAL	417,578	232,478	54,334	59,597	67,481

*United States Department of Commerce, *Bureau of Census, Twelfth Census*, 1900, Vol. I, Part 1 compiled from Table 92, 992–93.

TABLE 3

VOTE FOR GOVERNOR, 1892–1900*

COUNTIES	1892			1896			1900	
	Elias Carr Democrat	D. M. Furches Republican	W. B. Exum Populist	Cyrus B. Watson Democrat	Daniel L. Russell Republican	W. A. Guthrie Populist	C. B. Aycock Democrat	S. B. Adams Republican
Alamance	1,738	1,199	442	2,166	2,212	238	2,488	2,321
Alexander	586	436	385	881	620	244	892	1,027
Alleghany	814	328	1	744	601	5	784	607
Anson	1,348	263	283	1,681	1,158	626	2,015	522
Ashe	1,390	1,461	107	1,585	1,736	19	1,659	1,969
Beaufort	1,919	1,510	604	2,073	2,165	513	2,933	1,525
Bertie	1,698	1,322	369	1,372	2,009	586	2,675	996
Bladen	1,292	904	546	1,361	1,263	288	1,589	1,375
Brunswick	767	140	745	820	890	410	915	948
Buncombe	3,584	3,140	23	4,159	4,552	23	4,332	3,401
Burke	1,425	1,075	222	1,488	1,381	86	1,509	1,171
Cabarrus	1,442	620	825	1,490	940	852	1,915	1,550
Caldwell	1,193	582	285	1,290	964	138	1,248	1,272
Camden	496	499	95	511	584	45	545	567
Carteret	1,244	550	234	1,157	979	107	1,363	957
Caswell	951	1,498	453	1,310	1,699	49	1,421	1,313
Catawba	1,743	665	889	1,768	1,022	869	2,008	1,863
Chatham	1,609	372	2,240	1,698	1,469	1,211	1,755	1,894
Cherokee	687	804	37	759	988	25	778	1,080
Chowan	679	793	85	722	1,134	92	1,055	948
Clay	373	253	83	422	302	54	388	418
Cleveland	1,799	600	977	2,017	1,200	752	2,652	1,172
Columbus	1,618	755	648	1,420	1,014	731	2,178	1,201
Craven	1,483	1,657	249	1,656	2,867	228	2,611	932
Cumberland	2,389	1,001	1,436	1,955	2,261	525	2,719	1,629
Currituck	820	386	106	778	475	121	1,002	374
Dare	332	331	—	409	463	1	524	406
Davidson	1,928	1,830	424	1,881	2,372	176	2,406	2,275
Davie	738	1,073	231	747	1,303	158	959	1,367
Duplin	1,502	970	817	1,551	1,145	868	2,125	1,297
Durham	1,500	1,233	679	2,092	1,858	370	2,765	2,170
Edgecombe	1,760	1,074	580	1,807	2,736	410	3,758	385
Forsyth	2,903	2,377	453	2,685	3,780	226	2,913	2,432
Franklin	1,786	890	1,398	2,204	1,898	913	3,021	1,831
Gaston	1,634	1,146	379	1,891	1,559	263	2,514	1,584
Gates	889	545	372	877	767	243	1,232	603
Graham	323	260	6	359	344	1	396	343
Granville	1,406	1,589	505	1,896	2,196	363	2,540	1,527
Greene	1,035	567	239	1,005	1,021	221	1,474	774
Guilford	2,815	2,500	406	3,417	3,393	154	4,071	3,343
Halifax	3,328	1,124	593	1,997	3,979	272	6,618	877
Harnett	1,242	567	657	1,264	1,024	463	1,515	1,339
Haywood	1,507	949	49	1,878	1,039	33	1,736	1,244

VOTE FOR GOVERNOR, 1892-1900—*Continued*

COUNTIES	1892			1896			1900	
	Elias Carr Democrat	D. M. Furchess Republican	W. B. Exum Populist	Cyrus B. Watson Democrat	Daniel L. Russell Republican	W. A. Guthrie Populist	C. B. Aycock Democrat	S. B. Adams Republican
Henderson	842	1,172	75	1,005	1,452	41	1,121	1,468
Hertford	665	867	149	879	1,436	369	1,368	429
Hyde	864	14	716	881	810	205	971	905
Iredell	2,274	1,500	635	2,524	2,008	428	2,779	2,319
Jackson	966	576	164	1,002	872	148	1,118	1,025
Johnston	3,145	917	557	3,074	1,834	424	3,777	—
Jones	659	307	371	659	704	148	906	694
Lenoir	1,426	943	475	1,598	1,501	260	2,101	1,123
Lincoln	992	563	453	1,125	1,034	231	1,341	1,288
Macon	850	520	229	1,009	889	132	1,044	1,059
Madison	1,135	1,805	118	1,309	2,275	48	1,176	2,370
Martin	1,485	1,009	346	1,479	1,382	211	2,002	990
McDowell	1,062	732	64	1,075	949	121	1,174	1,034
Mecklenburg	3,887	1,961	550	4,439	3,748	627	5,095	1,627
Mitchell	714	1,311	32	618	1,855	15	413	1,940
Montgomery	988	834	202	984	1,204	155	1,341	868
Moore	1,693	1,373	750	1,739	1,910	536	1,890	1,875
Nash	1,081	347	1,348	1,578	1,571	1,397	2,957	1,360
New Hanover	2,447	1,326	187	2,218	3,145	75	2,963	3
North Hampton	1,455	1,027	819	1,660	2,312	218	2,438	1,096
Onslow	1,177	298	477	1,150	671	310	1,548	637
Orange	1,117	875	804	1,245	1,238	498	1,471	1,469
Pamlico	497	413	398	503	649	343	657	599
Pasquotank	869	1,216	187	938	1,510	123	1,502	926
Pender	901	957	132	1,089	1,159	186	1,260	276
Perquimans	521	816	285	684	1,006	127	959	732
Person	1,259	1,404	319	1,681	1,399	20	1,607	1,286
Pitt	2,083	1,123	1,444	2,538	2,462	521	3,433	2,096
Polk	507	563	—	477	715	1	534	650
Randolph	2,113	1,870	535	2,263	2,711	251	2,468	2,513
Richmond	1,740	1,074	469	1,849	2,462	382	1,645	185
Robeson	2,270	1,121	1,129	2,176	2,282	1,294	4,100	557
Rockingham	9,881	1,881	905	2,503	2,428	200	2,913	1,946
Rowan	2,327	848	787	2,495	1,428	660	3,157	1,519
Rutherford	1,799	1,550	254	2,049	1,945	147	2,389	2,092
Sampson	1,370	1,266	1,585	1,270	1,258	1,561	1,356	1,950
Scotland	—	—	—	—	—	—	1,065	25
Stanly	1,079	270	221	1,102	494	351	1,453	837
Stokes	1,230	1,570	191	1,407	2,052	40	1,519	1,944
Surry	1,998	1,683	47	2,083	2,540	8	2,154	2,594
Swain	580	395	185	739	531	69	540	816
Transylvania	522	506	6	600	649	3	596	607
Tyrrell	248	275	241	305	489	109	591	410
Union	1,827	475	851	1,784	1,001	988	2,379	660

VOTE FOR GOVERNOR, 1892-1900—*Continued*

COUNTIES	1892			1896			1900	
	Elias Carr Democrat	D. M. Furchess Republican	W. B. Exum Populist	Cyrus B. Watson Democrat	Daniel L. Russell Republican	W. A. Guthrie Populist	C. B. Aycock Democrat	S. B. Adams Republican
Vance	930	1,301	838	1,093	1,815	270	1,304	944
Wake	3,792	1,673	3,035	4,491	4,801	774	5,732	4,448
Warren	802	1,295	944	922	2,171	309	2,133	1,069
Washington	576	423	414	591	1,270	159	976	571
Watauga	928	829	94	1,041	1,172	33	1,055	1,411
Wayne	2,283	1,580	964	2,719	2,336	381	3,828	1,878
Wilkes	1,755	1,921	116	1,778	2,828	96	1,435	2,257
Wilson	2,032	406	1,277	1,552	1,443	1,052	2,916	1,430
Yadkin	1,044	1,234	163	1,017	1,641	79	1,011	1,821
Yancey	917	601	146	1,030	978	28	986	1,081
TOTAL	135,519	94,684	47,840	145,266	153,787	31,143	186,650	126,296

North Carolina Manual, 1913, 1005–6.

TABLE 4

VOTE ON THE SUFFRAGE AMENDMENT, 1900*

COUNTY	FOR AMENDMENT	AGAINST AMENDMENT	COUNTY	FOR AMENDMENT	AGAINST AMENDMENT
Alamance	2,353	2,388	Lenoir	2,122	961
Alexander	826	1,042	Lincoln	1,255	1,315
Alleghany	717	614	Macon	913	1,127
Anson	2,124	496	Madison	970	2,497
Ashe	1,483	1,983	Martin	1,889	993
Beaufort	3,012	1,456	McDowell	1,124	1,059
Bertie	2,649	944	Mecklenburg	5,110	1,557
Bladen	1,430	1,220	Mitchell	477	1,954
Brunswick	849	992	Montgomery	1,329	870
Buncombe	4,170	3,707	Moore	1,840	1,876
Burke	1,507	1,170	Nash	2,996	1,336
Cabarrus	1,893	1,578	New Hanover	2,967	2
Caldwell	1,128	1,354	North Hampton	2,469	1,095
Camden	551	552	Onslow	1,531	671
Carteret	1,332	908	Orange	1,406	1,493
Caswell	1,437	1,277	Pamlico	569	491
Catawba	1,928	1,896	Pasquotank	1,542	892
Chatham	1,708	1,976	Pender	1,255	294
Cherokee	707	1,103	Perquimans	964	679
Chowan	1,138	917	Person	1,658	1,221
Clay	302	454	Pitt	3,414	2,042
Cleveland	2,701	1,185	Polk	542	636
Columbus	2,231	1,234	Randolph	2,318	2,509
Craven	2,662	955	Richmond	1,636	193
Cumberland	2,713	1,768	Robeson	4,015	704
Currituck	1,012	413	Rockingham	2,898	2,045
Dare	531	380	Rowan	3,067	1,716
Davidson	2,235	2,278	Rutherford	2,304	2,103
Davie	938	1,378	Sampson	1,302	2,061
Duplin	2,072	1,361	Scotland	1,803	7
Durham	2,689	2,212	Stanly	1,417	858
Edgecombe	3,781	374	Stokes	1,406	1,977
Forsyth	2,810	2,561	Surry	2,013	2,643
Franklin	2,970	1,836	Swain	449	858
Gaston	2,482	1,581	Transylvania	596	620
Gates	1,215	596	Tyrrell	632	400
Graham	356	374	Union	2,396	822
Granville	2,459	1,610	Vance	1,343	913
Green	1,571	666	Wake	5,668	4,478
Guilford	3,941	3,358	Warren	1,807	1,356
Halifax	6,280	899	Washington	1,037	547
Harnett	1,466	1,387	Watauga	919	1,436
Haywood	1,281	1,549	Wayne	3,838	1,816
Henderson	1,202	1,389	Wilkes	1,351	2,240
Hertford	1,407	397	Wilson	2,855	1,443
Hyde	976	844	Yadkin	968	1,843
Iredell	2,683	2,373	Yancey	751	1,173
Jackson	1,019	1,064			
Johnston	3,853	1,749			
Jones	941	665	TOTAL	182,217	128,285

*North Carolina Manual, 1913, 1016–18.

FURNIFOLD SIMMONS' LETTER TO
UNITED STATES SENATOR JETER C. PRITCHARD

PRINTED IN THE *News and Observer*, OCTOBER 30, 1898

HONORABLE JETER C. PRITCHARD,
Marshall, N. C.

Sir:

I am informed that in your speeches and your statements to the President asking for Federal troops you deny that there is in any part of North Carolina negro rule or domination.

Now I desire to ask you some questions and I insist that you answer them over your own signature.

1st. Do you deny that there is a negro candidate running for Congress in the Second Congressional District and that he is the regular Republican nominee?

2nd. Do you deny that there is a negro candidate running for solicitor in the Second Judicial District and that he is the regular nominee of the Republican party?

3rd. Do you deny that there is a negro collector of customs at the port of Wilmington; that there are from 15 to 25 negro postmasters in Eastern North Carolina all of whom, both negro collector and postmasters, were appointed by President McKinley with your approval and consent?

4th. Do you deny that the negro COLONEL James H. Young, was until he resigned that position to accept the position of colonel of the Third Regiment of negro troops, a director of the White Blind Asylum, and that he was appointed to that position by Governor Russell?

5th. Do you deny that this same negro Colonel, James H. Young, was, until he resigned to accept the position aforesaid, fertilizer inspector, with a big salary and with white men working under him, and that he was appointed to that position by the Fusion Commissioner of Agriculture, at the insistence of Governor Russell?

6th. Do you deny that there is in the Fourth Collection District of North Carolina a general storekeeper and gauger, who is a negro, and who was appointed by Mr. Carl Duncan, the Republican Collector of the District, and your appointee and political manager in the East?

7th. Do you deny that the register of Craven County is a negro and that he was elected by the Republicans of that County?

8th. Do you deny that the deputies of this negro Register of Deeds as well as three deputies of the Republican Sheriff, of that county, are negroes?

9th. Do you deny that the Register of Deeds of New Hanover County is a negro and that he was elected by the Republican party?

10th. Do you deny that the present coroner of Craven County is a negro and that one of the members of the Board of County Commissioners is a negro, and that they were both elected by the Republican party?

11th. Do you deny that there are scores of negro constables and deputy sheriffs in New Hanover, Craven, Halifax, Edgecombe, Bertie, Warren, and a number of other Eastern counties, all of whom were elected by the Republican party?

12th. Do you deny that there are FORTY negro magistrates in the county of New Hanover, and that they were all either appointed by the Fusion Legislature of 1895, or elected by the Republican party?

13th. Do you deny that there are THIRTY-ONE negro magistrates in Edgecombe County, and that they were all either appointed by the Fusion Legislature of 1895 or elected by the Republican party?

14th. Do you deny that there are SIXTEEN negro magistrates in Bertie County, and that they were all either appointed by the Fusion Legislature of 1895, or elected by the Republican party?

15th. Do you deny that there are TWENTY-SEVEN negro magistrates in Craven County and that they were all either appointed by the Fusion Legislature of 1895, or elected by the Republican party?

16th. Do you deny that there are SEVENTEEN negro magistrates in Granville County and that they were all either appointed by the Fusion Legislature of 1895, or elected by the Republican party?

17th. Do you deny that there are TWENTY-NINE negro magistrates in Halifax County and that they were all either appointed by the Fusion Legislature of 1895, or elected by the Republican party?

18th. Do you deny that there are SEVEN negro magistrates in Caswell County, and they were either appointed by the Fusion Legislature or elected by the Republican party?

19th. Do you deny that in the various Eastern Counties there are negro magistrates to the number of nearly THREE HUNDRED, including those above specified, and that they were all either appointed by the Fusion Legislature of 1895, or elected by the Republican party?

20th. Do you deny that until your party within the last ten days removed from office, for political effect, there were FOURTEEN negro policemen in the city of Wilmington, all of whom were appointed by the Republican party?

21st. Do you deny that one of the members of the Finance Committee of Wilmington is a negro appointed by the Republican party?

22nd. Do you deny that there are negro policemen and negro aldermen in the city of New Bern appointed by the Republican party?

23rd. Do you deny that under the gerrymander of the Fusion Legislature of 1895, although there is a white majority in the town of Greenville, your party so divided up the wards in that town that the negroes have FOUR members of the Board of Aldermen, while the white majority have only TWO?

24th. Do you deny that there are THREE negroes running for the Legislature in Edgecombe County, all of whom were nominated by the Republican party, and have been endorsed by Fusion Populists?

25th.   Do you deny that there are TWO negroes running for the Legislature in Halifax County, both of whom were nominated by the Republican party, and have been endorsed by the Fusion Populists?

26th.   Do you deny that there are two negroes running for the Legislature in Granville County, both of whom were nominated by the Republican party and have been endorsed by the Fusion Populists?

27th.   Do you deny that there is a negro running for the Legislature in Vance County, one in Craven County, one in Pasquotank County, one in North Hampton County, one in Warren County, and in several other Eastern Counties, who were nominated by the Republican party, and have been endorsed by the Fusion Populists?

28th.   Do you deny that the Republican party has this year nominated in various counties in the East negroes for register of deeds, treasurers, coroners, constables, county commissioners, and magistrates?

29th.   Do you deny that there are upon the Republican ticket for the County of Craven, a negro for the Legislature, a negro for the Register of Deeds, a negro for Treasurer, and negro for Coroner, a negro for County Commissioner, and a negro for standard keeper, all of whom were nominated by the Republican party and are its regular candidates, and that the white Republican candidates for sheriff and clerk in that county have promised the negroes that, if elected, they will appoint negro deputies?

30th.   Do you deny that there are several hundred school committeemen in North Carolina, appointed by the Republican party and have authority over white as well as colored schools?

Now what constitutes negro domination may be a question of opinion or taste. What the people want to know is not what constitutes negro domination in your opinion, but your unequivocal statement of the facts with reference to negro office holding in the East and negro candidates on the part of your party, so that they may decide for themselves whether there is negro rule in Eastern North Carolina.

F. M. SIMMONS*

*Rippy (ed.), *Furnifold Simmons, Statesman of the New South; Memoirs and Addresses*, 522–32; also *News and Observer*, October 30, 1898. [It should be noted that there is a difference in "running for" offices and "winning" offices.]

Special
Administrative
Aide   AJ:MM:MS

POST OFFICE DEPARTMENT
First Assistant Postmaster General
Washington 25, D. C.

July 11, 1945

Miss Helen G. Edmonds,
    Box 622, North Carolina College,
    Durham, North Carolina.

My dear Miss Edmonds:

Receipt is acknowledged of your letter of June 20, 1945, requesting historical information concerning the various appointed postmasters in North Carolina.

The heavy increase in postal business during the present emergency makes it inadvisable to perform the extensive research and clerical work involved in supplying information of this nature.

It is regretted that favorable consideration cannot be given your request at this time.

Very truly yours,
C. B. Uttley
Acting First Assistant Postmaster General

THE SUPREME COURT'S RECORD ON OFFICE-HOLDING CASES DURING THE FUSION PERIOD

Ewart v. Jones—116, p. 570.
Cook v. Meares—116, p. 582.
Stanford v. Ellington—117, p. 158.
Wood v. Bellamy—120, p. 212 (Famous Hospital Case).
Lusk v. Sawyer—120, p. 225 (Famous Hospital Case).
Person v. Sutherland—120, p. 225 (Famous Hospital Case).
Ward v. Elizabeth City—121, p. 221.
*Caldwell v. Wilson—121, pp. 423, 425, 480.
Cromartic v. Parker—121, p. 198.
Shennonhouse v. Withers—121, p. 376.
Harris v. Wright—121, p. 172.
Barnhill v. Thompson—122, p. 493.
†*Houghtaling v. Taylor*—122, p. 140.
Holt v. Bristow—122, p. 245.
Ryan v. Lipscomb—122, p. 655.
State Prison v. Day—124, p. 362 (Famous Prison Case).
Wilson v. Jordan—124, p. 683.
Cherry v. Burns—124, p. 761.
Cunningham v. Sprinkle—124, p. 638.
‡*Abbott v. Beddingfield*—125, p. 256.
‡*McCall v. Webb*—125, p. 243.
‡*McCall v. Zachary*—125, p. 249.
‡*McCall v. Gardner et al.*—125, p. 238.
Ledford v. Green—125, p. 254.
Herring v. Pugh—125, pp. 437, 743.
‡*White v. Hill*—125, p. 194 (Basis of the impeachment).
‡*Greene v. Owen*—125, p. 212.
‡*Bryan v. Patrick*—124, p. 651.
‡*Railroad v. Dortch*—124, p. 663.
‡*Dalby v. Hancock*—125, p. 325.
‡*Gattis v. Griffith*—125, p. 332.
§*White v. The Auditor*—125, p. 674 (Basis of the impeachment).
White v. Murray—126, p. 153.
§*Mott v. The Commissioners of Forsyth*—126, p. 866.
Mott v. Griffin—126, p. 775.
Wilson v. Neal—126, p. 781.
Dowtin v. Beardsley—126, p. 119.
Baker v. Hobgood—126, p. 149.
Mitchell v. Alley—126, p. 84.

*Faircloth dissenting.
†Douglas dissenting alone.
‡Clark dissenting alone.
§Clark and Montgomery dissenting.

BIBLIOGRAPHY

PRIMARY SOURCES

(1) FEDERAL DOCUMENTS

Congressional Record, Fifty-first Congress.
Congressional Record, Fifty-fourth Congress.
Congressional Record, Fifty-fifth Congress.
Congressional Record, Fifty-sixth Congress.
United States Bureau of Census, *Negro Population, 1790–1915*, Washington, D. C., 1918.
United States Congress, *Biographical Directory of the American Congress*, 1774–1927, Washington, D. C., 1928.
United States Department of Commerce, *Bureau of Census, Eleventh Census*, 1890, Washington, D. C., Vol. 1, Part 1.
United States Department of Commerce, *Bureau of Census, Twelfth Census*, 1900, Washington, D. C., Vol. 1, Part 1.
United States Statutes at Large, Vols. XXIV, XXVI.

(2) STATE DOCUMENTS OF NORTH CAROLINA

Code of 1883.
House Journal, 1893, 1895, 1897, 1899, 1901.
North Carolina Supreme Court Reports, Vols. 16, 110, 116, 117, 119, 120, 121, 122, 123, 124, 125, 126, 133.
Private Laws, 1874–1875, 1875–1876, 1878–1879, 1880–1881, 1883, 1885, 1887, 1889, 1891, 1893, 1895, 1897, 1899, 1901.
Public Documents, 1895, 1897, 1899, 1901.
Public Laws, 1868, 1868–1869, 1875–1876, 1876, 1877, 1878–1879, 1880–1881, 1883, 1885, 1887, 1889, 1891,1893, 1895, 1897, 1899, 1901, 1903.
Public and Private Laws and Resolutions, Adjourned Session, 1900.
Report of the Bureau of Labor Statistics, 1887, 1889, 1900.
Senate Journal, 1893, 1895, 1897, 1899, 1901.
Trial of David M. Furchess, Now Chief Justice, and formerly Associate Justice of the Supreme Court of North Carolina, on Impeachment by the House of Representatives for High Crimes and Misdemeanors. Published by Order of the General Assembly. Raleigh, N. C.: Edwards and Broughton, and E. M. Uzzell, State Printers, 1901.

(3) MANUSCRIPTS

Charles Brantley Aycock Papers, North Carolina Historical Commission, Raleigh, N. C.
John Spencer Bassett Letters to Herbert Baxter Adams. Photostatic copies of the

private correspondence of Herbert Baxter Adams, Duke University Library, Durham, N. C. (Original correspondence preserved at Johns Hopkins University Library, Baltimore, Md.)

Marion Butler Papers (Shorter Collection). University of North Carolina Library, Chapel Hill, N. C.

Locke Craig Letters, Papers, and Scrapbook. Duke University Library, Durham, N. C.

John C. Dancy Papers .Papers are in possession of John C. Dancy, Jr., Director of the Urban League, 606 E. Vernor, Detroit, Mich.

Governors' Appointments and Commissions. The Governors' Letter Box, 1897–1901. North Carolina Historical Commission, Raleigh, N. C.

Charles N. Hunter Papers. Duke University Library, Durham, N. C.

Daniel L. Russell Executive Papers, 1897–1901. North Carolina Historical Commission, Raleigh, N. C.

Daniel L. Russell Papers. University of North Carolina Library, Chapel Hill, N. C.

Furnifold M. Simmons Papers. Duke University Library, Durham, N. C.

Edward Chambers Smith Papers. Duke University Library, Durham, N. C.

Cyrus Thompson Papers. University of North Carolina Library, Chapel Hill, N. C.

Alfred M. Waddell Papers. University of North Carolina Library, Chapel Hill, N. C.

(4) Autobiographies, Biographies, and Memoirs

Brooks, Aubrey L. *Walter Clark, Fighting Judge*. Chapel Hill, N. C.: University of North Carolina Press, 1944.

Clawson Memoirs, Recollections of Thomas W. Clawson on the Wilmington Race Riot of 1898. Deposited in the North Carolina Historical Commission, Raleigh, N. C., May 26, 1944.

Collins and Goodwin, *Biographical Sketches of the General Assembly of 1895* (North Carolina). Raleigh, N. C.: Edwards and Broughton, Printers and Binders, 1895.

Connor, R. D. W., and Poe, Clarence. *The Life and Speeches of Charles Brantley Aycock*. New York: Doubleday, Page and Company, 1912.

Daniels, Josephus, *Editor in Politics*. Chapel Hill, N. C.: University of North Carolina Press, 1941.

————. *Tar Heel Editor*. Chapel Hill, N. C.: University of North Carolina Press, 1939.

Fuller, Thomas O. *Twenty Years in Public Life, 1890–1910*. Nashville, Tenn.: National Baptist Publishing Board, 1910.

Jones, May F. (ed.). *Memoirs and Speeches of Locke Craig, Governor of North Carolina; 1913–1917; A History, Political and Otherwise*. Asheville, N. C.: Hackney and Moale, 1923.

Kirk, J. Allen, *A Statement of Facts Concerning the Bloody Riot in Wilmington, North Carolina, Thursday, November 10, 1898*. Duke University Library and University of North Carolina Library.

Rippy, Fred (ed.), *Furnifold Simmons, Statesman of the New South; Memoirs and Addresses*. Durham, N. C.: Duke University Press, 1936.

Waddell, Alfred M. *Some Memories of My Life*, Raleigh, N. C.: Edwards and Broughton Company, 1908.

(5) Party Documents of North Carolina and Miscellaneous Items

Amendment Catechism. Raleigh, N. C., 1900.

Constitution of the Farmers' State Alliance of North Carolina, 1889. Raleigh, N. C.: Edwards and Broughton Printing Company, 1889.

Constitution of Louisiana, 1898. New Orleans, La., 1898.

Democratic Handbook, 1894. Raleigh, N. C.

Democratic Handbook, 1898. Raleigh, N. C.

Democratic Handbook, 1900. Raleigh, N. C.

North Carolina Manual, 1913. Issued by the North Carolina Historical Commission, compiled and edited by R. D. W. Connor. Raleigh, N. C.: E. M. Uzzell and Company, State Printers, 1913.

People's Party Handbook, 1896. Raleigh, N. C.

People's Party Handbook, 1900. Raleigh, N. C.

People's Party Handbook of Facts: Campaign of 1898. Raleigh, N. C.

Republican Party Handbook, 1892. Raleigh, N. C.

Republican Party Handbook, 1898. Raleigh, N. C.

(6) Pamphlets

Address to the Populist Party of North Carolina, by W. M. A. Guthrie, 1896. (University of North Carolina Library)

The Brightest Day of Republicanism, Address by the Honorable Jeter C. Pritchard to the Republican State Convention at Greensboro, North Carolina, August 28, 1902. (Duke University Library)

Chairman Simmons Says the Democrats Made No Promises on the Suffrage Question in 1898, n.p., n.p., 1900. (University of North Carolina Library)

Citizens and Voters, A Circular Issued by the People's Party of North Carolina, 1898. (State Library, Raleigh)

Comments by the State Democratic Committee on the Handbook Issued by the People's Party State Executive Committee. N.d., n.p., n.p. (University of North Carolina Library)

Comparative Vote for Governor and Chief Justice and Treasurer and Members of Congress, 1892 to 1894, Josephus Daniels, State Printer and Binder, Presses of Edwards and Broughton, Raleigh, N. C., 1894. (University of North Carolina Library)

Comparative Vote for Governor and Members of Congress, 1892 to 1894, also vote for Treasurer of North Carolina, 1896, n.p., n.p. (University of North Carolina Library)

Comparative Vote for Governor, 1900, and for Members of Congress, 1898 and 1900, 1900, n.p., n.p. (University of North Carolina Library)

Dr. Cyrus Thompson's Great Speech, Delivered in Clinton, North Carolina, August 19, 1898. (North Carolina Historical Commission)

Great Speech of George Rountree, Esq., Delivered in the House of Representatives of North Carolina on the Subject of the Constitutional Amendment, Adjourned Session, June, 1900. (University of North Carolina Library)

Is The Democratic Party Honest? A Statement of Facts Issued by the People's Party State Central Committee, 1898, [1900]. Raleigh, N. C. (State Library, Raleigh)

Manhood Suffrage in North Carolina and the Proposed Constitutional Amendment, *February 6, 1900,* by Marion Butler. (University of North Carolina Library)

Negro Smith Scores the Populist Johnson, The [1899]. (University of North Carolina Library)

North Carolina Pamphlets, 1880–1899, Vol. VI, No. 73. (Duke University Library)

On the Proposed Amendment to the Constitution of North Carolina, Speech of the Honorable Jeter C. Pritchard of North Carolina in the Senate of the United States Congress, January 22, 1900. (University of North Carolina Library)

Opinions of a Lawyer on the Constitutionality of the Proposed Amendment, by W. M. A. Guthrie of Durham, April 21, 1900. (Duke University Library)

Position of the Negro in American Life by John Spencer Bassett, Address, May, 1900, at Winston-Salem Negro Normal School, Winston-Salem, North Carolina, Duke University *Pamphlets,* Vol. 1, No. 8, (Duke University Library)

The Problem of the Hour: Will the Colored Race Save Itself from Ruin? Address delivered by Julian S. Carr at the Commencement Exercises before the Trustees, Faculty, and Students of the North Carolina College of Agriculture and Mechanic Arts for Negroes, Greensboro, N. C., May, 1899. (Duke University Library)

Proposed Franchise Amendment, Some Constitutional Discussions with Declarations, The, 1900. (Duke University Library)

Proposed Suffrage Amendment: The Platform and Resolutions of the People's Party, The, Platform of April 18, 1900. (University of North Carolina Library)

Senator Butler's Position on the Proposed Constitutional Amendment and the Simmons-Goebel Election Law. N.p., n.d. (University of North Carolina Library)

Some Correspondence Between the State Chairman of Two Political Organizations, (Marion Butler, Populist, to Furnifold Simmons, Democrat). N.p., n.d., n.p. [1900]. (Duke University Library)

Speech Delivered by S. B. Adams, Chairman State Republican Executive Committee at Asheville, North Carolina, August 25, 1906, together with the Platform of the Republican Party, Adopted at Greensboro, July 10, 1906. (University of North Carolina Library)

Speech of the Honorable Charles B. Aycock Accepting the Nomination for Governor, April 11, 1900, Raleigh. (Duke University Library)

State Democratic Executive Committee: To The People of North Carolina, October 6, 1892, Raleigh, 1892. (Duke University Library)

To the Democrats of North Carolina, by James W. Wilson, 1902. (*Also Included in Some Campaign Letters of 1902*), 1902, Raleigh. (Duke University Library)

United States Shall Guarantee to Every State in the Union a Republican Form of Government: Speech of Hon. Jeter C. Pritchard of North Carolina in the Senate of the United States Congress, March 1, 1900. (University of North Carolina Library)

(7) PERIODICALS

African Methodist Episcopal Zion Church Quarterly, December, 1896; December 1898; December, 1900. Salisbury, N. C.: African Methodist Zion Press.

Butler, Marion. "The Election in North Carolina [1896]," *Review of Reviews,* Vol. XIX, November, 1896.

————. "The People's Party," *Forum,* Vol. 28, February, 1900.

Connor, Henry G. "A Saner Citizenship," Address, *Trinity College Historical Papers*, Series IV, 1900.

Crowell, John, "A Program of Progress: An Open Letter to the General Assembly of North Carolina of 1891," *Trinity College Publications*, No. 3.

Independent, "The Election of 1900 in North Carolina," Vol. 52, August 9, 1900.

————. "North Carolina's Red Shirt Campaign," Vol. 52, August 2, 1900.

Outlook, The, "The Constitutional Amendment in North Carolina," Vol. 65, August 11, 1900.

————. "North Carolina Race Conflict," Vol. 63, November 19, 1898.

————. "Republican Party in North Carolina and the Amendment," Vol. 65, August 11, 1900.

————. "Restricted Suffrage on Trial in North Carolina," Vol. 73, April, 1903.

Snyder, Carl, "Marion Butler," *Review of Reviews*, Vol. 14, October, 1898.

Tourgee, Albion, "Shall White Minorities Rule?" *Forum*, Vol. 7, 1899.

Waddell, Colonel Alfred M. "The North Carolina Race War," *Collier's Magazine*, Vol. 22, No. 8, November 26, 1898.

Weeks, Stephen. "The History of Negro Suffrage in the South," *Political Science Quarterly*, Vol. IX, 1894.

West, H. L. "The Race War in North Carolina," *Forum*, Vol. 26, January, 1899.

(8) Newspapers with the Location of Files

Asheville Citizen. (Democratic) Duke University Library.

Causasian, The, Clinton, 1892–1899; Raleigh, 1900. (Populist) Duke University and State Library, Raleigh.

Charlotte Observer. (Democratic) Duke University Library.

Durham Sun. (Democratic) Duke University Library.

Elizabeth City North Carolinian. (Republican) State Library, Raleigh.

Greensboro Patriot. (Democratic) Office of the Patriot.

Lenoir Topic. (Democratic) University of North Carolina Library.

New Berne Daily Journal. (Democratic) University of North Carolina Library.

News and Observer, The, Raleigh. (Democratic) Duke University Library.

Progressive Farmer, The, Raleigh. (Populist) State Library, Raleigh.

Raleigh Blade, The. (Republican) Single issue in possession of Mrs. Thomas S. Eaton, Henderson, North Carolina.

Union Republican, The, Winston. (Republican) Duke University Library.

Warren Record. (Republican) Duke University Library

Wilmington Messenger. (Democratic) University of North Carolina Library.

(9) Personal Interviews

Attorney James Hunter Young Carter, Winston-Salem, North Carolina.

Mr. John C. Dancy, Jr., 606 East Vernor, Detroit, Michigan.

Mr. J. E. Dickson, 602 North Mangum Street, Durham, North Carolina.

Mrs. James Youman Eaton, Henderson, North Carolina.

Mrs. Thomas S. Eaton, Henderson, North Carolina.

Mrs. Martha Young Ray, Winston-Salem, North Carolina.

Mr. Thomas Rivera, 403 Umstead Street, Durham, North Carolina.

Dr. Leon F. Sarjeant, 743 North 44th Street, Philadelphia, Pennsylvania.

Judge Armond W. Scott, Twelfth Municipal District Court, Washington, D. C.
Mrs. Hattie E. Shepard, 2004 Fayetteville Street, Durham, North Carolina.
Dr. James E. Shepard, North Carolina College for Negroes, Durham, North Carolina.

SECONDARY SOURCES

(1) PUBLISHED WORKS

Appletons' Annual Cyclopedia, New Series, Vols. XIX, XX, 1894, 1895; Third Series,
Vols. I, 1896; III, 1898; IV, 1899; V, 1900; VI, 1901. New York: D. Appleton
and Company.
Ashe, Samuel A. *History of North Carolina*, Vol. II. Raleigh, N. C.: Edwards and
Broughton Printing Company, 1925.
Buck, Solon J. *The Agrarian Crusade; A Chronicle of the Farmers in Politics.* New
Haven, Conn.: Yale University Press, 1921.
————. *The Granger Movement; A Study of Agricultural Organization and Its
Political, Economic, and Social Manifestations, 1870–1880.* Cambridge, Mass.:
Harvard University Press, 1913.
Caldwell, A. B. (ed.). *History of the American Negro*, North Carolina Edition, Vol.
IV. Atlanta, Ga.: A. B. Caldwell Publishing Company, 1921.
Connor, R. D. W. *North Carolina: Rebuilding an Ancient Commonwealth 1584–1925*,
Vol. II. New York: American Historical Society Inc., 1929.
Daniels, Jonathan. *Tar Heels: A Portrait of North Carolina.* New York: Dodd, Mead
and Company, 1941.
Franklin, John Hope. *The Free Negro in North Carolina.* Chapel Hill, N. C.: Uni-
versity of North Carolina Press, 1943.
Fuller, Thomas O. *Bridging the Racial Chasm.* Memphis, Tennessee, 1916.
————. *A Pictorial History of the American Negro.* Memphis, Tenn.: Pictorial
History, Inc., 1933.
Gobbel, Luther. *Church-State Relationships in Education in North Carolina Since 1776.*
Durham, N. C.: Duke University Press, 1938.
Hamilton, J. G. deR. *History of North Carolina Since 1860 (History of North Carolina*,
Vol. III). Chicago, Ill.: The Lewis Publishing Company, 1919.
Haworth, Paul L. *The Hayes-Tilden Disputed Presidential Election of 1876.* Cleveland,
Ohio: The Burrows Brothers Company, 1906.
Hayden, Henry, *The Story of the Wilmington Rebellion.* Wilmington, North Carolina,
1936.
Haynes, F. E. *Third Party Movements in the United States Since the Civil War.* Iowa
City, Iowa: State University of Iowa Press.
Henderson, Archibald. *North Carolina, The Old North State and the New*, Vol. II.
Chicago, Ill.: The Lewis Publishing Company, 1941.
Hicks, J. D. *The Populist Revolt, A History of the Farmers' Alliance and the People's
Party.* Minneapolis, Minn.: University of Minneapolis Press, 1931.
History of the General Assembly of 1895, January 9—March 13, 1895. (North Carolina).
Raleigh, North Carolina, 1895.
Johnson, Edward A. *A History of the Negro Soldiers in the Spanish American War and
Other Items of Interest.* Raleigh, N. C.: Capitol Printing Company, 1899.

Lefler, Hugh T. (ed.). *North Carolina History Told by Contemporaries.* Chapel Hill, N. C.: University of North Carolina Press, 1934.

Newsome, Albert, and Lefler, Hugh. *The Growth of North Carolina.* New York: World Book Company, 1942.

Otken, Charles H. *The Ills of the South: or Related Causes Hostile to the General Prosperity of the Southern People.* New York: G. P. Putnam's Sons, The Knickerbocker Press, 1894.

Simkins, Francis B. *Pitchfork Ben Tillman, South Carolinian.* Baton Rouge, La.: Louisiana State University Press, 1944.

————. *The Tillman Movement in South Carolina.* Durham, N. C.: Duke University Press, 1926.

Smith, Samuel D. *The Negro in Congress, 1870–1901.* Chapel Hill, N. C.: University of North Carolina Press, 1940.

Sprunt, James, *Chronicles of the Cape Fear River 1660–1916,* Second ed. Raleigh, N. C.: Edwards and Broughton Printing Company, 1916.

Thompson, Holland. *From Cotton Field to Cotton Mill: A Study of Industrial Transition in North Carolina.* New York: The Macmillan Company, 1906.

————. *The New South.* The Chronicles of American Series. New Haven, Conn.: Yale University Press, 1919.

Thorne, Jack (pseudonym of David Fulton Bryant). *Hanover: The Persecution of The Lowly. A Story of the Wilmington Massacre.* Published by M. C. L. Hill, N.d., n.p.

Turner, Joseph K., and Bridges, John. *History of Edgecombe County, North Carolina.* Raleigh, N. C.: Edwards and Broughton Printing Company, 1920.

Turner's North Carolina Almanac, 1895, 1897, 1898, 1899. Raleigh, N. C.: James H. Ennis Publisher, 1896, 1897, 1899, 1900.

Wager, Paul W. *County Government and Administration in North Carolina.* Chapel Hill, N. C.: University of North Carolina Press, 1928.

Wallace, David D. *The South Carolina Constitution of 1895,* Columbia, South Carolina, 1927.

Who's Who in America, Vol. 23, 1944–1945, Chicago, Ill.: The A. N. Marquis Company, 1944.

(2) Unpublished Works

Lacy, Dan. The Beginnings of Industrialism in North Carolina, 1865–1900. Unpublished M.A. thesis, University of North Carolina Library, Chapel Hill, N. C., 1935.

MacLeod, John B. The Development of North Carolina Election Laws, 1865–1894. Unpublished M.A. thesis, University of North Carolina Library, Chapel Hill, N.C., 1946.

Smith, Florence E. Populism and Its Influence in North Carolina. Unpublished Ph.D. dissertation, University of Chicago Library, Chicago, Ill., 1929.

Weaver, Phillip J. The Gubernatorial Election of 1896 North Carolina. Unpublished M.A. thesis, University of North Carolina Library, Chapel Hill, N. C., 1937.

(3) Periodicals

Bassett, John Spencer. "Slavery in the State of North Carolina," *Johns Hopkins University Studies in Historical and Political Science,* Vol. XVII, Nos. 7, 8, 1899.

Branson, E. C. "The Jungle of County Government in North Carolina," *County Government and County Affairs in North Carolina*, The North Carolina Club Year Book 1917–1918 (1919).

Delap, Simeon. "The Populist Party in North Carolina," *Trinity College Historical Papers*, Series XXIV, 1922, Duke University.

Farmer, Hallie. "Economic Background to Southern Populism," *South Atlantic Quarterly*, Vol. XXIX, 1930.

Gilbertson, E. "Forms of County Government in North Carolina," *County Government and County Affairs in North Carolina*, The North Carolina Club Year Book, 1917–1918 (1919).

Hamilton, J. G. deR. "Reconstruction in North Carolina," *Columbia University Studies in History, Economics and Political Law*, Vol. LVIII, No. 141, 1914.

Hicks, J. D. "The Farmers' Alliance in North Carolina," *North Carolina Historical Review*, Vol. II, 1925.

Holt, W. S. "Historical Scholarship in the United States, 1876–1901: As Revealed in the Correspondence of Herbert Baxter Adams," *The Johns Hopkins University Studies in Historical and Political Science*, Series LVI, No. 4, 1938.

Johnson, Frank, "Suffrage and Reconstruction in Mississippi," Mississippi Historical Society *Publications*, 1902.

Kendrick, Benjamin B. "Agrarian Discontent in the South, 1880–1900," *American Historical Review*, 1925.

McIntosh, A. C. "County Government in North Carolina," *National Municipal Review*, Vol. 14, 1925.

————. "The County Government System of North Carolina," *County Government and County Affairs in North Carolina*, The North Carolina Club Year Book, 1917–1918 (1919).

Mabry, William A. "Negro Suffrage and Fusion Rule in North Carolina," *North Carolina Historical Review*, Vol. XII, 1935.

————. "The Negro in North Carolina Politics Since Reconstruction," *Historical Papers of Trinity College Historical Society*, Series XXIII, 1940.

————. "White Supremacy and the North Carolina Suffrage Amendment," *The North Carolina Historical Review*, Vol. XIII, No. 1, 1936.

Mitchell, Broadus. "The Rise of Cotton Mills in the South," *Johns Hopkins University Studies in Historical and Political Science*, Vol. 39, No. 2, 1921.

Noblin, Stuart, "Leonidas Lafayette Polk," *North Carolina Historical Review*, Vol. XX, Nos. 2, 3, 1943.

Poe, Clarence. "Suffrage Restriction in the South: Its Causes and Consequences," *North American Review*, Vol. 175, 1902.

Popular Government, Vol. II, June, 1932, No. 2. Published quarterly by the Institute of Government, University of North Carina.

Ricaud, A. G. "Daniel L. Russell," *North Carolina Bar Association Report*, Vol. X, 1908.

Stephenson, Gilbert. "County Offices in North Carolina," *County Government and County Affairs in North Carolina*, The North Carolina Club Year Book, 1917–1918 (1926).

Taylor, Rosser. "Slaveholding in North Carolina: An Economic View," *The James Sprunt Historical Publications*, Vol. XVIII, Nos. 1–2, 1926.

Thompson, Holland. "The Southern Textile Situation," *South Atlantic Quarterly*, Vol. 29, No. 2, April, 1930.

Whitener, Daniel. "North Carolina Prohibition Election of 1881 and Its Aftermath," *North Carolina Historical Review*, Vol. XI, No. 2, 1934.

Willard, M. S. "County Finances in North Carolina," *County Government and County Affairs in North Carolina*, The North Carolina Club Year Book, 1917–1918 (1919).

INDEX

T

Printed in the United States
1399400002B/77-130